Ethics or the Right Thing?

Corruption, Care, and Family in an
Age of Good Governance

HAU
Books

Director
Anne-Christine Taylor

Editorial Collective
Deborah Durham
Catherine V. Howard
Vita Peacock
Nora Scott
Hylton White

Managing Editor
Nanette Norris

Editorial Officer
Jane Sabherwal

HAU Books are published by the
Society for Ethnographic Theory (SET)

www.haubooks.org

Ethics or the Right Thing?

Corruption, Care, and Family in an Age of Good Governance

Sylvia Tidey

Hau Books

Chicago

Cover: Monday morning roll call in Kupang, Indonesia
Credit: Sylvia Tidey

Cover design: Ania Zayco
Layout design: Deepak Sharma, Prepress Plus
Typesetting: Prepress Plus (www.prepressplus.in)

ISBN: 978-1-912808-64-9 [Print]
ISBN: 978-1-912808-66-3 [PDF]
ISBN: 978-1-912808-65-6 [Electronic]
LCCN: 2021931401

Hau Books
Chicago Distribution Center
11030 S. Langley Ave.
Chicago, Il 60628
www.haubooks.org

Hau Books publications are printed, marketed, and distributed by The University
of Chicago Press.
www.press.uchicago.edu

Printed in the United States of America on acid-free paper.

To my parents,

Michael Tidey and Chris Hooghuis

Contents

Acknowledgements

It is unimaginable to me now, that I ever thought that writing a book would mean starting with the first sentence and ending with the last. I have found that the process of writing a monograph is nothing like I once envisioned, which was something akin to a competitive skier making her way down an Alpine slope. Surely, she might expect some troublesome obstacles during her descent but, eventually and inevitably, a combination of natural ability and gravity would get her past the finish line in a speedy fashion. I have since learned that there is nothing inevitable—nor speedy—about the process. I also realized that natural ability, in fact, means hard work and practice. Most importantly, I now know that the force of gravity that finally gets you to writing that final sentence (which, incidentally, is likely nowhere near the final page of the book) actually consists of the influence, insights, support, and love given by many people along the way. I owe them all a tremendous debt of gratitude for the completion of this book.

Care and family form the central thread of the story in this book, but also in my own life. Many of the insights regarding the importance of a caring responsibility towards intimate others, as well as the fragility of family ties comes from being a part of a tight-knit extended family myself. For reasons of brevity, I cannot thank every one of you, so I will limit myself to my awe-inspiring aunties: Jannie, Francesca, Martha, Jacqueline, Patricia, and Suzanne. Being accustomed to having strong aunties made doing fieldwork in Kupang feel almost like a homecoming, for there I found myself absorbed into another loving network of aunties. Lele, Ince, and Tina: thank you for welcoming me into your homes and lives, and for teaching me how to not be an idiot.

I would furthermore like to give Melan, Remon, Ongen, Om Adi, and Nabila an emphatic *cium Savu* for all the kindness you have shown me. I would like to give an especially heartfelt thank you to Opa Leo Nisnoni and Rudi Rohi, for their friendship, companionship, and engaging conversations.

The dissertation project on which this book builds formed one part of a much larger ambitious research program funded by the Royal Netherlands Academy of Sciences, *In Search of Middle Indonesia*. I will forever be grateful for the endless patience my two supportive advisors, Henk Schulte Nordholt and Gerry van Klinken, showed me throughout my Ph.D trajectory. I am also thankful for all the scholars connected to the program for fostering a truly unique collaborative atmosphere: Basri Amin, Wenty Minza, Suzanne Naafs, Amalinda Savirani, Patricia Spyer, Ben White, Mario Rutten, Mohtar Mas'oed, Pratikno, Tamrin Amal Tomagola, Cornelis Lay, Pujo Semedi, Ratna Saptari, Bart Barendregt, Gerben Nootebom, Noorhaidi Hasan, Erwan Purwanto, Joe Errington, Chris Brown, and Jane Newberry.

At the Amsterdam Institute for Social Science Research, where I completed my Ph.D and postdoc, I would like to express my thanks in particular to Anita Hardon, Tina Harris, Niko Besnier, Ward Berenschot, Michiel Baas, Annemarie Samuels, Lex Kuiper, Stine Grinne, Oliver Human, and Megan Raschig.

I also want to thank my colleagues at the University of Virginia, where I have been fortunate enough to have found several welcoming academic homes. In the Department of Anthropology, I am especially grateful to the mentorship provided by China Scherz, Adria LaViolette, Eve Danziger, Kath Weston, and Lise Dobrin. In the Global Studies Program, I thank Richard Handler, Phoebe Crisman, Tess Farmer, David Edmunds, Gabi Kruks-Wisner, Pete Furia, and Helena Zeweri for their support. I also want to thank my fellow members of the CLEAR-Lab, especially David Singerman, Dan Gingerich, Sandip Sunkhtankar, Mike Gilbert, and Deborah Hellman, for offering a stimulating interdisciplinary setting for thinking about corruption.

Some of the most invigorating contexts for the pursuit of scholarly curiosity are unexpected ones. The 2016 Wenner-Gren symposium on the anthropology of corruption is one such example. I want to thank Akhil Gupta, Sarah Muir, Aaron Ansell, Diana Bocarejo, Ilana Feldman, Kregg Hetherington, Julia Hornberger, Smoki Musaraj, David Nugent, John Osburg, Italo Pardo, Jane Schneider, Anu Sharma, Cris Shore, Alan Smart, and Dan Smith, for a truly rewarding and joyful few days in Sintra. I hope that you recognize parts of your own work and our thinking together in this book.

Another such context that showed me how to combine intellectual pursuits with joy is the one I will refer to as "Team Phenomenology," which is the moniker given to the weekly Zoom gatherings for those with phenomenological inclinations, which was initiated by the phenomenal Jason Throop in the early days of the Covid-19 pandemic. I will borrow this term to refer to that ragtag group of anthropologists, who have come together in various formations in various workshops and panels, and AAA hotel bars, and who share an interest in phenomenological anthropology and similar pursuits. Besides Jason, I give my heartfelt thanks to Ellie Ochs, Sandro Duranti, Joel Robbins, Cheryl Mattingly, Bob Desjarlais, Linda Garro, Doug Hollan, Jarrett Zigon, Abby Mack, Aidan-Seale Feldman, Yael Assor, Devin Flaherty, Christopher Stephan, Thomas Schwartz-Wentzner, Rasmus Dyring, and Cre.

I also want to express my gratitude to another intellectually indispensable group of people, most of whom tend to remain invisible to an author: editors and peer reviewers. I will always remember and appreciate the time and effort Tom Boellstorff and Niko Besnier took to teach a very junior scholar how to improve article manuscripts. I hope to be able to emulate the academic generosity you extended to me. I also want to thank Vita Peacock for being a responsive and supportive editor throughout the process of developing this manuscript. Finally, and in spite of the many popular jokes about "reviewer two," I want to thank all the anonymous reviewers who have offered constructive criticism and helpful reviews of my work. I have learned so much about writing, structuring, and arguing a point from your mostly uncompensated willingness to help a fellow scholar. I intend to be equally helpful to those on whose manuscripts I have the fortune of giving input.

I am also forever grateful to my longtime friends, who at this point feel like family. Kim and Rosalie, I cannot wait for our next trip. I am lucky to count you as my friends. Yenkit, Dylan, Waiman, Claudio, Mart, and Koen: I know I can count on your Groninger down-to-earthiness and ruthless mocking to keep me grounded always. Sanne, Marloes, my sounding board, Annemarie, Mila, Maria, Brigid, Josh, Antonia, Natalie, and Eric: thank you for your enduring friendship.

I want to express my gratitude to my closest family members, to whom I owe everything. I want to thank my dad, Michael, for passing on his stubborn defiance to me. I thank my mom, Chris, for showing me that life can always get better. I want to thank my parents-in-law, Sandy,

David, and Janelle, for giving me a family on this side of the Atlantic. I want to thank Flora, Gino, Shainy, and AJ for reminding me that family takes unexpected shapes and forms. I thank Bianca and Naresh, for reminding me, and their daughters, what a loving home looks like. And to my nieces, the amazing Rani and Nisha: I am honored to be your *tante*. Being an aunt is a great responsibility. I promise to channel the very best of all the great aunties I have had in my life to love and encourage you.

Finally, to Jarrett Zigon, who is always already the ultimate love of my life. My *lekker ding*. Thank you for embarking on an unconventional life path with me. Thank you for agreeing that family is where we—and a certain fluffy cat named Lucy—are. I never imagined life could be this good. Thank you for knowing that, in the end, love might really just be all we need.

Introduction

The trial begins on Wednesday, February 25, 2014. The small room in Kupang's Corruption Court is packed.[1] Standing trial is Daniel Adoe, who served as the mayor of Kupang between 2007 and 2012. Family members of the accused, most of whom have not been able to meet with him since his arrest and detainment months before, are eager to show their support and offer the comfort of their physical presence. Many journalists have also gathered to cover the city's biggest corruption case to date. Photos from *Pos Kupang*, the local newspaper covering the trial closely, shows a frail, stooped, grey-haired man who bears little resemblance to the virile, black-haired, confidence-exuding victor of Kupang's first-ever direct mayoral elections, one who ran on a pro-democracy and anti-corruption platform less than a decade earlier. Adoe's claims of ill health impede the start of the trial several times and will continue to obstruct any smooth and swift court activities in the months to come. Indeed, a mere thirty minutes into the reading of the indictment, Adoe raises his hand to request a suspension of the proceedings due, again, to illness. The judge acquiesces and adjourns the session. Adoe shuffles

---

1. *Pengadilan Tindak Pidana Korupsi*, or *TiPiKor* for short. After the establishment a successful anti-corruption court in Jakarta (2004), the national legislature formed *TiPiKor* throughout Indonesia in 2011. Many of these regional corruption courts have been criticized by civil society organizations for perpetuating corruption (Butt 2012a).

out of the courtroom, one arm supported by his daughter, the other by a court employee.[2]

Adoe was charged, along with thirteen others, with the embezzlement of IDR 1.4 billion ($100,000) in state funds that were supposed to be used for the procurement of books by the Department of Education, Youth, and Sports. According to the testimony of an auditor from the Financial Supervisory and Development Board,[3] far more money was put aside for the procurement of those books than their actual cost, the difference going into the pockets of those involved. The others charged include various city-level government officials, members of the procurement committee tasked with evaluating competing bids, and the contractor who eventually won the contract. Adoe was facing the most severe indictments since the prosecution accused him of having abused his official position by, first, appointing all members of the procurement committee while lacking the official authority to do so, and, second, by influencing the committee in their determination of the winning contractor. The prosecution asked for a prison sentence of one year and three months as well as a fine of IDR 50 million ($3,575).

The final verdict by the panel of judges on July 10, 2014 turns out to be more severe than that. In addition to the fine, they also sentence him to prison for two-and-a-half years. The judges conclude that Adoe not only abused his position but did so at the expense of the state and thus deserved a longer prison sentence than what was requested by the prosecution.[4] After deliberating with his defense team for a few days, Adoe declines to appeal the verdict and accepts the sentence.

This account of Daniel Adoe's fall from grace after rising to power on a wave of anti-corruption promises is an all too familiar one in Indonesia. Indonesia joined the so-called third wave of democratization (Huntington 1991) rather belatedly when President Suharto stepped down

---

2. In my description of the trial and its charges and verdict, I draw on the many articles published in the local newspaper, *Pos Kupang* (2013) and gathered on the website: "Alleged Corruption Around the Procurement of Books."

3. The board is known locally as the BPKP (*Badan Pengawasan Keuangan dan Pembangunan*).

4. Adoe was charged with violating Article 3 of Law No. 20/2001 regarding the abuse of one's authority, opportunity, or position for the purpose of profiting on behalf of oneself, another, or a corporation in a way that harmed the state or the country's economy.

from power in 1998 after more than three decades of authoritarian rule. This political transformation occurred, in part, because of mass student protests that demanded sweeping reforms, democratization, and an end to corruption (Bünte and Ufen 2009; Lee 2016; H. Schulte Nordholt and Hoogenboom 2006). To be more precise, they demanded an end to the unholy trinity of *korupsi*, *kolusi*, and *nepotisme*—better known by its popular acronym KKN. Suharto's resignation ushered in a period of political reforms in promotion of democratization, or *reformasi*, under the ideological banner of "good governance," a move prompted and supported by the wider international development and financial community.

In this process of reformation, combatting corruption took center stage. Structural measures to change the institutional framework in which corruption had become so entrenched were implemented (Robison 2006). These included a devolution of economic and political power from Jakarta to the provinces, a process that unfolded so rapidly that the World Bank labeled it Indonesia's *big bang* and turned the nation from "one of the most centralized systems in the world into one of the most decentralized" (Hofman and Kaiser 2004). In 1999, the Indonesian government also introduced parliamentary elections, liberalized press laws, and allowed political parties and trade unions to operate freely. In 2002, it established the Corruption Eradication Commission (KPK), auditing bodies, and anti-corruption courts. This otherwise impressive march toward democratization, however, has been accompanied by some undemocratic disappointments. Post-Suharto Indonesia has also seen a continuation of military influence, a consolidation of local oligarchies, a revival of ethnic and regional sentiments, and an inability to ensure the rule of law (Bünte 2009). The hoped-for transition to the liberal, democratic principles suggested by the idea of good governance seemed thwarted by a continuation of bad practices.

Indonesia's predicament resonates with broader concerns about the state of democracy across the globe and the ways in which corruption threatens it. Over the last three decades, questions of ethics have informed international debates around governance, perhaps most obviously indicated by the *good* of the good governance approach. These questions have mostly been aimed at countries of the Global South and posed by international financial and development institutions attempting to help shape postcolonial state governments (Hough 2013; B. C. Smith 2007). In contrast, a concern with ethics did not figure prominently in earlier modernization efforts or structural adjustment policies during the Cold War era—Suharto's unparalleled corruption and cronyism could go unchecked as long as Indonesia continued to experience economic growth and remained a staunch political ally of the United States.

The current preoccupation with the quality of governance carries an explicit ethical charge that characterizes post-Cold War liberalism more generally (Hetherington 2018; Guilhot 2005; Moyn 2010). This movement towards what former United Nations High Commissioner for Human Rights, Mary Robinson, has termed "ethical globalization" (2003) is particularly clear in the context of military and humanitarian interventions, where the moral-political ideology exemplified by human rights and good governance has become the dominant mode of political imagining (Asad 2003; W. Brown 2001; Zigon 2013a). One consequence of this surge of global ethics (Sampson 2005) is that anti-corruption efforts have come to be seen as crucial for ensuring that newly democratized countries transition to a desired state of liberal democracy.

The supposed equivalence of anti-corruption, democracy, and the governmental good has proven to be, however, a tenuous one. Not only have anti-corruption efforts failed to deliver on their promise of curbing corruption around the world (Kaufmann 2009; Sampson 2009), the assumed equivalence of democracy and good governance does not even hold in the supposed heartlands of liberal democracy. Indeed, Western democracies are thought to be "in crisis," "under threat," "in decline," or even "dying" (Levitsky and Zieblatt 2018; Przeworski 2019; Van Beek 2019). Their legal remedies for things like emoluments, collusion, and nepotism increasingly lag behind popular condemnations of such practices. In many democratic nations, the threat of authoritarianism seems evermore real. For these reasons, it is necessary to reassess the relationship between corruption, democracy, and the idea of good governance.

In taking on such a reassessment, this book is not a dismissal of the importance of problematizing corruption or trying to work towards a kind of good in governance. Indeed, given that dissatisfaction with corruption figures so prominently in people's complaints about their governments all over the world (Muir and Gupta 2018), attending to the specifics of corruption offers valuable insights into existing visions of what counts as just, fair, and truly good in schemes of governance. The book is, therefore, an ethnographically grounded investigation into what the *good* in governance can look like outside of the dominant, contemporary configurations of ethical globalization that have become so hard to *unsee* and *unthink*. I turn to the effects of anti-corruption efforts in the nascent democracy of Indonesia to show how the good governance model itself enables a continuation of existing, as well as the emergence of novel

4

forms, of corruption. Spurred by these unanticipated and contradictory effects I ask: what if anti-corruption efforts actually make governance worse? If we look beyond hegemonic understandings of corruption and conceptions of the governmental good, what shapes can *good* governance take and how does corruption figure within it?

I attend to these questions from the vantage points of civil servants—who are often considered to be the main culprits of everyday, petty corruption—in the Indonesian city of Kupang, the capital of the eastern Indonesian province of East Nusa Tenggara (*Nusa Tenggara Timur*, or NTT for short). At the time of my research in the late 2000s, Kupang was majority Christian with close to 300,000 inhabitants (BPS 2008: 35). While I was conducting my fieldwork in 2008, the international anti-corruption agency Transparency International awarded it the dubious title of being Indonesia's most corrupt city. By attending to the social construction of corruption in the situated context of Kupang's civil service, I argue that corruption is not antithetical to good governance or outside of processes of democratization, but rather, it is intimately implicated with them.

Corruption as Political Failure?

I first came to know Daniel Adoe in 2007 during his first year in office, when he graciously allowed me to conduct my ethnographic research on the effects of post-*reformasi* administrative changes within all city-level government offices. His unexpected victory seemed to signal a decisive break with the clientelism and favoritism that had characterized his predecessor's twenty-one years in office. Adoe had managed, against all odds, not only to defeat the favored candidate, who had the full support of the then mayor and the biggest political party behind him, but to do so with a supporting coalition of political parties that mostly consisted of Muslim parties. In a Christian majority city within a country with the world's largest Muslim population, this was no small feat.

A popular concern with corruption played an important part in Adoe's victory. People in Kupang were tired of the *korupsi*, *kolusi*, and *nepotisme* (KKN) they associated with the former mayor and his favored candidate, dismissively characterizing them as "corruption buddies" or "collusion buddies" (Tidey 2018). They preferred to cast their vote for a candidate who ran on an explicit anti-corruption platform and offered the promise of progress and to keep the city's workings "clean." Adoe's election caused concern for those cronies who remained in city government and who now wondered how the unexpected change would affect their career advancement. For others, including poor market vendors, minibus drivers, and women doing laundry in the Dendeng River, Adoe's election held the promise of progress—or at least something better.

Nevertheless, by the time I started my fieldwork during Adoe's first year in office, traces of disappointment had started to cloud the initial excitement in Kupang. The disappointment was palpable among the civil servants with whom I spent much of my time. Some of their apprehension stemmed from the mayor's perceived incompetence. But while being critical of Adoe's political effectiveness, they were also engaging in self-reflection. As we have seen in, for example, Nigeria and India, (Gupta 1995; D. J. Smith 2007: 7–9), corruption narratives and complaints in Kupang were closely tied to the ways in which people tried to make sense of the state, city, and themselves. And in these processes of sense-making, civil servants found the city of Kupang, the province of East Nusa Tenggara, and Indonesia as a whole wanting, especially when compared to an idealized West, like the United States or the Netherlands, which they imagined to be "already developed" and "free from KKN." Perhaps most difficult for them was what they concluded about themselves: the persistence of corruption in an age of anti-corruption, lower-level civil servants, department heads, and politicians would all claim, meant that people in Kupang were simply "still stupid" (*masih bodoh*) and "not yet ready" (*belum siap*) for a new, democratic state system.

These self-accusations reflected a general feeling of humiliation the Kupangese felt towards their own city and society. The province of East Nusa Tenggara is among Indonesia's poorest. In 2011, it ranked thirty-first (out of thirty-four) on the country's Human Development Index with almost a quarter of the population living below the national poverty line (WFP Indonesia 2013). People in East Nusa Tenggara joke that the acronym by which their province is known, NTT, actually stands for *Nanti Tuhan Tolong* (God will help later), *Nasib Tak Tentu* (unfixed/uncertain fate), or *Nusa Tetap Tertinggal* (the island left behind). When Transparency International named Kupang Indonesia's most corrupt city in 2008 (Melayu Online 2009; Tempo 2009), it confirmed the self-Orientalizing critique Kupangese already possessed—that they were, indeed, "still stupid" and "not yet ready" for democracy, a conclusion that prompted further reflections about the state of democracy in Indonesia in general. It was not just the people that were ill-prepared for democracy,

Kupangese would tell me. Kupang, NTT, and even Indonesia as a whole were simply "not yet developed" and "still transitioning." This view of Indonesia's democratization process and the suspicion that corruption was to blame for the failure of the country's development also captured a more general scholarly disappointment about the trajectory of the post-*reformasi* Indonesian state (Aspinall et al. 2020; Bünte and Ufen 2009; H. Schulte Nordholt and Hoogenboom 2006). In spite of far-reaching reforms to stimulate democratization, critics claim that instead of having achieved the preferred end-stage of meaningful or liberal democracy, Indonesia is stuck in a protracted transition. Its democracy is thus categorized as predatory, of low quality, and illiberal.[5] Of particular scholarly concern is the lingering influence of hierarchical power dynamics on contemporary Indonesian politics, variously described as clientelism, patrimonialism, or neo-patrimonialism, or the continuing presence of asymmetrical power relations.[6] While there is some disagreement as to the extent to which this signals a continuation of more traditional power arrangements or suggests a particular modern reconfiguration of power and politics (e.g., Barker and Van Klinken 2009), the general consensus is that it interferes with achieving good governance. This is unsurprising, for hierarchical and asymmetrical power arrangements directly contradict liberal intellectual and political ideals, which consider individualism, freedom, and egalitarianism to be central to conceptions of meaningful personhood, justice, and the social good (Haynes and Hickel 2016; Piliavsky 2014). From this perspective, the possibility that hierarchy and patronage might be central to certain understandings of the good is absurd. The dissatisfaction and the related self-accusations people in Kupang voiced in the aftermath of *reformasi* thus fits well within the larger development narrative, in which corruption, and specifically the presumed inherent exploitative character of asymmetrical power relations, figures as the main obstacle to successful democratization.

---

5. This description of Indonesia is seen in the work of Aspinall and Mietzner (2019); Bünte and Ufen (2009: 6–7); Diprose, McRae, and Hadiz (2019); Hadiz (2008); Malley (2000); Mietzner (2009); Robison (2002); and Törnquist (2008).

6. For examples of how these relations are used to view Indonesia's protracted transition to flourishing liberal democratic conditions see Aspinall and Berenschot (2019); Choi (2009); Hadiz and Robison (2013); Schulte-Nordholt (2004); and Webber (2006).

In many ways, the contemporary preoccupation with corruption as an impediment to good governance is not unique to Indonesia and fits within a more general post-Cold War liberalism (Guilhot 2005). However, we would be wise to remember that long before the current neoliberal interest in good governance, corruption functioned as the symptom of a vestigial pathology of the body politic, a condition that weakened processes of political liberalization (Hetherington 2018). Most notably, perhaps, it was used to explain the failure of those states that gained independence after World War II to achieve the end stages of capitalism and development as set out in modernization theory (Pierce 2016: 17). This explanation fit seamlessly with the long-held belief that corruption was endemic to the non-Western Other (2016: 10–12). In this sense, good governance and its emphasis on anti-corruption is but the latest re-enactment of a steadfast fantasy of progress that fuels the logic of liberalism (Edelman 2004; Zigon 2013a). Such fantasies of progress are projected not just temporally but also geographically onto non-Western *elsewheres*, with little questioning of the ethical assumptions that ground good governance, or how these assumptions compare with other ethical foundations of governance outside of liberalism. These fantasies of progress, with their not-so-hidden ethical assumptions, have been central to establishing and maintaining global political-economic power dynamics and inequalities (e.g., Brown 2001; Guilhot 2005; Moyn 2010; Zigon 2017).

Perhaps paradoxically, Kupangese frequently use the familiar liberal language of development and democracy to articulate their complaints. Although this suggests that they hope to fulfill the fantasy of progress described above, the lived experience of this dissatisfaction and disappointment is much more complex. As Sarah Muir and Akhil Gupta (2018) have suggested, corruption might be best understood as a category of transgression. The transgressive character of corruption comes from its elision of definitions and evoking of questions about justice, equity, and appropriate relationships between power and economic resources. Viewed as such, the existent disappointment and dissatisfaction in Kupang capture how a program meant to improve governance in fact negatively impacts expectations of what counts as just, equitable, and good in connection to the distribution of resources. Complaints about corruption in Kupang, then, not only signal a failure of political transition, but more importantly a transgression of care; a dereliction of the caring responsibility of the state to ensure possibilities for its people to forge worthwhile lives. Good governance, in short, makes life worse.

The Rise of Good Governance

A particular vision of the good began to take shape in international policy circles during the years before Suharto's resignation and then influenced the particular administrative form of Indonesia during the *reformasi* years. The Indonesian concern with corruption dovetailed with a renewed interest that international development institutions displayed toward corruption in the 1990s, in which anti-corruption efforts came to be closely tied to good governance (Guilhot 2005). For decades, international institutions such as the World Bank and the International Monetary Fund (IMF) had little concern for corruption, favoring instead a strict economic approach to development.[7] In Indonesia this meant that Suharto's extravagant corruption could go uncontested, as long as Indonesia continued its economic development and remained an ally of Western powers in the Cold War.

However, with the end of the Cold War and the so-called victory of liberal democracy, and the recognition that modernization efforts and structural adjustment programs had failed to deliver stable markets and democratization, the focus of development shifted from the narrowly economic to the role of corruption and governance (Hough 2013, 12–30; B. C. Smith 2007: 1–16). The most dramatic denouncement of corruption happened when James Wolfensohn, then president of the World Bank, referred to the "cancer of corruption" in his address during the bank's annual meeting on October 1, 1996. His speech and the subsequent launch of the Corruption Action Plan Working Group effectively solidified the importance of anti-corruption efforts for international development and financial institutions, where it had been steadily growing for a number of years. For example, the non-governmental organization Transparency International—known for its annual publications of the *Corruption Perceptions Index* and *Bribe Payers Index*—had been pushing for the necessity of attending to corruption since its foundation in 1993. Furthermore, the United Nations, IMF, and the Organization for Economic Co-operation and Development (OECD) had also started to prioritize the importance of tackling corruption (Bukovansky 2006). By the late 1990s and early 2000s, most multilateral and nongovernmental

---

7. Although we should recall that political scientists deployed patrimonialism and neo-patrimonialism to explain the failure of African and Asian states to modernize in the 1970s and 1980s (see Joseph 1987a; Crouch 1979).

organizations had incorporated anti-corruption as a central part of their rhetoric and reform programs.

The definitions of corruption that prominent international institutions generally employ tend to be markedly concise and characterize corruption in a Weberian vein—a transgression of the boundaries between the public and private realms.[8] For example, the World Bank describes corruption as "the abuse of public office for private gain"; the IMF defines it as "the abuse of public power for private benefit"; Transparency International stresses "the abuse of entrusted power for private gain"; and the OECD calls it "the active or passive misuse of the powers of public officials (appointed or elected) for private financial or other benefits" (Hough 2013: 2).

It is worth noting that despite the sheen of universality and timelessness exuded by such definitions, the understanding of corruption solely in terms of transgressing public-private boundaries is relatively new. As Bruce Buchan and Lisa Hill (2014) argue in their comprehensive overview of the changing usages and meanings of corruption throughout Western political thought, it was not until the late eighteenth-century that understandings of political corruption came to be restricted to the abuse of public office for private gain.[9] Until that point, the rather narrow view of corruption as a matter of public office was accompanied by a more expansive definition of the "degenerative"—a general social,

---

8.   Weber's main intellectual pursuits revolved around questions regarding the creation and maintenance of legitimate political orders. In the context of advancing modernity and capitalism in the late-nineteenth and early twentieth centuries, he described a slow evolutionary process of rationalization transforming traditional societies into bureaucratic or legal-rational societies. In such societies, legitimacy of the social order stems from clear rules, a high level of professionalism and expertise, meritocracy, the separation between the private household and public office, and the subordination of passions and personal interests to rationalism and logic. Definitions of corruption as the misuse of public office—employed by international financial and development institutions—come from this line of thought (Rubinstein and Von Maravić 2010).

9.   See also Muir and Gupta (2018b: 5): "As an array of scholars have argued, the public/private distinction grew out of but diverged from European medieval political theology and became fundamental to the ideological and bureaucratic structures of modern states and markets (Arendt 1958; Corrigan and Sayer 1985; Habermas 1991; Kantorowicz 1958; Marx 1978; Polanyi 1944; Weber 1978)."

political, and moral decay. While different in scope, these two conceptions of corruption were interconnected as moral and societal decay offered fertile ground for discrete public-office misdemeanors that, in turn, further tainted the moral and political fabric of societies. It was only with the emergence of the rationalities of liberal democratic governance and political economy in the late eighteenth-century, that the interrelatedness between public office and degenerative corruption came undone, and a paricular understanding of the former notion of corruption emerged as the dominant definition.

Furthermore, by the late eighteenth-century, changes in political organization, attitudes toward commercial activity, and imperial expansion and colonialism encouraged a progressivist view of history that radically departed from the pessimistic, eschatological view that characterized earlier classical and medieval thought (Buchan and Hill 2014: 147–148). This meant that the long-reigning idea of inevitable, degenerative corruption and certainty societal decay gradually made way for a teleological view, and an understanding of corruption as something that could be overcome through technocratic reforms (Pierce 2016: 9–15). This shift can be seen as foreshadowing the many ways in which successive incarnations of development schemes in general, and anti-corruption efforts in particular, would be "rendered technical" (Li 2007: 123) or "projectized" (Sampson 2005: 109).

Accompanying this change in temporal understandings of corruption was a shift in the spatial sense of where corruption was to be found. In the context of empire and colonialism, the sources of corruption were no longer understood to come from within the body-politic of the metropole, but rather from the territories where a persistent primitivism threatened the advanced motherland (Pierce 2016: 12). If in the tradition of Western political thought, concerns with corruption entailed focus on the state of one's own political community, from the late eighteenth-century onwards, a set of Orientalist prejudices maintained a contradistinction between an honest and industrious North against a South lacking those qualities (Taussig 1999: 78).

This hierarchical positioning of West/North above the rest of the world continued to reverberate in concerns with corruption throughout the twentieth century, particularly in the post-Cold War development of good governance principles. During the period of decolonization, as countries throughout Asia and Africa gained independence, it was thought that so-called traditional and cultural tendencies worked to favor kin, clan, or other intimate groups through hierarchical exchange patterns, or the selfish desires of rulers seeking to satisfy their own appetites for riches (Bayart 1993; M. Crouch 2008; R. Joseph 1987)—these were the obstacles to the teleological progress of modernization, development, and democratization. In Indonesia, the current resurgence of an analytical interest in hierarchical power asymmetries to explain Indonesia's failure to democratize—couched in terms of clientelism and (neo)patrimonialism—suggests a continuing reluctance to question the narrative of developmental progress and its liberal political limitations. The presumed incompatibility between patronage and liberal democratic political arrangements only works to further compound already imagined spatial distinctions. This incompatibility is strengthened by the tendency to view corruption in Western liberal democracies as incidental rather than endemic or systemic (Anders and Nuijten 2007: 3). The annual publication of Transparency International's annual *Corruption Perceptions Index* forms perhaps the most visible example of the persistent confluence between perceptions of corruption and "longstanding racialized sociogeographic distinctions of development and modernity" (Muir and Gupta 2018: 11), and thus contributes significantly to the perception of the "corrupt," non-Western Other.

The definition of corruption as the abuse of public office for private gain, its spatial and temporal focus, suspicions of hierarchical political arrangements, and faith in technocratic solutions have particular historical, geographical, and intellectual origins. Nonetheless, they have managed to quickly gain the force and air of the eternal and universal. This is buttressed in part by the disciplinary approaches that have influenced anti-corruption policy. When international financial and development institutions began to prioritize the problem of corruption in the 1990s, their understanding of the problem and their policy solutions were heavily influenced by the ideas and recommendations of political and developmental economists (see Rose-Ackerman 1978; Tanzi 2000). These ideas, firmly rooted in the traditions of rational choice and economic liberalism, were characterized by a great skepticism about the influence of the state in economic and social life, as well as particular presuppositions regarding human behavior (Bukovansky 2006; Hough 2013: 23–24). These included, for example, assumptions that politicians and public officials tend to be guided by self-interest and profit-maximization. Accordingly, larger governments were thought to offer more opportunities for rent seeking. Economic liberalism includes a suspicion of states, which are assumed to meddle in markets and thereby hinder economic growth and development. When it came to the formulation of policy regarding anti-corruption, it thus made sense to single out governments, public officials, and their interference in the economy as the main source of corruption. The problem of corruption and the framing of anti-corruption efforts, therefore, took shape in terms of corruption as a problem of the public sector supported by a liberal economic distrust of the state.

Consequently, the solution to corruption was initially to encourage a "lean" state approach that focused on decreasing the size of governments. This approach was perhaps most emphatically voiced by the Nobel Memorial Prize winner Gary Becker, who built popular press articles out of ideas like: "If You Want to Cut Corruption, Cut Government" (1995) and "To Root Out Corruption, Boot Out Big Government" (1994). Nevertheless, this lean-state approach and emphasis on economic liberalization failed to deliver convincingly on its promise of combating corruption and there is little evidence that anti-corruption efforts have mitigated or tackled the roots of corruption (Hough 2013: 22). As Steven Sampson notes, "Despite hundreds of millions of dollars, and hundreds of programmes, projects, and campaigns, conducted by an army of anti-corruption specialists, experts, and trainers, we have very little evidence of any decline in corrupt behaviour, or even a decline in public perceptions of corruption" (2009: 171).

In fact, opportunities for corruption can flourish alongside anti-corruption efforts (E. Brown and Cloke 2004; Shore and Haller 2005: 9). For instance, some of the most spectacular corruption cases in Indonesia have involved officials in the upper echelon of the Corruption Eradication Commission (KPK), which was created in 2002 to investigate large-scale corruption cases (Butt 2012b). Furthermore, the privatization of state businesses that form a part of the economic reforms that international financial institutions demand as a conditionality for aid have occasioned many opportunities for illicit enrichment (E. Brown and Cloke 2004: 288). Even from the perspective of rational choice theory, this is perfectly plausible—why, after all, would a private sector or other non-public sector employee be any less incentivized by rent-seeking opportunities than her public sector counterpart? Finally, the lean-state approach to corruption proves difficult to pursue when the countries that persistently score highest (indicating lower rates of corruption) on Transparency International's *Corruption Perceptions Index*— such as Denmark, Sweden, and the Netherlands—have notoriously big governments (cf. Tanzi 1998: 23).

By the late 1990s, a renewed appreciation of the state took hold in international development and financial institutional circles. Accordingly, the focus on anti-corruption started to shift from focusing on government size to the quality of governance (Hough 2013: 31–47). The lean-state approach consequently made way for the ideal of good governance, following the reasoning that states that are well governed foster environments inimical to corruption. While many buzzwords of good governance (e.g., efficiency, accountability, and transparency) have infused the discourse of policy and practice the world over, the implementation of good governance generally involves reforms in four areas: constitutional, political, administrative, and public policy (B. C. Smith 2007: 6). Good governance at a constitutional level requires strengthening the rule of law and the accountability of political leaders, ensuring respect of human rights, and decentralizing political authority. Politically, good governance advocates political pluralism, political participation, and anti-corruption. At the level of administration, good governance expects accountable and transparent public administration as well as effective public management. Finally, at the level of public policy, good governance is driven by a distinctly neoliberal approach to economics and politics.

Despite an ostensible reevaluation of the role of the state in the management of a country's affairs, neoliberal economics continue to dominate the policy dimension of good governance and preferences for lean governments persist. Although the good governance approach appears to leave more space for nuanced and country-specific anti-corruption measures than the earlier lean-state approach, corruption and governance are still viewed as institutional design flaws that can be remedied through technocratic intervention and changes in incentive structures (Bukovansky 2006; Hough 2013: 34–35). As Ed Brown and Jonathan Cloke (2004: 287) write, "it is clear that the general thrust of anti-corruption programmes within the 'good governance' agenda are sharply contradicted by the wider economic restructuring policies prescribed by the same institutions." In spite of the supposedly new appreciation of the role of the state in the good governance approach, anti-corruption measures still suffered from an earlier "anti-state slant" (2004: 286) in which good governance equals lean states.

For the more pessimistic voices within the anthropology of corruption, the continued hegemony of neoliberal thought suggests that good governance is merely the latest form of "aid conditionality" (Blundo and Olivier de Sardan 2006b: 6) and anti-corruption simply "the new stick to beat non-Western governments into compliance with the economic and political agenda of the United States and the dictates of global capitalism" (Shore and Haller 2005: 19). However, such a singular and malevolent view of good governance does not fit entirely with what has now grown into a veritable anti-corruption industry that intersects with movements for global ethics, corporate governance, public administration accountability, and transparent management, as well as other projects that involve the promotion of democracy, economic development, and state-building (Sampson 2009). Such a complex amalgam of projects, plans, and ideologies—whose complexity is perhaps better characterized as a "corruption/anti–corruption complex" (Muir and Gupta 2018: 7)—is likely to contain multiple perspectives and intentions, including sincere ones to do good.

It thus appears that the range of possibilities for what can count and be recognized as either good or corrupt is rather limited, and does not stretch beyond public sector reforms and increasing market competitiveness. It is therefore necessary to move beyond these limitations, and consider alternative possibilities for visions of a governmental good within a more complex moral-ethical constellation.

Ethics and Corruption

During Daniel Adoe's corruption trial, the prosecutors conducted another inquiry involving the mayor's son, Adi Adoe, who was said to have received a cash sum of IDR 600 million ($43,000) after the completion of the book procurement project. Minus other evidence, prosecutors needed a contractor's testimony and they pressed him repeatedly. He admitted asking Adi to notify him whenever new projects came up because Adi was the mayor's son, leaving open that it was merely a proactive initiative by an entrepreneurial businessman and not part of a quid pro quo. The contractor also admitted giving Adi money, but only as a *reward* for his help. This admission still was not enough for the prosecutors to pursue a case against Adi, however, because according to his lawyer the contractor had drawn on his personal funds rather than project funds to make the payment, which was not illegal in any way. The lawyer, furthermore, told the local newspaper *Pos Kupang*: "If you want to entrap Adi Adoe you can only do that if [the contractor] admits there was an element of extortion. But the facts of the trial reveal that the IDR 600 million from the contractor were given as an

15

expression of gratitude [*ungkapan terima kasih*] to Adi Adoe" (Lewan-meru 2014).[10]

This failed pursuit of potential charges against Adi Adoe is sugges-tive of both the legal and ethical limitations of anti-corruption measures, and the limited persuasiveness of good governance as a superior kind of "global ethics." Against prosecution attempts to prove a quid pro quo, the defense lawyer played the legal definitions of corruption off ethically more opaque understandings of corruption expressed in terms of grati-tude. In doing so, the lawyer deftly took the good governance definition of corruption and translated it into an alternative governmental good: one characterized by relationality, gift exchange, and care.

Well aware of the fact that in order for actions to become prosecut-able as corruption they have to be proven to transgress the boundaries of the law, the lawyer made clear that the money given to Adi Adoe originated from his client's perfectly legal personal funds, thereby pre-empting the possibility for framing the monetary transaction as corrup-tion. But he did more than disprove the allegation of an illegal or illicit exchange. For at the same time, he portrayed the transfer of money as an ethical act. By invoking the specter of an extreme form of exchange—extortion—only to immediately deny its relevance, he diminished the negative moral charge of the transfer. By subsequently referring to the transfer of money as an "expression of gratitude", he managed to embed his client's potentially illegitimate actions into the well-accepted ethics of interpersonal gift exchange.

What this maneuvering shows is the tenuousness of the connections between legality, legitimacy, and ethics, which the easy entwinement of anti-corruption legislation with the moral charge of good govern-ance fails to acknowledge. In so-called modern societies, the rational-legal authority Weber identifies with legality equates to legitimacy (D'Entréves 1963). In such societies, legitimacy and the law overlap to such an extent that they appear to be the same thing. The legality of anti-corruption efforts, then, can easily be conflated with the presumed legitimacy of good governance. Italo Pardo (2013; 2018) disputes such easy conflations and reminds us that "the production of the law must take into account the moralities and ethical principles which inform the definition of legitimacy at the grassroots, for legislation that enjoys le-gitimacy is authoritative, therefore, effective legislation" (2013: 124). In

---

10. Lewanmeru (2014) pursued the story in a succession of articles in *Pos Ku-pang* between April-June 2014.

other words, legitimacy has a legal as well as a moral component, and for the law to carry authority it needs the legitimization that occurs through a resonance with existing ethical notions and practices.[11] In Kupang, the absence of authority of anti-corruption legislation is explained in part by a lack of resonance with any *singular* ethical component. For anti-corruption efforts fit uneasily with other—sometimes conflicting and sometimes overlapping—notions of what is just and good in this eastern Indonesian city, where the most dominant notions of just and good are best described in terms of an ethics of care and exchange.

When anti-corruption efforts arrived in Kupang's government offices in the early 2000s, they did not form one coherent (practical, governmental, and even ethical) project. They also did not land on a tabula rasa devoid of ideas and practices of a governmental good. As Stephen Collier (2005) has argued, neoliberalism does not so much bring its own values to any particular new context as co-opt and transform already-existing values in its own image. We should therefore be mindful of the multiple mediations (Gupta 1995; Mani 1990) through which the state, or in this case civil service corruption and ideas of a governmental good, comes to be constructed. In order to imagine alternative visions of such a good, we need to closely attend to how connections between corruption and ideas of the good (and the just) take locally distinctive forms without losing sight of the complex, multiply mediated manners in which they are constituted, and from there disclose a more complex ethical picture of morality, the good, and the just.

Delineating these locally distinctive forms has long been the strength of anthropology. For example, some of the discipline's earliest engagements with corruption emphasized moral economies (Scott 1977), local rationalities, cultural logics, and the social and symbolic dimensions of politics, power, and economics, thus recasting what some might view as corruption in terms of reciprocity, gift exchange, or patronage (e.g., Harrison 2006; D. J. Smith 2007: 10). Still, while such a focus on moral economies and local rationalities forms an important contribution to general discussions of corruption in which little room is left for ethical excess and complexity, portraying corruption in terms of (local) cultural logics does little to problematize Orientalist stereotypes, or the hegemony of the progress narrative of liberalism. Neither, it should be added, does it address the unquestioned acceptance of a distinction between

---

11. For more ethnographic approaches to situating corruption within discussion of the law and morality, see Nuijten and Anders (2007).

public office and the private sphere that we have already seen as central to international anti-corruption efforts.

However, over the last decade-and-a-half, an increasing number of anthropological studies have emerged in which the intersection between corruption, morality, state, and capitalism is addressed more explicitly (Shore and Haller 2005). These studies emphasize the many different types of corruption (Blundo et al. 2006); the embedded patterns of personal relations and gift giving within changing state configurations (Ansell 2014; Musaraj 2020; Osburg 2013; Rivkin-Fish 2005); the frictions between morality and legitimacy (Pardo 2000; Tidey 2016); how claims to legitimacy are tied to the ability to exercise authority (Harrison 2006); and the wide geographic range of corrupt practices (Hetherington 2011; Hornberger 2018; Sharma 2018; Schneider and Schneider 2005; Yang 1994)—including in the supposed heartlands of Weberian bureaucratic rationality, which contradict the assumptions that corruption is incompatible with legal-rational modernity (MacLennan 2005; Shore 2005; 2018).

We can apply these insights to the hierarchical asymmetrical power dynamics, that many scholars of contemporary Indonesian politics and governance view as the main obstacle to the country's transition to liberal democracy. Since liberal conceptions of modern politics place egalitarianism, disinterestedness, and individualism at the heart of good democratic practice, it becomes almost impossible to consider such power dynamics as anything but unjust and exploitative. Indeed, the often-preferred term of clientelism for such hierarchical arrangements points exactly to an individual profit-seeking model of transactionalism that is devoid of morality and meaning beyond an exchange of goods or service for political support. The recent revitalization of anthropological studies of patronage and hierarchy (Ansell 2010; Haynes and Hickel 2016; Keeler 2017; Peacock 2015; Piliavsky 2021) demonstrate something different. Besides refuting the assumption that patronage and modern democracy are incompatible, they remind us that patronage points to a moral way of organizing transactions. Rather than working from the calculus of rational choice, patronage operates on the moral logic of relatedness (Piliavsky 2014: 21–27). All this is to say, informed by a particular relational morality, it is not surprising that many people turn to hierarchy as a source of hope and a desirable social good.

The moral richness of the many vernacular terms that overlap with and yet exceed the English word "corruption" offers further insight into the locally distinctive forms that connections between corruption and ideas of the good can take. For as Steven Pierce (2016: 4) reminds us: "taking the term 'corruption' as transparent and straightforward implies that it has a universal set of meanings, but its vernacular application … maps onto a distinctive local moral field [and] the use of the term lies at the center of how moral questions about the distribution of public goods are negotiated." This is illustrated by the many vernacular words that share semantic similarities to *corruption*, but have a more elastic ethical charge. Vernacular terms such as the Arabic *wasta* (Benstead, Atkeson, and Shahid 2020), the Chinese *guanxi* (Smart 1998; Yan 1996) or the Russian *blat* (Ledeneva 1998; Rivkin-Fish 2005) cover a semantic field that ranges from interpersonal connections to nepotism. They offer no indication of their legitimacy beyond that of the specific social context in which they occur. The Indian word *brashtaachaar*, furthermore, occupies the same semantic field as *corruption* in the sense that it points to violations of the law and social norms, and yet it also invokes the moral obligation of elites to look after the poor (Gupta 2012: 80). Something similar occurs in Nigeria, where the word corruption can mean both the abuse of public office for personal gain and a wide range of confidence schemes perpetrated in order to obtain some kind of advantage, with the latter generally being considered far more morally questionable than the former (D. J. Smith 2007). What these vernacular terms indicate is that their use in particular social and cultural contexts does not easily fit with a priori legal codes that presume universal validity. Moreover, their moral status is not static and unambiguous.

When it comes to the legitimacy of practices that might be considered corrupt, international financial and development institutions cannot have the final say. With the moral status of potentially corrupt practices open to interpretation, there is some agentive possibility of giving ethical shape to this interpretation. This is something Beatrice Jauregui (2014) shows well in her discussion of the ethics of illegality surrounding the Indian practice of *jugaad*. Similar to the vernacular terms expressed above, *jugaad* occupies a broad semantic field. As a highly polysemic term it should roughly be understood as a resourceful approach to achieving material or social goals, or a kind of "making do." Depending on the context in which it occurs or who deploys it, *jugaad* connotes innovation, provision, or corruption. Its lack of a fixed and stable meaning indicates that its moral status is contested and ambiguous, and best characterized as what Jauregui calls "contronymic," or as having the capacity to contain two opposing meanings at once. The contronymic character of *jugaad* facilitates a kind of provisional agency that makes it possible for people to creatively, and in an improvisational manner, make legitimate what might otherwise be considered corrupt. And this improvisational play with contronymy would be impossible without a close familiarity with the particular complexities of the situation in which different configurations of corruption and ideas of the just and good contrast, collide, and (temporarily) overlap. To paraphrase Dorothy Zinn (2019) when she says that seeing the Italian practice of *racommandazione* as sheer bribery misses the associated poetics that are key to understanding it (Shore and Haller 2005: 7), considering *jugaad* as mere corruption misses the poetics of provisional agency that allows it to become virtuous rather than immoral.

Throughout this book, I attend to this creative and poetic aspect of corruption in relation to the larger structural complexity that characterizes the corruption/anti-corruption complex (Muir and Gupta 2018). Contronymy helps to make sense of, for example, a lawyer's masterful maneuvering of legality, legitimacy, and ethics but does not suffice to capture the institutional and discursive ethical complexities, contradictions, and overlaps that constitute the social worlds within which the civil servants of Kupang need to navigate the confusing anti-corruption measures. These social worlds are better described in terms of what Jarrett Zigon (2009; 2011b: 62–72) calls a moral-ethical assemblage.

Such moral-ethical assemblages are not made up of one all-encompassing and totalizing morality and its ethical practices, and neither does it provide a space for a singular "global ethics" to clash with a singular local morality. Instead, these assemblages bring together a wide range of institutional, public discursive, and embodied moralities that coalesce to constitute the particular social-moral worlds in which people go about their everyday lives for the most part in an unreflective and unreflexive manner. In such social worlds, civil servants do not merely need to creatively navigate the contronymy of potentially corrupt practices, but rather their moral-ethical assemblic constitution. How, for example, should an ambitious civil servant respond to an acquaintance's request for a civil service position when doing so is justifiable via the logic of family care, might fit a national ideal of state organization, but otherwise offends his own professional standards? The complexity of this moral-ethical assemblage entails that certain practices can have the moral status of corrupt, ethical, right, or perfect—sometimes simultaneously. It is precisely the complexity of this creative enactment that can sometimes lead to certain practices being considered corrupt from the narrow perspective of good governance, while being experienced as the right thing to do by civil servants.

An Ethnography of Care in Indonesia's Most Corrupt City

This book is based on thirteen months of ethnographic fieldwork in Ku-pang between 2007 and 2010. Since then, the rapid advance of internet connections in Kupang, along with an increase in smartphone owner-ship, ensuing Facebook accounts, and messaging applications enabled me to stay up-to-date on developments in the city. For example, I fol-lowed Daniel Adoe's trial and conviction, as well as the changes in the lives of my guest family, friends, and other interlocutors. In Kupang, I had joined a household (the Kaho family) whose members had roots in the nearby island of Savu. Living alongside the Kaho family proved pivotal for the two interrelated strands that would make up my field research: an in-depth study of the effects of anti-corruption efforts on Kupang's civil service from within its bureaucracy, and an intimate ac-quaintance with the central role that the joys, demands, and obligations of family belonging play in the everyday life of Kupang.

When I first embarked on my fieldwork, I hoped to conduct an eth-nography of Kupang's bureaucracy: conducting participant observation and interviews while working alongside civil servants within Kupang's government offices. I feared this hope would remain unfulfilled. The very things that make bureaucracy fascinating for anthropologists—such as its performative formalism, opaque internal dynamics, impenetrable red tape, and subtle forms of discrimination and exclusion (Handelman 1981; Herzfeld 1992; Gupta 2012)—also make it a notoriously difficult arena for them to access. Anthropologists have therefore mostly taken to studying bureaucracy obliquely through the material culture, such as the documents, writing practices, and auditing activities that comprise bureaucratic knowledge production (Das 2004; Feldman 2008; Hull 2012b; Tarlo 2001).[12] Indeed, my desire to access the ranks of Kupang's civil servants would have been much more difficult, if not impossible, but for my guest brother, Valentino (who plays an important role in chapter three). When I arrived in Kupang, Valentino had just graduated from a prestigious national-level civil service preparatory academy and started his first civil service job as an aide to the recently elected mayor Daniel

---

12. A notable and encouraging exception to these indirect approaches are the various advances into ethnographic studies of bureaucracy conducted by China Scherz (2011), Hadi Nicholas Deeb and George E. Marcus (2011), both of which appeared in the same 2011 issue of *PoLar* on the anthropo-logical study of bureaucracy.

Adoe. Valentino arranged for me to have an audience with the mayor to request his permission to conduct research within any city-level department under his mayoral command. During his early tenure, Adoe appeared eager to steer city-level civil service toward what he viewed as a more developed and democratic direction. Granting a foreign researcher, who was interested in post-reformasi (italicized) good governance efforts, permission to participate in everyday office life and conduct interviews within his departments aligned with his intentions.

With the mayor's permission, I spent approximately three months apiece in the following departments: Governance; Information and Communication; Human Resources; and Public Works. In these, I participated in the general, everyday duties of the civil servants. I chose the first three departments because they were located in the same building as the mayor's office and would therefore enable me to witness what was turning out to be a contentious aftermath of an unexpected election victory. I selected Public Works because of its reputation as a particularly "wet" (i.e., corrupt) department. I joined meetings, roll calls, trainings, and the actual tenders for construction projects; followed the processes of drafting formal documents and the hiring of new civil servants; and accepted invitations for parties, short trips, and aerobics classes. With a team of student assistants from the local Undana University, I closely followed the 2008 East Nusa Tenggara gubernatorial elections. I also conducted formal and informal interviews with lower- and upper-level civil servants, temporary employees, department heads, journalists, and contractors within and outside the offices in Indonesian—interviews that became increasingly sprinkled with Kupang vernacular.

Having a guest brother who had just started working for the mayor was an example of the kind of fortuitous happenstance that characterizes the undetermined and open-ended method of ethnographic fieldwork, which sets it apart from methods aimed at producing more standardized forms of knowledge (Armstrong and Agulnik 2020; Hazan and Hertzog 2011; Rivoal and Salazar 2013). The Kaho family, however, would likely offer a different explanation for my relatively smooth entry into Kupang's civil service. The immersion in family life that formed the second strand of my research in Kupang familiarized me with the importance of helping others through material gifts and non-material support, all in the service of maintaining social ties. Variously framed by my guest family members as "Kupang custom" or "Eastern character," social and moral life in Kupang hinges, in part, on the continual responsibility one has towards intimate others when they are in need and when one is in a position to fulfill their obligation. From this perspective, my access to the bureaucracy was less serendipitous as it was the expected result of having already been invited into an existing network of kin, and enjoying the accompanying caring responsibility displayed towards others within such networks.

The continued interweaving of these two strands of my research, disclosed a different story about corruption and its discontents, from the international-institution narrative regarding monadic individuals who engage in corruption for reasons of self-interest to the detriment of the efficient and effective functioning of government. The story that materialized was one of everyday people in Kupang routinely helping each other out in an economically precarious part of Indonesia while becoming uncertain about the moral status of their acts and afraid of legal repercussions due to an increased scrutiny of corruption. In this account, anti-corruption is not experienced as a guarantor of a good life but as a threat to it—interrupting the caring responsibilities that make life livable in a poor province whose nicknames suggest it is *left behind*, doomed to an uncertain fate, and in need of divine help. The central challenge, therefore, is not how to entice people to adhere to new rules and regulations in order to ensure a narrowly defined prescriptive and universal good, but how to ensure that anti-corruption efforts do not impede possibilities for forging worthwhile lives. The ensuing struggle is to distinguish good relationality from badly responding to expectations of and obligations towards intimate others. To put this differently, it pertains to how to distinguish corruption from care. Making sense of the adverse effects of anti-corruption efforts inspired by the idea of good governance, requires emplacing these efforts and their effects within a perspective that prioritizes the centrality of care.

To that end, let us reframe the projects of good governance and anti-corruption in terms of care, or lack thereof. In order to do this, it is helpful to draw on Elizabeth Povinelli (2011: 160), who writes, "to care is to embody an argument about what a good life is and how such a good life comes into being." Povinelli poses this definition in the context of her long-term investigation into possibilities, under the conditions of what she calls late liberalism, for a social and political *otherwise*. By late liberalism she refers to its crisis of legitimacy as a theory of political governance and self-evident relation to democracy and capitalism. These interconnected questions of care and the good life amidst the crisis of liberalism are relevant for people in Kupang, who increasingly struggle to live with the direct effects of the tension inherent in the project of good governance, where the liberal democratic promise is corroded by its economic liberal assumptions and practices. As we have seen, despite the *good* in the programmatic aims of good governance, its suggestions for the good life are all tied to an economic and political preference for lean governments. In Kupang, this translates to fewer job opportunities, fewer possibilities for socioeconomic ascent, and more policing of caring behavior. Rather than embodying an argument of what a good life is, good governance actively appears to prevent possibilities for a good life from coming into being. Couched in this perspective of care, we see a disconnect between a particular governing ideal that has lost sight of the importance of care, and a set of living practices for cultivating the good life in which care figures prominently.

This friction between larger caring impulses and situated notions of what counts as a good or worthy life, has similarly figured prominently in various ethnographies of biopolitical, humanitarian, and developmental care published over the last decade (e.g., Feldman 2019; Garcia 2010; Gupta 2012; Stevenson 2014; Ticktin 2011; Zigon 2019).[13] What these studies have in common, and shared by the argument put forth in this book, is that large care initiatives are often experienced as *uncaring* by

---

13. For example, Lisa Stevenson (2014) highlights the troubling discrepancy between the Canadian bureaucratic state's concern with biopolitical care around the epidemics of tuberculosis and suicide and its cruel indifference to the particular lives of Inuit in the Canadian Arctic. Angela Garcia (2010) shows the disconnect between the therapeutic impetus of heroin detoxification clinics and the impossibility of alleviating the pain of intergenerational material and cultural dispossession along the Rio Grande in New Mexico. Jarrett Zigon (2019) depicts harm reduction programs all over the world as more akin to clinics for normalization than as providing a community of users who care for one another in an attuned manner. In the realm of humanitarian care, Miriam Ticktin (2011) addresses how in France humanitarian immigration practices carried out in the name of compassion work to reproduce rather than address existing racial and gendered inequalities. In Palestine, Ilana Feldman (2019) describes the inability of humanitarian aid practices equipped to deal with emergencies to meet the challenges of Palestinian refugees experiencing the chronic condition of loss and displacement into camps. Finally, in his work on bureaucratic structures and institutions in India, Akhil Gupta (2012) masterfully dissects how care is not only arbitrary in its consequences but also that this very arbitrariness is produced by the very mechanisms that are supposed to alleviate social suffering.

those subjected to them. Instead of allowing people to feel cared for or about, these initiatives feel indifferent, anonymous, excluding, stigmatizing, isolating, and erratic to those who experience them. What adds to this experience of care's absence is the contrast between the ways in which these larger caring initiatives envision persons—be they patient, addict, asylum seeker, refugee, or civil servant—as individualized and disconnected from their histories, material conditions, and relations with others, and people's actual and experienced entanglements within material and cultural surroundings, intergenerational continuities, historical developments, and particular lifeworlds with the human and the non-human, the living and the dead. To put this differently, the disconnect between a supposedly caring governing impulse and situated conceptions on what constitutes a good life stems in part from a misrecognition of human beings as atomized rather than as relational.

This is a misrecognition that extends to contemporary liberal democratic modes of governance. Here it is rooted in the long-standing liberal distrust of inequality and relatedness, given its ideological valuation of egalitarianism and disinterestedness. However, as Anastasia Piliavsky (2014) points out, all political arrangements imply some form of relational morality, even liberal democratic ones where, paradoxically, a pretense of asociality exists alongside the expectation that voters will cast their votes out of selfless social mindedness. In liberal democratic political conditions, a state's caring promise is that in return for their participation in a system of representative democracy, citizens will be able to attain some version of the good life. However, for many people currently living under such conditions, like those still enduring the far-reaching austerity measures implemented by many European countries in the time of the Great Recession, it seems that the liberal democratic state is increasingly failing in the fulfillment of its caring promise. A recognition of the fundamental relational character of people, as well as modes of governance, is thus a pressing one that extends far beyond the confines of Kupang.

In this book, the idea of care begins with the assumption that humans are essentially relational beings with an inherent capacity for openness to the world, others in it, and the possibilities such openness affords. If we can trace a rational, individualist understanding of personhood back to liberal political philosophy, this relational understanding has its roots in the phenomenological tradition of continental philosophy. I draw, in particular, on the work of Martin Heidegger (2008: 235–244; 349–381). In contrast to a cognition-focused Cartesian view of human beings that places a distance between subjects and the external world of objects that fits so well with the monadic individualist conception of human beings in good governance ideology, Heidegger presents us with an understanding of human beings as inextricably and ecstatically in worlds with others. Human beings' mode of being-in-the-world with others is not characterized by separation, but by a basic and constant "standing out" (*ekstasis*) spatially and temporally towards other beings, things, and events in the present, past, and future. It is this basic human ecstatic relationality that Heidegger refers to as care. We can roughly understand this to mean that care points to people's tendency to orient themselves to, and concern themselves with, their worlds and those in it; projecting themselves into future endeavors while being shaped by past conditions. Care, then, does not in itself convey any kind of sentimentality, value, or good, but simply refers to the "out-standing" and relational way in which human beings exist in their worlds with others. To put it simply, to be human is to be concerned and care for the world and others with which one is inextricably intertwined.

There are ethical implications to understanding care in terms of such human, ecstatic relationality—particularly in light of the failures of anti-corruption efforts. As proposed in the previous section, good governance is but one institutional morality in a larger and much more complex moral assemblage that also includes "custom," "character," older corruption regulations, ideologies of nation-building, religious teachings, along with many other examples of embodied, discursive, and institutional moralities. These assemblages offer people what Webb Keane (2016: 27) calls *ethical affordances*, meaning "any aspect of people's experiences and perceptions that they might draw on in the process of making ethical evaluations and decisions, whether consciously or not." In this study of the contradictory effects of anti-corruption efforts, my main interest lies not in which rules are bypassed, but rather in the question of what people do when ethical demands present themselves. Put another way, given the various affordances offered by the complex moral-ethical assemblic context of everyday life in Kupang, what stokes people's *moral engines* (Mattingly et al. 2018)? What propels them to act in certain ways and not others? As this book sets out to show, an ethics of care and exchange—or an ethics characterized by a caring responsibility that is tied to helping out in material and non-material ways—finds far more resonance along this moral-ethical assemblage than the rule-based prescriptive morality of good governance.

This book roughly covers the period of Adoe's mayoral tenure, a period in Kupang marked by an initial excitement and hope regarding the promise of *reformasi* that then gave way to disappointment and resignation. It looks at how civil servants and others in Indonesia's supposedly most corrupt city unreflexively re-inhabit their lifeworld after a moral breakdown (Zigon 2007) occasioned by these anti-corruption efforts. These attempts cannot be properly understood without taking into account, that one of the most difficult things for many Kupangese in the aftermath of the implementation of anti-corruption efforts, was how to clearly and unambiguously distinguish corruption from care in their everyday practices. Thus, a central component of my aim of considering alternative possibilities for governmental goods beyond the dominant one proposed in good governance programs, is to ethnographically consider the way in which accusations of, complaints about, and attempts to avoid engagements with KKN connect to violations of expectations of care for others. While most of the ethnographic examples I describe here concern small-scale, interpersonal situations—some of which take place within the walls of government offices, others on the front porches of people's homes—the insights we can gain from these are helpful for understanding the larger question of why anti-corruption efforts have not noticeably decreased corruption in Indonesia (and elsewhere), and why good governance initiatives may, in fact, make governments worse.

At the heart of answering such questions lies the recognition that care, as grounded in a foundational human relationality, forms an indissoluble part of any form of a governmental good. Where good governance approaches go wrong is that the understandings of corruption and the anti-corruption measures they put forward in an eagerness for *leanness* and faith in technocratic reforms are disconnected from such questions of care; indeed, they disregard the Heideggerian insight described above: to be human is to be a caring being. Furthermore, its one-size-fits-all, top-down approach fails to account for the complexity of the moral-ethical assemblage of any locality where it arrives. Therefore, in contrast to conceiving of any governmental good a priori, let us dive into this assemblic complexity, and spend some time with actual people and their attempts to navigate the blurry, murky, opaque landscape of post-*reformasi* bureaucracy, and contemplate care and corruption with them in order to think an alternative to the false promise of good governance.

CHAPTER ONE

Kupang, the Giving City

From the Back to the Front

The crown jewel in Kupang's complex of city-level government branches, offices, and institutions is the mayor's office. Its modern and majestic two-storey building is home to several of the city's departments and the offices of hundreds of civil servants. In front of the building is a large open space known as a *lapangan*. In more fertile parts of Indonesia, such an area would be covered in luscious, green grass, but in arid Kupang, there are only paving stones painted green. Twice a week, all the civil servants gather on this site: on Monday mornings for an obligatory communal assembly and on Friday mornings, in their best athleisure wear, for a weekly aerobics session.[1] At its far end, gold metal letters affixed to a concrete base seem to beam out Kupang's city motto to all those gathered there: *Kupang Kota Kasih*, or "Kupang the Giving City."

Indonesians are prone to clever portmanteaus and other forms of word play, so it is not surprising that the *kasih* (giving) part of the motto actually forms an acronym that spells out the city values: work, safety, health, beauty, and harmony. In a city where acts of giving to others is an important responsibility and care is prized in relationships with intimate others, it is not surprising that at first glance the city's motto also

---

1. While attending these events is obligatory, it is not uncommon for civil servants to skip them.

emphasizes giving. But the motto does not refer to the city's citizens as giving but, instead, frames the city itself as giving. Why would that be? What is it that a giving city *gives*?

For the civil servants who gather on the *lapangan* twice a week, what the city gives above all else is employment. Because Kupang has a relatively small private sector, the state is the main source of reliable work and the competition for government jobs is steep. The desirability of a civil service position stems in part from its material rewards. Beyond the salary, there is: a monthly rice allowance based on an employee's family size; health insurance; the possibility of getting a loan at the bank or credit at car and motorcycle dealers; and a guaranteed pension. The association with material benefits leads young men with civil service positions to dress in their civil service uniforms when they go to a girlfriend's parents to ask permission to marry. In other words, the giving city provides the means for making a life.

Along with the material benefits, there is also the matter of social standing. As *Pak* Marinus, an upper-echelon official in the Kupang Department of Public Works pointed out to me during an evening I spent with his family in their comfortable home: "Here in Kupang, your social status is higher if you're a civil servant. Even though you can just manage to make ends meet, this job comes with prestige (*gengsi*). You have more status." Telling me about his childhood growing up as the youngest of a family of eight in the neighborhood of Fontein, which was decidedly lacking in *gengsi*, he made clear to me that the importance of this opportunity for status cannot be overstated. His parents were uneducated and poor. His father made some money by occasionally hauling stones at building sites and by searching for medicinal plants in Timor's interior to sell in Kupang. Family parties were as much part and parcel of life in Kupang then as they are now. His parents, nevertheless, rarely attended such parties as guests but, instead, tended to work in the background—cooking and cleaning in exchange for some money or food.

One night at a neighbor's family party, while arranging some firewood to heat the cooking pots, Marinus's father pulled him aside and gestured towards the guest area, where chairs were precisely lined, facing a little improvised stage on which the MCs and other speakers would give their speeches. He told Marinus that he hoped one day his children would be able to sit there among the other guests. He did not entertain the possibility that his children could make it to the front row, or even up on the stage, for such honorary spots, he presumed, were only for very important civic officials. It would be enough if they could just sit in *the front*, for this would mean his children would no longer be involved with the labor in the back, such as getting water from the well and doing dishes. Instead, they would be *respected guests*. Currently a high-ranking civil service official and a beloved MC who often finds himself not just among the invited guests and sitting in the front but standing up on the stage, Marinus often recalls his father's words. His move from a family in the back and behind the scenes to a prominent person at the center of social life, was entirely facilitated by his employment as a civil servant of the giving city. The giving city, then, not only provides the financial means to make a life, it opens the possibility for a socially meaningful life.

Comparable stories abound in Kupang. For instance, a middle-aged lower-level civil servant recalled the awe he felt as an eight-year-old boy, shoeless in dirty clothes, when a government official visited his little village on the island of Rote. It was his first encounter with someone from the government and he was struck by the man's appearance: washed face, coiffed hair, shiny shoes, and well-pressed uniform on which no stain or tear could be detected. "This," he thought, "really *was somebody*." Similarly, while reminiscing about his childhood growing up in Kupang, Cornelis Lay, a professor at the prestigious Gadjah Mada University in Yogyakarta, Java, also underscores the transformative power of a civil service job. As he describes it, a common response people have whenever someone manages to obtain an elusive civil service position is to exclaim: *Su jadi orang nah!* (Now he's really become someone!) (Lay and Van Klinken 2014: 168). Further east in Biak, Papua, civil servants also form an important prototype for a valued category of personhood—they are not "just anyone" (Rutherford 2003: 45).

These examples of what Michel Trouillot (2001) calls "state encounters" suggest that the giving city offers people not only the means for earning a livelihood but more importantly the means for pursuing a good life that is locally worthy. It bestows upon those lucky enough to become civil servants the possibility of achieving a particular form of valuable personhood—of really becoming *someone*; the kind of person who can take up the responsibilities of care that are expected of accomplished adults in Kupang. From the perspective of people living in the giving city, then, the good governance preference for lean states means limiting the opportunities for people to take on those caring responsibilities and the vaulted status of personhood otherwise unavailable. How can such limitations be considered a good thing? Conversely, how can attempts to expand access to the giving city's resources ever be constructed as something corrupt?

This chapter pursues the question of how to understand the unanticipated effects of anti-corruption efforts within the logic of the giving city. Responding to recent calls in anthropology to attend to the disaggregation of the state (Gupta 2012), I here demonstrate that the effects of anti-corruption campaigns are a lot less surprising if we recognize the state in Kupang to mean a giving city than if we assume a state's coherence, unity, or singular intention. Singling out what is often assumed to be a mere part of the state that usually gets subsumed under the wider encompassing category of the nation-state—that is, the city—as that which constitutes the very meaning of the state in Kupang, might seem somewhat counterintuitive. Of course, as Akhil Gupta (2012: 70) reminds us, those "presumptions regarding the ontological sameness of states motivate many cross-cultural comparisons of states."[2] Indeed, it is such presumptions of a cross-cultural sameness that make possible comparisons between them regarding, for example, their levels of corruption listed in the *Corruption Perceptions Index*, and from which general and generalizable ideas of good governance can take form. Yet, these presumptions of sameness are the product of studies of the state that are always partial, fragmented, and often focused on particular branches, institutions, or representatives of the state (2012: 54). This partiality, then, hardly justifies generalizations to universality or reifications of the ontological status of states. In the case of civil service corruption in an age of good governance, such presumptions impede any understandings of how anti-corruption efforts fail to curb corruption and even facilitate the emergence of new forms of it.

The idea of a giving city has much more resonance in Kupang than conceptions of the state rooted in ideas of coherence and vertical encompassment. Taking a historical view, we see that Kupang belongs to a wider network of suzerainty and sovereignty, which in pre- and post-independence Indonesia has always been contingent, based not on loyalty or nationalist sentiment but on strategies of gift exchange and state

---

2. This agreement centers around assumptions that states are social imaginaries that operate within a bounded national territory (Gupta 2012: 61); have a monopoly on the legitimate use of force (Weber 1946); possess the primary claim to authority and legitimacy over and against other social institutions (Corrigan and Sayer 1985: 7); and employ a notion of scale that ensures the vertical encompassment of hierarchical levels into a coherent whole (Ferguson and Gupta 2002a). They are "unitary organization(s) acting with singular intention" (Gupta 2012: 46).

expansion. The ethnographic examples then show that Kupang does not sit within the nested hierarchy of a vertically encompassed state (Ferguson and Gupta 2002a). Instead it is one node in what I call, drawing on Rupert Stasch's (2009) work on the central role of alterity in social relations, a wider *state-of-otherness*—a conception of the state in which belonging is always tinged with suspicion, and where closeness and distance are created, maintained, or kept at bay through a logic of care and exchange.

Consequently, in a giving city, visions of a governmental good differ from those of a neoliberal state. What comes to count as corruption from the perspective of the neoliberal state can be viewed as care from the perspective of the giving city. If we want to understand the ethical and practical confusion around the effects of anti-corruption in civil service in Kupang and begin to imagine an alternative governmental good, we need to grasp the tension between the ethos of good governance and the actual giving city with its ethos of care and exchange. This tension can be seen by looking at two cases of civil servants being hired illegally and asking: what comes to count as corruption when the giving city comes up the against neoliberal state?

Kupang, a Gifted City

Kupang, located on the southwestern edge of the arid island of Timor, serves as the capital and sole urban district (*kota*) of the East Nusa Tenggara province, where the overall opportunities for employment are scarce and where most of the population relies on subsistence agriculture in a region that has one of the lowest average rainfalls in Indonesia. Thus the "hungry season," or *musim lapar* (McWilliam 2002: 39), is a regular occurrence, leaving people from all over the province and beyond to migrate to Kupang in search of educational and professional advancement.[3] The overwhelming presence of the state contributes to its attraction, and indeed, its reputation as a giving city is closely tied to it being a site for the redistribution of state resources.

---

3. West Timor is part of the Indonesian province of East Nusa Tenggara. The eastern part of Timor, along with the small exclave of Oecusse in northern West Timor, form the sovereign state of East Timor (*Timor Leste*), which gained independence from Indonesia following a referendum supervised by the United Nations and its bloody aftermath.

Until 2010, Kupang formed the administrative center of three distinct levels of government: the municipality (*kota*) of Kupang, the regency of Kupang, and the East Nusa Tenggara province.[4] Given the presence of these three levels of administration in one city, the state apparatus is the largest provider of direct, indirect, formal, and informal employment (Tidey 2012).[5] The state also dominates the urban landscape as the most eye-catching structures are government buildings and the smaller government offices are found among the houses and shops throughout the city's sprawling neighborhoods. Even when not in the direct vicinity of a government building of some sort, the state leaves its imprint. Office vehicles, for example, are used by civil servants for purposes other than work. You will find their red-numbered plates on cars and mopeds parked in front of Kupang's sole night club on a Saturday night, by the beach at Tablolong, south of Kupang, on a Sunday afternoon, or parked overnight outside a government official's home. In other words, as we saw with the role the civil service uniform might play in a proposal of marriage, the material and visual representations of the state are woven into even the most intimate parts of everyday life in Kupang.

In spite of this, we should refrain from viewing such visible and material representations as the successful construction of what Philip Abrams (1988) calls the mask of the state, or of an achieved vertical encompassment into the larger Indonesian nation-state (Ferguson and Gupta 2002). From within the logic of the giving city, instead of the vertical imposition of the state, we see how the state is expanding and contracting along ever-changing webs of sovereignty and suzerainty. Rather than an image or mask of state coherence and unity there is an uncertain and fragile condition maintained through longstanding logics and practices of gift exchange. From the perspective of the *longue durée*, good governance forms only its latest iteration.

---

4. Indonesia is divided administratively into four levels. *Propinsi* (provinces) form the first-order administrative level, *kabupaten* (regencies) and *kota* (municipalities) the second-order administrative level, *kecamatan* (districts) make up the third-order administrative level, and *desa* (villages) and *kelurahan* (urban communities) make up the fourth-order administrative level. Provinces, regencies, and municipalities have their own local governments and parliaments.

5. In 2010, the *kabupaten* (regency) of Kupang moved its administrative center and departments to the town of Oelamasi, approximately thirty-five kilometers outside of Kupang.

Colonial Occupation

The Republic of Indonesia's boundaries were largely set during the time of Dutch colonial occupation. Within its current borders, there are over seventeen thousand islands and hundreds of ethnic and linguistic groups (Ricklefs 2008). Achieving a sense of unity amidst this diversity, to echo Indonesia's national motto of "Unity in Diversity" (*Bhinneka Tungal Ika*), is no small feat. While some Indonesian historians point to the former great empires of Majapahit and Mataram in order to claim precolonial historical precedents for Indonesia's national unity—suggesting that West Timor and other eastern Indonesian islands functioned as vassal states to these empires—historical evidence offers little to suggest they were ever anything more than trade partners to these early states (Farram 2010: 4).

The rise of Hinduism, Buddhism, and subsequently Islam that so influenced political organization in Java did not have any significant impact on Timor, which contained, instead, a dynamic and shifting political system that consisted of a religious center with four territories around it. There, and in the other islands that currently make up East Nusa Tenggara, political systems were not characterized by long-lasting stability, but by shifting and changing alliances that were made and re-made through intermarriage, internal warfare, and headhunting internal warfare, and headhunting (Cunningham 1962; Ormeling 1956; Nordholt 1971). This does not mean that Timor and the other islands that now make up the province of East Nusa Tenggara were not in contact with other parts of the archipelago, Asia, and the wider world beyond. The abundance of high-quality sandalwood had indeed attracted traders from at least the thirteenth century onwards. In this way, Timor was shaped as a hub in trade networks that extended far beyond the Indonesian archipelago.

The sandalwood trade that connected Timor to faraway lands also attracted Europeans to the region, and their arrival would ultimately pose the biggest change to existing Timorese political systems. After their conquest of the Malay city of Malacca in 1511, the Portuguese were the first to establish a permanent settlement in the Lesser Sunda Islands by building a fortress on the island of Solor, north of Timor, in 1561 (Farram 2010: 35). The Dutch East India Company (VOC), embarked on a series of assaults on this stronghold from 1613 until 1646, when they finally occupied the fortress. In 1653, the Dutch shifted their stronghold and the hub of their activities from the Lesser Sunda regions to Kupang, naming their new castle Fort Concordia (Boxer 1947: 1–5). This move took place in accordance with an agreement the Dutch had made earlier with the Helon ruler of the Kupang area to establish a presence in Kupang Bay and participate in the sandalwood trade (Nordholt 1971: 167). Remnants of Fort Concordia still overlook Kupang Bay; the surrounding area now a military base. Throughout the seventeenth and eighteenth centuries, the Dutch continued to compete with the Portuguese and the Topasses—a Eurasian population loosely allied with the Portuguese—for control of the sandalwood trade and, thereby, territorial control of Timor. By the end of the eighteenth century, the island was divided into three: the Dutch controlling the western part, the Topasses the center, and the Portuguese the eastern part (Farram 2010: 37).

Until the late nineteenth century, however, the presence of the Europeans in Timor did not radically interfere with the existing dynamics of political (and religious) systems. The Dutch scholar Jacob van Leur (1967) suggests that European entities in Southeast Asia were at best on equal footing with indigenous ones and mostly had to adapt to existing systems of power. Many Topasses married the daughters of local rulers to forge alliances, whereas the Dutch and Portuguese relied on contracts and agreements. For the Timorese, the alliances with European newcomers offered opportunities for advancement in ongoing intra-island rivalries. The Dutch only exercised authority in their stronghold in Kupang and its immediate surroundings, and they populated this area with clusters of loyal immigrants from the nearby islands of Rote and, to a lesser extent, Savu. They engaged in military action with the help of Rotenese troops only when provoked by the Portuguese, Topasses, or rebellious Timorese, but otherwise made no attempts at territorial control of Timor outside of Kupang and had no significant presence there. This started to change when, between 1893 and 1916, the Dutch and the Portuguese set out to end hundreds of years of disputes and enmity by establishing a border between the western and eastern parts of the island (Farram 2010: 52). While this boundary issue played out, however, sentiments in the Netherlands regarding how to rule the colonies were in flux, mirroring a general new imperialist trend among colonial powers at the time. The period of Dutch rule in Timor that can be best described as a "policy of non-interference," or abstention, had effectively come to a close by the end of the nineteenth century (2010: 62).

The early twentieth century saw the rise of Dutch pacification campaigns that attempted to establish Dutch suzerainty throughout the entire Indonesian archipelago.[6] In order to accomplish this, they employed military interventions and short contracts between the Dutch and indigenous rulers. In western Timor, ongoing warring and head-hunting between indigenous states, and not infrequent rebellion against the Dutch, spurred a series of Dutch military campaigns to bring about the "peace and order." Additionally, the Dutch drastically reduced the number of kingdoms there, seeking to create a legible system of indirect or native rule consisting of kings (*raja*), administrators, and village heads who could act as an effective intermediary between the Dutch administration and native population (Farram 2010: 104).[7] This Dutch attempt to create a stable, legible, and effective layer of indirect rule did not fit well with the far more fluid reality of Timorese politics and, in fact, helped exacerbate the existing intra-island battles for political power. For example, the internal strife and competition impeded the authority some *raja* had over their new subordinates while various rulers fought over who would fill a particular *raja* position. Finally, the Dutch indirect system of rule failed to take into account the fact that those rulers with authority over the greatest number of territories, the ritual lords, had no executive power, whereas secular lords with executive power exerted their influence over a smaller territory (2010: 104–106). In short, these attempts to implement political change did not succeed in upending existing power relations or unambiguously establishing Dutch suzerainty.

In a similar vein, the moral component that accompanied the intensification of Dutch control in the early twentieth century—named the Ethical Policy—also ended up undermining Dutch colonial rule. Claiming that their reinvigorated interest in imperialist expansion was at least partly motivated by a "moral duty" to repay a "debt of honor" to the Indonesian people for the enormous wealth the Netherlands had extracted from Indonesia, the Dutch professed concerns for the welfare

---

6. Besides formalizing their authority, the Dutch also sought to implement taxation, expand their administration, and construct roads and other infrastructure with the help of corvée labor.

7. For example, the small states surrounding Kupang, which had formed part of the Helon kingdom at the time of the Dutch arrival in the seventeenth century but had long since been overtaken by other rulers, united into the kingdom of Kupang. Nicolaas Isoe Nisnoni, a descendant of the notorious Sonbai kingdom, who the Dutch considered to be loyal and who was well-respected among Timorese kings, became the first *Raja* Kupang (see Farram 2010: 104–105).

of the Indonesian population (Ricklefs 2008: 183–184). Consequently, Timor saw the construction of roads, a telephone network, and airfields (Farram 2010). The Catholic Church and Protestant churches, whose presence had been stable but minimal since the arrival of the Dutch and the Portuguese in the area, also expanded steadily and a network of native schools emerged.

This rise of educational levels throughout the archipelago generated the first stirrings of nationalism. In Kupang, Malay-language newspapers with nationalist inclinations appeared in the 1920s. Around the same time, various political organizations modeled on those established in Java began to coalesce around a range of nationalist ideas.[8] Although the nationalist aspirations differed by group and the combined membership of these groups was but a fraction of the population of Kupang, Timor, and NTT, it is fair to say that the Dutch efforts at establishing suzerainty was not unequivocally successful. While the Dutch had hoped these efforts would increase Indonesians' support for their colonial suzerains, they, in fact, facilitated possibilities for nationalist imaginings outside Dutch colonial rule. Their attempts to foster a sense of belonging to the colonial state instead fueled fantasies of freedom.

When the Japanese easily defeated the Dutch during the Second World War and occupied the archipelago, they further destabilized

---

8. But, as Farram (2010: 109–127) notes, these groups differed in their ideologies and alliances. For example, the *Timorsch Verbond* (Timorese Alliance) aimed to expose Dutch misdeeds and injustices and its members ranged from moderate to more revolutionary. They sang *Indonesia Raya* at meetings, and allied themselves with the *Permoefakatan Perhimpoenan–perhimpoenan Politik Kebangsaan Indonesia* (PPPKI; Consensus of the Indonesian People's Political Associations), the union of nationalist groups under Sukarno, who would become Indonesia's first president. The more moderate members of the *Timorsch Verbond* went on to found *Perserikatan Timor* (Timor Union), a moderate group that expressed loyalty to the Dutch, although some of its members at times expressed a desire for independence. *Sarekat Rajat* (People's League) was a more radical and supposedly communist group with links to the national *Partai Komunis Indonesia* (PKI; Communist Party Indonesia), even though most of its members were hazy on what communism actually meant. The more youthful *Perserikatan Kebangsaan Timor* (Union of the Timorese People) was established in 1937 and it supported the demands made by *Gabungan Politik Indonesia* (GAPI; Indonesian Political Federation), a union of nationalist organizations, for increased equality between the Netherlands and Indonesia.

established authority and helped foster new nationalist dreams.[9] However, not everyone imagined a unified Indonesia stretching from Serang in the very west to Merauke in the very east that freedom fighters in Java and Sumatra were envisioning. Japan, while offering lofty promises of independence to nationalists in Java and Sumatra in order to secure their co-operation, planned on the resource-rich eastern Indonesia to remain a colony (Farram 2010: 143–188).

The Dutch, who returned after the end of the war in 1945 to attempt to reestablish their control of Indonesia, an endeavor they finally abandoned in 1949, similarly saw little reason for a unitary state. Hoping to counter the advance of the decidedly anti-Dutch Indonesian Republic that was founded in Java and Sumatra in 1949, they supported the establishment of an Indonesian Federation. In 1946, Timor, along with other parts of eastern Indonesia that the Dutch presumed to be loyal, formed the State of Eastern Indonesia (*Negara Indonesia Timur*, or NIT). While some factions in Timor scoffed at the idea of continuing relationships with the Dutch, giving NIT the nickname *Negara Ikut Tuan* (the state that follows its master), others feared Javanese domination and an Islamic takeover if Timor or the NIT were to join with the republic (Farram 2010: 192–243). A general suspicion of perceived Javanese influence and Muslim dominance continues to be a source of worry and complaint even today.[10] After the Dutch agreed to Indonesian sovereignty in 1949, and the various states that made up the federation merged into the Republic of Indonesia, NIT, fearing the prospects of becoming second-class citizens in a Javanese dominant and overwhelmingly Muslim state, was one of the last states to follow. The newly formed republic thus contained, from its inception, some fundamental internal divisions that belied its proudly proclaimed national motto: Unity in Diversity.

Postcolonial Kupang

These fears of marginalization did not disappear after unification, and attempts to allay them set a precedent for how the relationship between Kupang and the national government in Jakarta would function in the

---

9. They did so in part because they employed local nationalists and *rajas* in their ranks (see Fox 1977; Van Klinken 2014: 111–118).
10. As exemplified by the conviction of Basuki Tjahaja Purnama (better known as Ahok), the Christian former governor of Jakarta, on blasphemy charges in 2017.

following decades. During the 1950s, after the initial euphoria over independence had mostly dissipated, regional dissatisfaction with the central government started to grow. The discontent centered on corruption, a failure of Javanese management, president Sukarno's increasing support for the Communist Party of Indonesia (PKI), and suspicions of a budgetary favoring of Java at the expense of other regions. It fueled regional revolts and calls for increased autonomy in Aceh, other parts of Sumatra, Ambon, and Sulawesi.

One such revolt was the Permesta rebellion that originated in the eastern Indonesian city of Makassar in 1957 and whose proponents demanded increased autonomy for all of eastern Indonesia. The revolt spread to Kupang, where people had been growing increasingly frustrated with, among other things, the influx of Javanese former freedom fighters who received coveted positions in local civil service as payment in return and the central government's lax delivery of much needed services (Farram 2010: 260–263). The central government's response to such uprisings was to grant more regional autonomy and local control over state resources. In 1958, the province of Sunda Ketjil, consisting of some of the former NIT islands, became three separate provinces: Bali, West Nusa Tenggara, and East Nusa Tenggara.

The increased autonomy created a surge in civil service positions. After independence in the 1950s, the number of civil service positions was three times the number of the 1930s (Van Klinken 2014: 36). After the creation of East Nusa Tenggara, the number of provincial civil servants again tripled—from 438 in 1956 to approximately 1500 in 1958. Most of these were stationed in Kupang (2014: 135). As Gerry van Klinken has put it, the payoff for quashing regional rebellion was to turn the bureaucracy into a "massive job creation scheme" (2014: 37). In lieu of infrastructural developments or other projects aimed at improving the welfare of regional populations, the expansion of civil service functioned as a kind of "gift of primitive accumulation" under the ideological mantel of "state socialism" (2014: 10). In other words, we can see that what holds the Indonesian nation-state together is an emerging practice of exchange.

When Suharto replaced Sukarno (1967) as president by playing on anti-communist sentiments, the civil service initially shrank due to the purging of suspected affiliates of the Indonesian Communist Party. With the echoes of regional revolts still reverberating, however, Suharto's New Order regime was mostly preoccupied with the maintenance of political stability (Van Klinken 2014: 35–38). This meant that it kept personal taxation low and continued to send cash to the regions and expand the civil service, an endeavor greatly aided by the 1974 oil boom.[11] In 1978, for example, the central state gifted Kupang its official status as an "administrative city" (*Kota Administrasi*), which again occasioned further expansion of its civil service (Kota Kupang, 2021). Besides limiting the potential for regional rebellion, this expansion of jobs also helped secure the political loyalty of Indonesia's sizeable civil service corps.

Fears of insurrection as well as rewarding loyalty motivated the central government's decisions on regional budget allocation, an arrangement Hans Antlöv (2003: 143) characterizes as a "massive patronage system." The result: "loyalty was rewarded and predation on those outside its embrace was tolerated if not encouraged" (Bourchier 2015: 242). In other words, even with the New Order, the relationship between Kupang and the nation-state was still maintained by a political logic of exchange, in which money and employment were used to assure loyalty and inclusion into a less than stable nation-state. The giving city bestowed its gifts of employment, *gengsi* (prestige), and personhood, because of its relational entanglement with a giving state.

Reformasi-era Kupang

It is perhaps not surprising that the administrative changes implemented in the post-Suharto *reformasi* era, although heavily shaped by the conditions that came with IMF aid, do not seem to have altered the practices of exchange significantly. Just as post-independence Indonesia saw an increase in regional autonomy, so too did it see a *pemekaran* (blossoming) of newly autonomous regions. After 1998, the number of provinces rose from 26 to 33 (now 34), while the number of autonomous regencies and cities grew from 300 to 440 in 2005. Although the idea of *pemekaran* fits with the decentralizing mission of good governance, the subsequent expansion of the state apparatus and civil service seems to contradict

---

11. In 1979–1980, 89% of NTT's provincial budget consisted of transfers from the central government (Barlow, Bellis, and Andrews 1991: 262–263; cited in Van Klinken 2007: 275). Between 1975 and 1986, the government's share in NTT's RGDP doubled from 10.1% to 19.5%, overtaking trade. Agriculture's portion of the RGDP, meanwhile, had shrunk from 71% in 1970 to 53.9% in 1986. Meanwhile, between 1979–1980 civil servants received anywhere between 68% and 86% of the government budget (Barlow, Bellis, and Andrews 1991: 243; Van Klinken 2014: 138).

the dictates of an *efficient* and *lean* state so prized in good governance ideology. However, once again, we might view this expansion as a way to alleviate the threat of revolt. While Indonesia's post-independence period occasioned the *Permesta* rebellion, the post-*reformasi* era saw its own eruption of regional revolts (Van Klinken 2005; 2007). As before, granting more autonomy and increasing civil service proved to be an effective way of preventing secession and the spread of regional discontent.

While this logic of exchange might have long proven effective in preventing and soothing the regional rebellions that damaged the imagined unity of the nation-state, it does not unequivocally ensure a seamless (vertical) encompassment into that imagined unity. The introduction of a modern state-system from the early twentieth century did not so much culturally construct a state over and against a notion of society, as it continuously secured the fragile and uncertain integration of places such as Kupang into the fabric of the nation-state through repeated gifts—in the form of that expanding state apparatus and civil service. Concomitantly, this offered opportunities for social ascendancy to those who were "lowly born," thereby slowly erasing the privileged position the aristocracy had long held (Van Klinken 2014: 70).

Worth emphasizing here, is how the gift of locally worthy personhood is made possible by the city's integration into a larger state, works as gift-giving. The giving city can give because of the gifts it is given by the national government. While this logic of gift exchange as a means of tying different spatial nodes and hierarchical levels of government together has been analyzed quite productively through the lenses of neopatrimonialism and clientelism in the context of post-*reformasi* Indonesia (Berenschot and Aspinall 2019; Simandjuntak 2012), we should refrain from using terms that suggest an aberration from the ideal-typical visions of what states ought to look like. Rather, keeping in mind both Gupta's (2012) admonishment to treat the ontological sameness of states as a question rather than an established fact, and Danilyn Rutherford's call to allow for "alternative paths to modernity" (2003: 231), we can begin to see a kind of state in which gift exchange plays an important part of its ontological groundings.

Kupang and Timor's history of warring clans, trade relationships, strategic marriage alliances, ever-shifting and dynamic political partnerships, and post-independence state socialism show the managing of closeness and distance across a social field characterized by a fundamental alterity—an alterity that can be bridged through an active and continuous flow of gifts. Here we see that reflection of Rupert Stasch's

(2009) understanding that for the Korowai of West Papua *otherness* is central to social organization (in contrast to the idea that social bonds are the product of people's similarities or shared experiences). If our focus is otherness rather than unity, therefore, we see a state organization in Kupang based on the centrality of gift exchange and the place of the giving city within a wider political *state-of-otherness* that makes possible various relationalities of distancing and closeness.

Distancing and Closeness in a State-of-Otherness

The giving city of Kupang is the product of hundreds of years of accumulated relationalities of distance and closeness practiced through a logic of gift exchange. Successive cycles of state expansion have managed to both position Kupang within the larger constellation of the Indonesian nation-state and establish its reputation as a giving city that can bestow its gifts of employment and valuable personhood upon the citizens. However, the historical vicissitudes of the uneasy relationship between Kupang and the Indonesian nation-state continue, characterized by deep-seated feelings of mutual distrust and suspicion. In such a context, the regular state expansion and promise of an increase in civil service positions and other state resources offer the bare minimum of a conveyance of care necessary to secure a sense of national stability, while directly contradicting the neoliberal good governance preference for lean states.

Parading Personhood

As an example of the distance, otherness, and distrust that characterizes the relationship between Kupangese and the nation-state, let us first turn to the civil servants and their eager participation in events meant to celebrate national belonging. Recall that civil servants in Kupang are quite eager to inhabit the state uniform and then some are reluctant to take off their uniforms after work. Many eagerly don their national Civil Service Corps (KORPI) uniforms on the seventeenth of every month in commemoration of Indonesia's independence on August 17, 1945. While such representations and other performances of statehood can form important modalities through which states are culturally constructed (Sharma and Gupta 2006: 18–21), this is not necessarily what happens in Kupang. Rather than strengthening an image of the state as whole, coherent, separate from society, or contributing to the verticality and encompassment that lends states their superior authority and legitimacy, participation in performances of statehood and nationalism in Kupang works to encourage distancing between Kupang and Jakarta and strengthens the image of the giving city as a maker of valuable personhood.

To illustrate this, consider the civil servants working in the mayor's office during the week leading up to the massive parade the city organized to celebrate Kupang's fortieth anniversary as an administrative city in March, 2008. Kupang does not offer its citizens much in the way of excitement, so the few annual parades and the yearly city fair that takes place every August are highly anticipated events. For the city's anniversary celebration, all city-level departments participate. The parade is routed along Kupang's main thoroughfares and stretches from late morning to midafternoon. Although not every civil servant is obliged to join in, most in the mayor's office plan to do so. Some people work to design banners that display the name of their department. Others discuss the hair and make-up appointments they have made in preparation of the event. Those in the parade have to walk several miles while fully exposed to the sun, but this does not elicit complaints from the very people who normally grumble about having to stand out in the bright day in uncomfortable shoes during weekly assemblies, or walk the fifty yards from the office to the nearest food stand for some fried rice or instant coffee. Unlike assemblies, weekly aerobics sessions, and other tedious communal civil service activities, the parade is something everyone looks forward to.

On the day itself, I stand on the side of *Jalan Sudirman*, Kupang's main shopping street, with members of my guest family and neighborhood friends. The onlookers who line the streets are many rows deep. The vendors selling snacks, drinks, and toys are doing good business. I see department after department walk past. Civil servants, all well-coiffed, well-shod, and wearing big smiles, hold up their banners and wave as the people of the crowd look for familiar faces in the parade. This parade celebrating Kupang's status as an administrative city within the larger Indonesian nation-state was in many ways a performance of statehood and seeming celebration of national belonging. Its banners, uniforms, and little red and white Indonesian flags all form cultural representations of the state. In other contexts, such displays of state performance help conjure the mask of the state (Abrams 1988; Nugent 1994). In Turkey, for example, enthusiastic participation in similar state performances strengthen nationalist sentiments among participants and onlookers, even though this is not the immediate purpose of such performances (Navarro-Yashin 2002).[12] In Kupang, by contrast, because state formation was never fully achieved, participation in performances of state and nationalism actually work to produce distance in a state-of-otherness.

Danilyn Rutherford's (2003) ethnography of the Biak in the easternmost province of West Papua, an area historically even more tenuously incorporated into the Indonesian nation-state than Kupang, offers an illuminating comparison. The central problem Rutherford interprets concerns the Biak's abrupt switching of nationalist sentiments to Papua in the 1990s, after what appeared to be their solid integration into the Indonesian nation-state. Throughout most of the New Order rule, the island of Biak—like the city of Kupang—displayed an enthusiastic participation in the state's representational and discursive practices, projects and programs, such as diligently attending schools and universities, taking up employment in government institutions, being fluent in both the Indonesian language and its rhetoric of rule, and joining in the regime's projects and programs. Yet, despite this enthusiastic participation, such affect failed to take hold among the Biak and had, in fact, seriously frayed by the end of the New Order regime.

In order to understand this failure of hegemony among people who did not openly defy or attempt to subvert the regime but, in contrast, wholeheartedly participated in it, Rutherford stresses the particular fetishistic fascination Biak's have had historically and culturally with the "foreign" (*amber*). The foreign provides valuable goods and prestige to

---

12. To be sure, enthusiastic participation in nationalistic performances do not always strengthen the state image. While addressing the Peruvian government's response to a popular underground party in the 1950s, David Nugent (2018) stresses how in times of crisis, participation can actually serve to fuel suspicions of revolutionary inclinations. Furthermore, Alexei Yurchak (2006) described how in late-Soviet Russia, participation in the general form of authoritative discourse enabled a "performative shift" in which speech and discourse tended to slide away from constative meanings. However, these two authors address breakdowns and failures in state coherence and state formation in contexts where state formation seems to have been successful at some point—as Navarro-Yashin (2002) shows it still is in Turkey—and where performances of state were successful in producing the mask of the state. In Kupang, as suggested above, there is the possibility that state formation was never unambiguously achieved.

those with access. Both value and prestige can be bestowed upon others through intimate exchange and in turn become locally recognizable and exchangeable. Important to note is that accessing the foreign does not mean fully identifying with the perspectives of outsiders, but rather, to wear "foreign potency on [one's] skin" (Rutherford 2003: 17). Indonesians from other islands, American tourists, representative of the United Nations would all be grouped as *amber*. It is in the context of this fetishistic fascination with the foreign that Rutherford understands Biak's anti-national understandings of space, time, and self despite apparent signs of submission to national authority. Instead of radically rupturing understandings of subjectivity and relationality, these processes, practices, and materialities of nation-building became yet another potential source of *amber*. Apparent performances of national belonging, then, do not strengthen nationalist sentiments but imbue people with an elevated status.

These are important insights to keep in mind when considering Kupang's anniversary parade. The banners proclaiming department names, the uniforms, and the Indonesian flags all conjure the image of the state, but along with something else, something more important. This something else was conveyed in the shined shoes of those participating, the salon-styled hair, the elegant high heels, and the freshly applied lipstick. It was communicated by the smiles flashed to onlookers and the excited waves exchanged between the parade participants in the street and the audience on the sidewalks. It was expressed in the sigh my teenage guest brother, Yongki, let out when looking at the parade he said that he wanted to become a policeman. This *something else* that was culturally constructed in this performance of statehood was not so much the state but a locally valued personhood. In other words, the onlookers who had gathered to watch the parade that day did not see the Indonesian nation-state. They saw individuals who had really become *somebody*. The performativity in Kupang's parade did not so much produce a mask of the state as it indexed the nation-state as an elevated *amber* source of value that gives people personal prestige or *gengsi*. In this way, Kupang does not become more integrated into the nation-state but, rather, takes its distance from it.

Fragmented Field Administration

The continued presence of vertical structures of government within the supposed horizontalization of administration effected by decentralization serves as another example of this play of distancing and closeness between Kupang and the nation-state. Post-*reformasi* decentralization efforts have indeed transformed the old hierarchical structure of subordination—cities and regencies answered to provinces, provinces answered to the central government—into self-governing administrative regions with elected district heads and members of parliament. Cities, regencies, and provinces thus have a certain degree of autonomy in budgetary and governing matters. However, there are deconcentrated, "vertical agencies" under the direct control of the central government: responsible only to the central government, receiving their budgets from the central government, recruiting only from the central government's labor pool, and following the central government's policies. The coexistence of vertical government agencies under the central government's jurisdiction and decentralized, horizontal government agencies is aptly called "fragmented field administration."

While vertical agencies were ostensibly justified by the need to deliver certain specialized services, one city-level department head nevertheless considered their presence in Kupang to be the continuation of a supposedly passé *sentralisme*. The governor of the East Nusa Tenggara (NTT) once complained in a newspaper article about national officials being unwilling to coordinate their programs with regional administrations:

> If one is stationed in this area, one has to coordinate with the regional government whenever there are development activities. The provincial government of NTT forms an extension of the central government in the region, so every vertical official is obliged to coordinate with the regional government. If one does not wish to coordinate, one should not be stationed in NTT (Kupang News, 2011).

The uneasy coexistence of vertical and horizontal government structures contributes little to imagining a coherent and unified state. Instead, it exacerbates long-standing mutual antagonisms between Kupang and "Jakarta," which is no neutral metonym for the state, but used to signal the idea of national-level power wielded against unvalued places like Kupang. Rather than producing a smooth-running state apparatus in which a specialized vertical structure of governance offers expertise and professionalism to complement the complex everyday business of regional governance, the co-existence of vertical and horizontal governing structures only reinforces a sense that regional governments and officials remain inferior in status and power to their slightly elevated federal counterparts.

For their part, vertical officials see very little reason for cooperating with their regional counterparts. I saw this firsthand when trying to find budgetary information on Kupang by visiting the local office of the Ministry of Finance. The department head's carpeted office was outfitted with a sizeable executive desk, luxurious couches, and even an aquarium. He told me how vertical agencies differed from the local government offices, civil servants, and bureaucratic practices of Kupang. Vertical civil servants, he explained, were far more professional than those employed in regional administrations. Their salaries are higher but they work much longer hours than non-vertical civil servants, who, he assumed I had noticed, have a tendency of showing up late for work and leaving early. Vertical civil servants are transferred to new areas every few years to prevent rustiness and to keep them, he assured me, from getting entangled in, or used for, what he called the "unsavory dealings" that were said to be the norm in places such as Kupang: namely, nepotism, bribery, and laziness.

The head himself was from Jakarta, he explained, and he had previously been posted in Java and in Bali. He wistfully recalled his times there:

> In Bali or Java, when executing a construction project, you know that all the money will be spent on building the building. The money is put to good use. Here, however, by the time the money is spent the building is not yet completed or of poor quality. Somehow, along the way, people "eat the cement, eat the asphalt, eat the papers" (*makan semen, makan aspal, makan kertas*). It's unprofessional! *That* kind of stuff does not happen here, in a vertical institution.

Corruption in the construction sector is by no means unique to Kupang, as we will see in greater detail in chapter five, nor are the other ills mentioned by the national official. From someone who professed to be very unhappy with being stationed in what he considered to be a humiliating backwater, the tropes of corruption, unprofessionalism, and laziness were used to distinguish the professionally and ethically inferior regional administration from the superiority of the vertical agencies. Whereas the production and embodiment of differentiation between the higher reaches and lower levels of bureaucracy is one means by which states can produce the effect of vertical encompassment of the "local" (Ferguson and Gupta 2002a: 987–988), in this case it we see the opposite effect of distancing Kupang.

Construction Projects: Keeping it Local

This distancing effect is mutually produced. Kupangese officials and contractors active in the city-level construction sector so reviled by the Ministry of Finance, also prefer to conduct their business within the confines of the giving city. Most construction companies in Kupang are classified as small and are not equipped to take on larger-scale projects. A Public Works official explained to me how the department and local contractors nevertheless find ways to keep bigger projects in-house:

> Not many local companies have the manpower, machinery, or skills to handle large projects, therefore there is a risk that the large-scale and expensive projects get snatched away by big contractors from outside (*luar*), for instance Java. Public Works committees and local contractors have a mutual understanding of how to engage in business. They know one another, are familiar with each other's backgrounds, families, experiences in the field. Most importantly, they know how their bribing system (*suap-menyuap*) works. It is less clear how to socialize with (*bergaulan*) outside contractors, who are unaware of the construction customs in Kupang. So sometimes it's easier, and definitely more profitable, to cut up a large tender project into smaller pieces so our smaller companies can get it.

A solution to the problem of outside contractors monopolizing the large construction projects is turning those larger projects into smaller ones that local companies can execute. If kept within the local bribing system, state money allocated to construction projects tends to find its way to all sorts of people who are formally unrelated to the project through intricate networks that operate according to ideas of fairness and necessary distribution. Outsiders are likely unwilling to indulge these local unwritten "construction customs," thus keeping money out of local circulations of exchange and care. Neither the contractors nor the Public Works officials in Kupang are under the illusion that big outside contractors do not engage in some kind of *suap-menyuap* themselves, but they simply know how to "socialize" with big outsiders in such a way that they can tap into the vast money flows of big construction projects.

Practices such as cutting up large tender projects, then, help keep outsiders *out* and distanced.

Simmering underneath these practices is the long-held suspicion that Jakarta simply takes from regions (especially non-Muslim ones) without giving back, thus flouting the ethics of exchange and care that Kupangese hold dear. Whether by awarding civil service positions in Kupang and NTT to freedom fighters from Java and Sumatra in the immediate post-independence period, or today, by neglecting to invest in a region lagging economically, educationally, and in healthcare, people in Kupang expect very little from the capital. The tendency and preference for "keeping things local," however, is not one of simplistic contradictions between local and national, or even global, but is open to a creative alignment of the giving city with other nodes across this expansive state field of otherness. If a fear of missing out on the spoils of construction money encourages contractors and Public Works officials to keep outsiders at a distance, the logics of gift exchange are also employed to bring other outsiders closer.

The Windmill Project

In an effort to secure green and cheap energy in a city plagued by regular power outages, the newly elected mayor had a plan to construct windmills. Through channels that never became clear to me, Kupang had connected with representatives from a small Dutch municipality who were interested in helping Kupang erect a row of windmills. The project was not the result of any kind of bilateral cooperation, NGO intervention, or transnational program. It was simple mutual cooperation. Project representatives in Kupang hoped to profit from Dutch expertise with wind energy, whereas the Dutch delegation was motivated by a desire to do good, perhaps out of a Dutch moral duty to repay a long-standing debt of honor.

In order to assess possibilities for developing the windmills, the Dutch delegation of five middle-aged male civil servants visited Kupang in mid-2008. Besides formal planning meetings and field visits to potential suitable field sites, the visit also included various forms of *gengsi* and personal touches that helped establish professional ties deepened by personal bonds, not unlike those of *guanxi*-building banquets in China (Osburg 2013; Smart 1998; Yan 1996; Yang 1994) or mafia banquets in Sicily described by Jane and John Schneider (2005). They were welcomed with lavish formal ceremonies, fêted with dinner parties, and treated to enchanting entertainment. Upon request by the mayor, I did my best to aid the proceedings by acting as a translator. Unaccustomed to, but appreciative of, this mix of businesslike negotiations with pleasurable sociality, members of the Dutch delegation told me they were very committed to the windmill project. When I told the mayor about the Dutch enthusiasm, he seemed pleased. He asked me if the guests had enjoyed the Kupangese displays of respect and attempts at making them feel welcome, and was much relieved when I assured him that they had. Success in any business endeavor cannot be expected on the basis of formality alone. Establishing what the Public Works official called a "mutual understanding," or being able to "socialize," matters just as much if not more.

During the remainder of my fieldwork, however, I heard nothing more about the windmill project. I had, in fact, completely forgotten about it until, by coincidence, I ran into one of the members of the Dutch delegation in a restaurant in the Netherlands. When I asked him what had happened with the project, he said that after having assessed various possible locations, none were suitable for catching enough wind to generate electricity. They had, therefore, regretfully decided to pull out of the project. Despite the ultimate failure of the windmill project, this example illustrates that when improvement is needed, Kupang does not necessarily look to Jakarta, which is seen as a place of rejection, non-recognition, and lack of respect (*mutuality*). Rather, it looks across an assemblage of overlapping and competing sovereignties for potential alignment and cooperation along the logic of an ethics of care and exchange.

From the Matryoshka-Doll State to the Giving City

After taking a close look at the historical and recent development of the city of Kupang within larger contexts of sovereignty and suzerainty, and the various ways in which distance with Jakarta and closeness with transnational *elsewheres* is produced, the image of the state that emerges in Kupang is one that counters that of unity, coherence, and encompassment. Against this image, we can see the state in Kupang in terms of a giving city in a wider state field of otherness. Within this field, any connectedness with other branches, scales, and representatives of the nation-state, transnational states, and even supranational, state-like organizations cannot be assumed but needs to be accomplished anew through that logic and ethics of mutuality and exchange.

One implication of this is that anti-corruption efforts—or any efforts to bring about change under the banner of good governance as imposed from on high—will have unexpected and contradictory effects. Good governance initiatives depend on the visions of states, the legal-ethical authority and legitimacy of which stem, in part, from the seamless encompassment of localities into wider regions, nation-states, and, ultimately, the international community (Ferguson and Gupta 2002). In these Matryoshka-doll conceptions of the state, legal changes at the level of the nation-state ought to play out in local domains without losing their persuasiveness. Similarly, the ethical clarity of good governance should descend unadulterated. As we have seen so far, however, Kupang is not part of such a state. It is, instead, as a giving city, the working ideas of the good are embedded in a complex ethics of care and exchange. What, then, happens when the giving city comes up against a neoliberal state?

Corruption, Care, and *Honorer*

The post-*reformasi* decentralization of the Indonesian state apparatus set in motion a blossoming *(pemerkaran)* of new provinces and regions, thereby enabling an expansion of the civil service that contradicted the neoliberal ideological preference for lean states. To counter this fattening of the state in an era of a supposed trimming, the Indonesian government decreed a nationwide moratorium on hiring new civil servants in the months leading up to Kupang's first-ever mayoral elections in 2007. In Kupang, such a moratorium effectively contradicted its conceptions of the governmental good and its norms of conduct. In order to bypass the injunction from Jakarta, there arose the practice of hiring temporary office workers known as *honorer*. In this way, the city was able to maintain an ethics of care and exchange as the giver of valuable personhood. In doing so, it offered a different view on what counts as corrupt and as good in the giving city.

Honorer are well-known fixtures in Indonesian government offices. Officially, government departments employ *honorer* on the basis of necessity, as when the number of tasks exceeds what "full" civil servants at that department can handle. When the need for extra help has passed, departments are supposed to let their *honorer* go. *Honorer* are paid from a region's discretionary funds, or own-source revenue rather than the centrally allocated funds that are used for the salaries of civil servants.[13] Because of this, departments can exercise some discretion in hiring and firing of *honorer*.

It is easy to distinguish *honorer* from actual civil servants. The khaki uniforms of *honorer* do not display the Indonesian Civil Service (KORPRI) emblem that is so proudly displayed on those of the civil servants. *Honorer* also do not receive the complimentary monthly rice allowances that accompanies civil servants' salaries and are not entitled to health insurance or pensions. Nevertheless, given the general difficulty of finding employment in Kupang, *honorer* positions are highly desired. Even without the KORPRI emblem, the uniform still signals the enviable attained personhood Kupangese associate with civil service employment. Furthermore, although *honorer* positions are supposed to be short-term, in practice one can hold *honorer* positions for many years. For some, such positions even prove to be stepping-stones to "full" civil service employment. In fact, every year, city-level government accepts a number of *honorer* formally as actual employees with all accompanying benefits into civil service without requiring them to undergo the various arduous application procedures usually required of aspiring civil servants.

For the disgruntled head of the Ministry of Finance office in Kupang, the employment of this *honorer* loophole served as yet another example of local backwardness and a lack of professionalism, since, according to him, officials used this loophole to unfairly hire family members into positions for which they were neither needed nor qualified. As we will learn in the following chapters, some officials indeed admit to hiring family members as *honorer*. However, by invoking a responsiveness to family obligations they often describe this as an ethical rather than illicit act.

Max Weber (2006: 58–59) pointed out that bureaucrats operating under abstract rules and general norms might always exercise some creative discretion. When such rules and norms are deemed to be too rigid or run afoul of popular opinions regarding substantive justice, bureaucrats can flout formal and rational objectivity. Weber does not mean to imply that officials act in a completely arbitrary manner or are motivated solely by personal interests. Rather, their creative discretion takes place against a larger purpose, or *raison d'etat*, that is stifled by bureaucratic formalism

---

13. *Own-source revenue* refers to the revenue that is collected by regional governments (for example in the form of local taxes), instead of funds being transferred from the national budget to regional governments, and which these governments can spend as they see fit.

and rigid rules. In the case of *honorer*, the *raison* that Kupangese officials prize is the ethos of the giving city; an ethos that would be stifled under the rigid cap on new hires inspired by lean-state ideologies. Thus, when officials in Kupang employ the *honorer* loophole, they are, I suggest, using creative discretion regarding the hiring cap in recognition of the responsibility the giving city has to its people.

It is in this space of creative discretion that we can sketch the contours of what counts as the governmental good and as corruption in Kupang. For whereas some frame the continued hiring of *honorer* in defiance of the moratorium as a form of corruption because it represents an egregious instance of self-aggrandizement, others view the hiring of *honorer* as a form of much-needed care in economically precarious circumstances. Elsie, one of the aunties who lived in the house where I stayed during much of my fieldwork, held this latter view. After having pressed me for weeks to accompany her to the middle school where she worked as a lower-level administrator, I agreed to do so one morning in late 2008. She was eager for me to meet two *honorer* who had worked with her for a long time. While people in Kupang generally view civil servants as people who have "already become persons," for her, the two *honorer* coworkers embodied an unenviable precarious existence at the edge of subsistence. The reason she wanted me to meet them was because she hoped I might be able to find a beneficiary in the Netherlands who would want to offer them some financial assistance. As she told me, her coworkers had children but could barely afford to pay for their tuition fees, school uniforms, and schoolbooks. She hoped that I, a Dutch citizen, could help. In contrast to Indonesia, *Belanda* (the Netherlands), as she imagined, was a country that actually cared for (*peduli*) people. Not only did it offer unemployment benefits to its own citizens, it also offered all sorts of aid to people in far-away countries. To put it another way, for her, *Belanda* represented a hazy and opaque realm from which to draw financial aid, not unlike the Biak's sense of *amber*. As her sole line to that fabled *Belanda*, she hoped I would be able to find a willing sponsor who could offer financial aid, not to her coworkers themselves, but for their children's education.

One morning I met with the two *honorer*: Yohanes and Levy. *Pak* Yohanes was a forty-nine year old man, with a wife and two toddlers. He graduated from high school in the mid-1980s and had a checkered work history of temporary jobs in small stores and as a *honorer* in government offices. *Pak* Levy was forty-six years old and had a wife and six children between the ages of three and sixteen. After graduating high school, he made some money doing odd jobs, such as hauling stones at construction sites, until he landed his *honorer* position at the middle school in 2003. Both of them were indeed having a hard time making ends meet. Earning less than half of the lowest possible salary for a full civil servant—about IDR 1 million ($75)—they told me about the many concessions they made in order to ensure shelter and food for their families. Yohanes would forego paying a small daily sum for a *bemo* (a mini bus that serves as public transportation in Kupang) and instead walk to and from work every day instead. Levy and his family went without running water and electricity in their small house on leased land and would eat maize instead of the more expensive Indonesian staple of rice. In contrast to their full civil servant coworkers, who had obtained that elevated status, Yohanes and Levy exemplify the bare lives of temporary bureaucrats who maneuver on the edges of both the civil service and on the edges of subsistence without hope of edging away from it—except perhaps through aid from *Belanda*, a place where people are thought to care.

Without their meager *honorer* incomes, however, life would undoubtedly be more difficult still. Instrumental to the hiring of both Yohanes and Levy was the head of administration at the school, *Pak* Calvin. Yohanes told me that at the time he was hired "the school needed *honorer*. *Pak* Calvin's wife was related to mine. Therefore, he offered me the job." Levy explained that "*Pak* Calvin and I were in an organization together. That's why he knew I needed a job." We might point to the previous relationships these men had with the school's head of administration to mark these hirings as clear-cut cases of KKN—which is the Indonesian acronym for corruption, or *korupsi, kolusi*, and *nepotisme*). But it is important to point out that *Pak* Calvin did not seem to have hired these *honorer* for reasons of personal gain. What he did, instead, was use his authority and ability to tap into the own-source revenue funds to offer two acquaintances in need the means to earn living. He thus displayed the kind of caring responsibility that (as I will show in the next chapter) figures prominently in the ethics of exchange and care in Kupang. Instead of enhancing personal prestige by using the *honorer* loophole, he facilitated the availability of locally worthy, albeit precarious, personhood.

If this example serves to portray the hiring of *honorer* as a form of care in a wider national context where such care appears to be sorely missing, other examples suggest that the hiring of *honorer* can indeed constitute a form of corruption. This reminds us that even though the use of hiring *honorer* allows the giving city to dissent from the neoliberal state, as Weber pointed out, a *raison d'etat* is by no means unambiguous or agreed upon. Thus when I visited the Office of the People's Advocacy Initiative (PIAR), an anti-corruption agency in Kupang, in early November 2008, its tireless and outspoken director, Sarah Lery Mboeik, was quick to claim that the hiring of *honorer* had become one of the most troubling examples of KKN in the Indonesian civil service. Pulling out a thick file from a nearby bookcase, she covered the table in front of us with sheets of paper with rows of names, ages, and addresses. These papers, she explained, held the names and accompanying background information of 454 *honorer*, all of whom were hired in 2006, which was after the moratorium but before the first-ever direct mayoral elections. These *honorer* had been hired by longtime mayor, S. K. Lherik, who, Lery Mboeik suspected, had done this as a way of gathering support for his favored mayoral candidate Yonas Salean who nevertheless ended up losing the 2007 election to Daniel Adoe. The acceptance of these *honorer*, who would all have to be funded with own-source revenue funds that were thereby lost for other projects, had little to do with departmental needs, Lery Mboeik asserted, but everything with the upcoming mayoral elections. By defying the hiring ban and gifting hundreds of *honorer* positions, Lherik assumed he would secure the votes from recently accepted, as well as aspiring, *honorer*.

What bothered Lery Mboeik most about this was not the use of public funds for non-professional reasons, since hiring *honorer* had long been a way to dodge formal procedures and help out family or other relations. What distinguished current *honorer* hiring practices from the commonplace informality surrounding the allocation of *honorer* positions, and therefore drew her critical attention, was both the scale and motivations. She told me:

> *Kedekatan* (closeness) to someone big in office is always an important way to get in. Before [decentralization], being a part of someone's family helped someone to get in as a *honorer* and maybe to move up the ranks (*naik pangkat*). Now, however, receiving a lot of *honorer* before an election is a new tactic for candidates out of this idea of answering a favor (*balas–jasa*): if I get you a job you will recruit voters for me.

Lery Mboeik here paints a picture of shrewd and strategic elite civil servants who deploy the cultural logics of gift-giving to further their political careers. Such calculated use of *honorer* positions with the expectation of political return transposes the use of the *honorer* loophole from the realm of gift exchange with its ethics of care to that of pure market exchange. This is where we can see how the cultural contours of Kupangese understandings of a governmental good in contrast to corruption emerge. For while both examples of *honorer* hiring would constitute illegal practices from the viewpoint of the neoliberal state, only one of them would likely meet the threshold of KKN in the court of popular opinion. In both cases, the hiring of *honorer* facilitated a continuation of Indonesia's post-independence expansion of the civil service and that expansion worked as a means to ensure a sometimes rebellious region's loyalty. However, while school headmaster *Pak* Calvin flouted the rules in order to bestow the giving city's gift of worthy personhood onto others, former mayor Lherik did so for reasons of political prestige and advancement. Thus, *technically corrupt* acts can be understood in terms of an ethics of care and exchange when done in order to bestow others with a valuable, even if still precarious, personhood, or understood as KKN when exercised in order to make oneself (or one's protégé) into a more prominent person. This does not mean that the headmaster's gift could not reflect favorably on himself, nor that Lherik's actions did not benefit the lives of many. Virtue and charity are not mutually exclusive and this is where we see the potential slippage between corruption and care. When the neoliberal state comes up against the giving city in a general context of precarity, what comes to count as corruption and the governmental good is not decided in laws or national decrees, but instead within the logic of an ethics of care and exchange.

This did not make deciding what to do with the hundreds of newly hired *honorer* in the aftermath of the 2007 elections any easier for the new mayor, Daniel Adoe. The mayor's aide told me that the mayor was at a loss as to what to do with these *honorer*, whom he had to pay out of the limited discretionary funds. What would be easier than to fire them? Getting rid of these *honorer* would not only free up money, keeping them was illegal, since it contradicted the moratorium. However, as the aide said:

He also can't fire them because they have families and need to live. In Indonesia there is no welfare system, there are no unemployment benefits. If people in Kupang do not have a job they have no sources of income. How could one deprive someone, such as a *honorer*, of their sole source of money?

We might view the mayor's decision to keep the illegally hired *honorer* on the payroll simply as a form of charity. To some extent, charity is the clear corollary of neoliberalism that helps make up for some of its ethical shortcomings (Muehlebach 2012). In Kupang, however, such *charity* should be seen as a part of deeper rooted practices of care and exchange as well as a localized continuation of a longer-standing practices of state expansion in a particular context of precarity. In lieu of being able to count on a state or government as a guarantor of well-being or care (*peduli*), as we have seen in this chapter, people in Kupang wage their hopes on their giving city, on constructing mutual understandings with municipalities in other countries, or on unknown caring benefactors from far away.

Giving Personhood

My aim in this chapter was to offer an understanding of the unanticipated effects of anti-corruption efforts from within the social workings of the giving city. Central to this endeavor was questioning a priori presumptions regarding the ontological sameness of states. From this starting point, the state in Kupang emerged not as a coherent, unified, or singular state that facilitates cross-cultural comparison or invites effortless government interventions, but instead, a refracted and relational one. Attending to a conception of Kupang as a giving city offered us some insights as to why national anti-corruption efforts have failed. Kupang's position within a wider network of suzerainty and sovereignty in pre- and post-independence Indonesia has always been contingent, based not on loyalty or nationalist sentiment, but on strategies of gift-exchange and state expansion. Kupang is not within the nested hierarchy (Ferguson and Gupta 2002a) of a vertically encompassed state, but one node in a wider state-of-otherness—one in which relationality is always uncertain and tinged with suspicion, and where closeness and distance between different nodes are created and maintained—or kept at bay—through the an ethics of care and exchange. In a city where these practices of care and exchange form a long-standing part of belonging and relationality in a state field of otherness, visions of what counts as a governmental good differ from those of a neoliberal state. The good governance preference for lean states contradict the giving city's mandate to provide. What comes to count as corruption from the vantage point of the neoliberal state, furthermore, can come to be seen as care from the vantage point of the giving city.

It is telling that the "Kupang the Giving City" sign in front of the mayor's office faced inwards, towards the civil servants lined up on the *lapangan* for their exercises. If the giving city offers a locally worthy kind of personhood, it makes sense that it broadcasts its message towards those it has already made into *somebodies*. What the giving city gives, ultimately, is the means to achieve a locally meaningful personhood. To complement those anthropologists of the state who focus on the everyday practices, discourses, and performances that help culturally construct the mask of the state, I highlighted the cultural construction of personhood that simultaneously occurs. Here, it is worth recalling that Louis Althusser (1971), in his example of being hailed by an arm of a state apparatus, considered the structure of ideology to work as a doubly speculary process of mutual recognition between a subject and the state. In other words, he reminds us that as an image of the state as coherent and discreet is constructed, so too are the state's subjects constituted. While a neoliberal state might hail self-governing and self-sufficient individuals (Rose 1996), we might consider the possibility that a giving city hails the kind of person that can exhibit the caring responsibility that matters so much in Kupang.

CHAPTER TWO

Corruption as Caring Responsibility

Custom, Kin, and Corruption

When the anti-corruption activist Sarah Lery Mboeik met me in her office in 2008, she shared more than just her findings on former mayor Lherik's use of *honorer* to influence Kupang's mayoral elections. She also pulled out a file that she was convinced contained irrefutable proof of corruption by Lherik's protégé, Yonas Salean. Carefully placing two documents on the table in front of me, Lery Mboeik explained that I was looking at a photocopy of a young woman's acceptance form for a *honorer* position in the city's civil service *and* a photocopy of that same young woman's high school diploma. Pointing at the respective dates on the two forms, she emphasized that the young woman's start date as an *honorer* was a year before her high school graduation. Regulations for hiring civil servants strictly forbid accepting anyone without a high school diploma, suggesting someone with significant influence must have helped her bypass the regulation and obtain the position. The young woman in question happened to be Salean's niece, and at the time he was still a high-ranking city official. Lery Mboeik suspected that he had arranged this *honorer* position to help launch her into full civil service employment after graduation. Lery Mboeik felt certain that these forms, along with the family connection between the woman and Salean, would be sufficient for a legal case against Salean and expose him as indisputably corrupt.

When I had a chance to interview Salean a year later and asked him about these accusations, he had a very different view of his actions. After his humiliating defeat in the 2007 mayoral elections—in part because of his association with the corruption, collusion, and nepotism that Kupangese had been eager to leave behind—I had expected him to steer clear of any suggestion of corrupt behavior, all the more so because he was in the midst of plotting his political comeback. Much to my surprise, however, he did not deny Lery Mboeik's allegations of using his formal position to help out his niece. In fact, he fully justified his actions:

> That has happened, because the meaning of our life here in Kupang is that family is important. If we have problems or difficulties, it is, in the first place, family that is there for us. So, several family members have come [to me] and asked, for instance, about their child who wants to become a civil servant or *honorer*. I, then, order the Human Resources Department to look into them. Even though they are family, we don't want them to embarrass us who have leadership positions in civil service. Therefore, they [Human Resources] investigate if they indeed have the skills. If family members want to become civil servants, they ought to be given positions in line with their abilities.

While Lery Mboeik framed Salean's actions as indisputable proof of corruption, Salean placed his actions at very heart of the meaning of life in Kupang—to be there for family in times of trouble. What Lery Mboeik saw as legally improper, Salean saw as familial obligation. Although we might want to join Lery Mboeik in her suspicions of Salean's claim to moral righteousness, especially since he sidesteps the main point of her accusation regarding his niece's ineligibility for an *honorer* position based on her graduation date, these opposing interpretations highlight the corruption-care conundrum in Kupang.

For people in Kupang, the tension between what gets defined as KKN and the sense of obligation to intimate others represents the city's fragile incorporation into the modern Indonesian nation-state. With longstanding practices of gift exchange and state expansion, the boundaries between corruption, charity, and care are not neatly drawn nor consistently enforced. Salean's explanation does not just make sense to those looking to him as a potential patron, but is recognizable to anyone existing within a network of intimate others. It is therefore not at all certain whether most Kupangese would view this act of helping out a niece as corruption as Lery Mboeik does. While the last chapter invited us to rethink what a governmental good can look like given the operations of a giving city, this chapter asks, what comes to count as corruption in such a city?

In the giving city, a gift does not necessarily constitute corruption even if the exchange crosses those already blurred boundaries between public and private. One widespread example of this is the habit workers have of giving money back to the individual who doles out the pay. For instance, after they were handed their salaries every Friday, the laborers who worked on a construction project involving the Dendeng River next to the Kaho family home, would without fail give the project's treasurer some "bus money" or "cell phone credit money." Furthermore, a neighbor, who was in charge of handing out the monthly salaries to civil servants at the mayor's office, considered the many sums of "thank you money" she received every month a welcome supplement to her own income. My guest sister, Sinta, told me that this practice was so important that when her mother went out of town and asked Sinta to collect her salary, her mother would call on payday just to remind her about giving the treasurer back a small sum.

While this habit of giving money back to the person dispensing the funds would fit somewhere between "unwarranted payment for public services" and "gratuity"—categories of everyday corruption that Giorgio Blundo and Jean-Pierre Olivier de Sardin developed in their comparative study of corruption in West African countries (2006a: 72–80)—civil servants in Kupang saw no contradiction between their participation in practices such as these and their simultaneous fervent support of the anti-corruption project. Mere minutes after telling me about her mother's frantic exhortation to remember to pay the treasurer, Sinta herself exclaimed, without any apparent sense of irony, how she would rid the region of KKN if she were governor. When I asked Sinta whether she found this statement to be incongruous with her own practices (e.g., tipping the treasurer), she did not think so. Giving something back was not corruption, she explained, but simply "Kupang custom."

As for Salean's gift of an *honorer* position to his niece, the moral force of his explanation stems from helping a family member. Responding to family obligations or expectations does not by itself constitute KKN for many civil servants. As Rika, a middle-aged civil servant at the Department of Governance mused: "The strength of relatives (*kekuatan kerabat*) is very important. Kinship (*kekerabatan*) and familiarity (*keakraban*) matter. If someone close to you comes to you and says, 'this is my kid, can you help?' you do your best, you know?" Indeed, whenever I asked civil servants who they would hire if there were two candidates, equally qualified, but one was family, most responded without hesitation they would hire the family member. "You cannot," I was told, "refuse family." This does not mean that civil servants will always favor family members. As Rika remarked at some point during our conversation, "the important thing is that there has to be a balance." Even Salean claims only to accept family members who possess the right skills for a position. It simply means that having a prior relationship helps tip the balance.

The question of what comes to count as corruption in a giving city thus requires us to embed our understandings of corruption within a relational context, where balancing the requirements of one's relationships to (intimate) others matters in deciding whether or not one's actions meet the definition of corruption. This differs markedly from understandings of corruption in the ideals of good governance: discrete acts that transgress public-private boundaries. Such understandings leave little space for the possibility that responding to the expectations and obligations of relationality might constitute something permissible, customary, or even good. In fact, these understandings of a governmental good depend on public officials foregoing private relationality. In Kupang, whether something counts as KKN is not determined by the act itself, but by a line between acceptable and unacceptable ways of responding to relational expectations and obligations. Trying to make sense of corruption and its discontents does not, therefore, entail avoiding the pull of relationality altogether but does involve contemplating the question of *when* relational expectations and obligations might constitute corruption. This leaves the people of Kupang walking the fine line between corruption and care.

That uneasy boundary between corruption and care is certainly at play within existing institutional moralities. Throughout much of modern Indonesian history, corruption was conceptualized in terms of the *public interest*, which understands corruption not as discrete acts in themselves but in connection to ideas of a larger common good. The current *public office* approach to corruption is in fact a rather novel one that uneasily joined already those already in existence. Given Sinta's emphasis on Kupang custom and the insistence that one cannot refuse family, I take a responsive phenomenological approach (Mattingly 2018; Schwarz Wentzer 2018a; 2018b; Waldenfels 1994) to the relational intertwining of care and kin in Kupang. This allows us to better recognize the impossibility of refusing the pull of family expectations. We see this in the narrative of one family's intergenerational socioeconomic ascent, pulling insights from studies on eastern Indonesian kinship relations and social organization to propose that what emerges here is a "moral engine" (Mattingly et al. 2018). This engine drives ethical behavior in the form of caring responsibility towards family in times of hardship; time in which the greater good of the family takes priority over the particular desires of individual family members.

In what follows we see that corruption as a transgression of care finds various points of institutional, discursive and embodied moral resonance in the larger moral-ethical assemblage (Zigon 2009; 2011b: 62–72) of Kupang. This helps explain why the recent and enthusiastically received anti-corruption efforts, which do not pose questions of care, fail to convince civil servants in Kupang that responding to the pull of (familial) relationality constitutes corruption.

However, before I paint too rosy a picture of the resilience of family care in a part of Indonesia that is jokingly described as perpetually left behind, of having an uncertain fate, and in need of divine help, I also want to emphasize that there are limits to the certainty and reliability of familial care. Stasch (2009) reminds us that alterity is also ever-present among kin, such that the suspicion, disconnectedness, and distancing that we saw vis-à-vis the giving city's incorporation into wider networks of the state is similarly present in interpersonal relationships. Therefore, the expectation of caring responsibility among family members must also be negotiated through a process a process of distancing and closeness. Indeed, the material aspects of reciprocal care in the context of family parties show how suspicions of distance, estrangement, and not-belonging always accompany an ethics of care and exchange.

A Relational View of Corruption

The discrepancy I highlighted earlier between civil servants who profess an interest in curbing corruption and then partake in acts that may appear as corruption does not necessarily indicate insincerity or hypocrisy. As other anthropologists have shown, complaints about, and simultaneous participation in, corruption indicates the complexity of everyday life (Hasty 2005; B. C. Smith 2007). In the context of Kupang, the discrepancy stems from the existence of contrasting understandings of what corruption is and when it matters. We would do well, therefore, to keep in mind a reminder from the British political philosopher Mark Philp (1997), who says that corruption does not stand apart from its connection to normative visions of what the political realm *ought to be*.

For what comes to count as corrupt or correct (e.g., just and good) is not determined by the legal force of regulations set forward under good governance initiatives, but takes shape under the accumulated weight of other institutional, discursive, and embodied moralities (Zigon 2011a). These moralities fit together in ways that offer plausible *oughts* that differ from, or even contradict, newer legal stipulations brought forth by the ideals of good governance. In order to understand the seeming discrepancy between a disavowal of and complicity in corruption in Kupang, or the possibility that corruption overlaps with care, we need to attend to already existing institutional and discursive moralities regarding corruption and normative visions of the good. For those normative visions emphasize the importance of relationality and mutuality and therefore form a stark contrast with the understandings of corruption put forward in anti-corruption initiatives operating under the auspices of good governance.

In post-*reformasi* Indonesia, corruption is defined as discrete examples of misuse of one's formal duties or public role. This reflects the recent adoption of policies rooted in a *public office* understanding of corruption, and such an understanding tends to forego larger questions of a political good in favor of legalistic definitions of corruption (Philp 1997: 440). This public office understanding is characteristic of the now-hegemonic notion of good governance that has taken root in Indonesia and beyond. The rapid creation of new laws on corruption and the erection of institutional bodies to counter corruption that occurred in post-*reformasi*. Indonesia display this concern with an individual abuse of one's (governmental) position (e.g., the accumulation of wealth by government officials), the establishment of an anti-corruption commission to investigate corrupt acts by government officials, and the enforcement of administrative accountability through investigations of the actions of government officials.[1] While severing corruption from larger assembled

---

1. For example, Law 28/1999 on Government Executives Who Are Free and Clear from Corruption, Collusion, and Nepotism helped create the Indonesian Corruption Eradication Commission (KPK) to target the accumulation of wealth by government officials and investigate allegations of corruption (Art. 12 & 17). Article 43 of the Law 31/1999 on the Eradication of Corruption provides for the establishment of an anti-corruption commission to investigate corrupt acts of government officials. The additional establishment of a (national) ombudsman, furthermore, ensured the enforcement of administrative accountability through investigations of

discourses and dispositions allows for a clear recognition of instances of law-breaking and rule infraction, it inevitably reduces understandings of corruption to examples of individual motivation or pathology. And it does this without taking into account the ways in which norms, values, habits, obligations, and expectations bear upon embodied and relational human agency.

Contrasting with the public office understanding of political corruption is an understanding grounded in terms of *public interest*, or the subverting of the common good by private individuals (Philp 1997: 440). A public interest approach maintains the connection between corruption and assembled normative visions of good governance. Indeed, there is a range of terms that point to the interconnection of corruption and assembled normative discourses and dispositions.[2] The familiar concept of an *old boys network*, for instance, conjures a sense of comfortable, elite solidarity, comradery, and brotherhood to justify what some might view as unfair and unjust favoritism in what is supposed to be a meritocratic system of resource allocation. At the same time, there is the example of the Indian practice of *jugaad* (Jauregui 2014), which is understood to be a form of creative improvisation and suggests not so much a transgression of public-private boundaries (as public office definitions of corruption would have it) but rather a playful, ever-shifting moral boundary between inventively *making do* and abusing one's ability to manipulate circumstances for excessive gain.

Both of these examples signal a subversion of the public interest or common good, as well as a *violation* of how the political realm ought to operate. At the same time, they imply different visions of what an uncorrupted politics might look like. Cross-cultural concerns with corruption, therefore, require an openness to the idea that what counts as corruption and what counts as politics can differ; in some states political rule might be somewhat compatible with nepotism or patronage while in others "anything less than a perfect meritocracy and an absolute scrupulousness about financial matters may be deemed corrupt" (Philp 1997: 451). Such

---

the actions of government officials and by offering a public avenue for the voicing and solving of corruption-related complaints (M. Crouch 2008: 384–385).

2. As Philp notes (1997: 441–442), political scientists in the 1960s and 1970s saw politics and corruption according to the western values of democratic societies, and did so in a way that counters any lingering Occidental dominance regarding the nature of politics.

a focus on culture allows for ideas of politics, equity, and social justice to differ between a neoliberal state and a giving city like Kupang. If we turn to the way KKN is referred to in Indonesia, the contours of corruption that emerge here, match the public interest concern with questions of the common or normative good much more than a public office concern with discrete examples of the misuse of one's formal duties or public roles. What stands out with the acronym of KKN, which gained nationwide recognition during the anti-Suharto protests of 1997–1998, and which civil servants in Kupang were so quick to identify as the kind of corruption that needed to be eradicated, is that the first K (corruption) is deemed insufficient to describe the problem. Corruption is thus followed by a second K (collusion) and then the N for nepotism. The specific additions of *collusion* and *nepotism* imply that corruption in Indonesia has particularly problematic relational connotations. Indeed, when Amien Rais, the chair of Indonesia's oldest active Islamic organization, Muhammadiyah, first coined the term KKN in the early 1990s, he did so in direct response to the excessive corruption of the Suharto family, whose malfeasance consisted of self-enrichment from the distribution of favors, deals, and contracts in a wide web of family, friends, politicians, and business cronies (Williams 2017: 105–106). Rais denounced the Suharto family's KKN in an Islamic register of social justice and thereby managed to capture the larger societal discontent regarding social inequity emerging from the elite's illicit accumulation of wealth and the relational structure through which it occurred.

Nevertheless, it was not this relational character of corruption in itself that violated popular visions of the governmental good.[3] These practices failed to meet the popular standards of KKN only in times of economic peril. Rais's denouncement of KKN dovetailed with the economic downturn Indonesia experienced from the mid-1980s, when oil proceeds collapsed and Indonesia could no longer afford the protectionism and import substitutions that had driven its steady economic growth during the 1970s. The Suharto family and their cronies had profited richly from policies that guaranteed business and import

---

3. Suharto styled his personalistic type of rule in part after Javanese kings, and drew on Javanese conceptions of power to legitimize self-enrichment and the dispersion of economic and other opportunities among his family and anointed few (Robertson-Snape 1999: 597), which some Indonesians may have similarly accepted as legitimate.

monopolies (Robertson-Snape 1999: 594) but in an oil-subsidized economy there was not much popular pushback.[4] However, when the economy slowed down and the decreasing price of oil necessitated the sale of state assets, the Suharto family's continued profiting came to seem like a transgression. Enjoying the spoils of office seemed acceptable when everyone was benefiting from the economic bounty. But when the windfalls failed to reach beyond the elite few, there were charges of KKN. Likewise, the pro-*reformasi* protesters sought to curtail KKN in the wake of the 1997 Asian financial crisis. To put it another way, specific acts that were not seen as corruption came to be seen as KKN when the acts that benefited close relations seemed to thwart the common good.

This importance of a common good that connected all Indonesians resonates with how corruption was defined in Indonesia.[5] The constitution itself states that the national economy ought to be organized on the principles of the family, invoking a sense of intimacy between state subjects or employees in a collaborative effort of working towards a common good. Under President Suharto, this family ideology would receive

---

4. In fact, this economic inward-looking turn was in part prompted by protests—known as the Malari riots—against the corruption and nepotism facilitated by Indonesia's outward-looking economic policy (1999: 593).

5. A public interest view of corruption has a longer legal and ideological history in Indonesia. As Fiona Robertson-Snape (1999: 598) points out, "criminally corrupt" was long defined around the conception of public interest as: a) whoever by contravening the law commits acts, to enrich himself or another or a corporate body, which directly or indirectly injure the finances or economy of the State, or if it is known or suspected by him that such acts will do so; b) whoever with the intention of advantaging himself or another person or a body, abuses the authority, opportunity, or influence which he has by reason of his office or position, which directly or indirectly can injure the finances or economy of the state. This definition of corruption does not single out the abuse of public office or the transgression of public office norms. Instead, it emphasizes a violation of the public interest, which is here understood in terms of economic distribution—"the finances or economy of the s/State" (Robertson-Snape 1999: 598). Viewing KKN as transgressing the boundaries of the law in a way that neatly separates the public from the private thus ignores the more prevalent institutional moral sense (Zigon 2011a) that KKN is a matter of transgressing the opaque, vague, and shifting boundaries of economic fairness and equity in terms of the public interest.

an organicist twist so that during the New Order, the family served as an inspiration for a corporatist and integralist model of state organization. However, the importance of prioritizing a common good and interest also appealed to the Lenin-reading Sukarno, who likened the Indonesian state ideology of *Pancasila* (five pillars) to the supposedly shared Indonesian value of *gotong-royong* or "mutual cooperation" (Bourchier 2015: 70–71). In other words, both leftist and organicist visions of Indonesian state organization, generated institutional and public support (Zigon 2011a) for the idea that a public interest should be organized around ideas of economic distribution and was a matter of mutuality, collectivity, and cooperation.

The *kolusi* and *nepotisme* that characterize the Indonesian KKN thus signal a transgression of what is otherwise a prized and valued relationality. None of this implies that some degree of individual interest-maximization, or prioritization of one's own family over the national family, in itself would count as corruption. It merely suggests the need not to overlook the public interest or common good and to maintain some semblance of fairness in economic redistribution. Thus Suharto's self-aggrandizement and prioritization of his family and associates constituted KKN when they clearly came at the expense of the *national family*.

What is striking about the post-*reformasi* definition of corruption based on the public office, is that it disregarded the elasticity and valued aspect of relationality afforded by the earlier focus on the public interest. These efforts also offer no recognition of the occurrence of corruption outside of the confines of a public office. Furthermore, the emphasis on discrete acts committed by individuals who are government officials abandons consideration of the connection of discrete acts to larger questions concerning the common good, fairness, or equity. Moreover, it fails to account for the possibility that there could be a relational component to agentive actions that would be considered a good, as in the value of gotong-royong or "Kupang custom."

In short, these post-*reformasi* anti-corruption efforts enabled the prosecution of discrete, individual, and identifiable acts but did not allow for the contested relational character of KKN and the connection of discrete acts to larger questions of fairness in economic distribution. Put differently, they did not allow for questions of care to factor into considerations of what comes to count as corruption. Nonetheless, in the province thought to be *perpetually left behind*, questions of care remained at the heart of everyday existence.

Narratives of Kin and Care

Cornelis Lay, a professor of politics and government at one of Indonesia's most prestigious universities in Yogyakarta, Java,[6] once described what it was like to grow up in a relatively poor neighborhood of Kupang in the 1960s–1970s. Throughout his story, Lay constantly stresses the importance of family for a boy and young man of very modest means. He writes:

> When Kupang people said they were relatives or family, they didn't mean something genealogical, but something social. Blood relations were of course an important foundation, but not the most important. Social relations were much more decisive. Marriage relations, neighbors, mixing around and work were the points of reference for turning "relative" into a social concept. The denser the relationship formed, the more strongly we would say they were relatives (*saudara*). (Lay and Van Klinken 2014: 156)

Crucially, Lay emphasizes that family inheres not in biology-and-blood but is constituted by "something social," a density of relationships. He thus adds weight to recent claims made by anthropologists of kinship (in the flourishing post-Schneiderian landscape) who insist that kinship points to a "mutuality of being: people who are intrinsic to one another's existence" (Sahlins 2013: 2) or "people who live each other's lives and die each other's death" (Carsten 2004: 107). In order to further understand how corruption can slip into care and care into corruption, let us look at the existing social relationships of Kupang, which as Lay suggests, often come to be interchangeable with kin relationships.

I will focus here on an intergenerational narrative of socioeconomic ascent as told by various members of the Kaho family, with whom I lived during my field research in Kupang. Cheryl Mattingly's (2018: 40) argument that narratives offer an "existential picture of ethical responsiveness" greatly helps us understand the impossibility to refuse the pull of family expectations and obligation, and thus facilitates the reframing of potential instances of corruption as ones of care. Mattingly makes this proposal within her phenomenological approach to ethical drives,

---

6. Unfortunately, Dr. Cornelis Lay passed away on 5 August, 2020. I owe much of my research to his kind support, and I regret that I will not be able to share this book with him and receive his responses to it.

or *moral engines*, that impel people to act in certain ways in the face of an ethical demand. She suggests that narrative singularities and the construction of narrative selves—in tandem with the ongoing, improvisational, and ever-changing process of crafting narratives—offer valuable analytical insights into moral drives.

First, attending to narrative singularities and the selves that craft, construct, and experiment with narrative possibilities reveals uncertainty in response to ethical demands; responses that emerge at the points of friction between the norms and values that shape the social facticity of life and the existential excess that always accompanies every singular ethical demand.[7] This means that we are not engaging linear and coherent stories but witnessing inconsistencies, gaps, and contradictions. Mattingly's focus on the singularities that emerge from narrative selves invites us to take seriously "history on a smaller scale, the history of intentionality that comprises a personal life or small unit (like a household) who share life over time" (2018: 44).

So it is with the intergenerational narrative of the Kaho family that was shared with me by various members of the household. It indeed offers the "existential picture of ethical responsiveness" necessary to understand the porous boundary between corruption and care in Kupang (Mattingly 2018: 40). It does so in part by presenting the kind of care that consists of responsibility for intimate others as a moral engine. Therefore, I suggest that when "family" is used in Kupang as a shorthand as an explanation for something that might be categorized as corruption, we should understand it to convey a sense of caring responsibility that is especially pressing in times of need and precarity.[8]

Growing up in Kupang

I first got to know Viktor Kaho when we were both working on an international, collaborative research project devoted to economic, political,

---

7. For a wonderful exploration of possibilities and impossibilities afforded by narratives in the context of post-disaster recovery in tsunami-stricken Aceh, I point readers to Annemarie Samuels's *After the Tsunami* (2019).
8. I do not think this would contradict Mattingly's focus on narrative selves or call for attending to individuals, since her individual is not a (Kantian) autonomous, freely choosing, self-mastering "I," but a relational and responsive self who nevertheless bears historical singularity (Mattingly 2018: 40).

and social life in Indonesian provincial towns. Upon learning I planned to conduct my fieldwork in Kupang, he promptly suggested I stay in his family's house and live there with his sisters, brother-in-law, nieces, and nephews. I gladly accepted this invitation and made my entry into Kupang as a new and temporary member of the Kaho household. When I met him, Viktor was a lecturer at a prominent university in Java. Although born in poverty to parents who arrived in Kupang from the island of Savu, a small island between Timor and Sumba, he had managed to enroll in one of Indonesia's top universities and complete his studies there. He became lecturer at the same school while also emerging as an active member in the political party PDI-P, the party that delivered Indonesia's fifth president, Megawati Sukarnoputri, in 2001. Viktor was generally considered to be a close confidant of Megawati. In other contexts, his story of moving from humble beginnings to social prominence might earn him, deservedly or not, the label of being a *self-made man*. Neither he nor his sisters, however, would ever view him as self-made, for while his success was in part due to his hard work, it was also owing in part to the numerous instances of the sacrifice of others sacrificing to help him in small ways.

Viktor's parents, Paulus and Elisabeth, had both already passed away by the time I arrived in Kupang. They were born in the 1920s and in their twenties, independent of each other, migrated to Kupang, where they eventually met and married. Paulus and Elisabeth built a modest house on a small plot of land in the neighborhood of Fontein, located west of the town center along the Dendeng. This plot of land was a gift from a kind "uncle," a fellow Savunese "big man" named Simon Bubu, who was the boss of Kupang's harbor workers in the 1940s. He managed to parlay his influential position in Kupang's import-dependent economy into substantial personal wealth. During the 1950s, he bought land all over Kupang, where he allowed his political allies and laborers to build houses (Van Klinken 2014: 212).

The family house Paulus and Elisabeth built reflected their limited economic means. Viktor's sister, Ina, remembers how the family would scramble to find pots and other receptacles to catch the water leaking through the roof every time it rained. Still, the little house was home to them as well as their five daughters and only son.[9] It stood virtually

---

9. Ever since Lévi-Strauss (1983) introduced the concept of "house societies" into anthropology in order to overcome some of the complexities around the applications of lineage and descent theory, houses have formed an

unchanged on the slopes of the Dendeng river until the early 2000s, when Viktor had a new house more befitting the family's increased social-economic status built on the same plot of land where his parents' home had stood. Although at that point Viktor lived in Java with his wife and children and would therefore not use it himself—and his father only spent one year in the newly built house before he passed away in 2006—he had created a home for three of his sisters, a brother-in-law, and four nieces and nephews.

As Paulus and Elisabeth raised their children through the 1950s–1970s, there were limited job opportunities in Kupang. Viktor recalls often going hungry to the point of fainting. The constant lack of food was not unique to his family nor just a characteristic of Fontein. Notwithstanding the areas where the better-off government officials lived, shortages of food were so common throughout Kupang that in everyday conversation neighbors most often asked each other about food: "What are you cooking?" or "Have you cooked yet?" If someone had nothing to eat, a neighbor would send a child over with what little food they could spare.

Making ends meet and feeding a family of eight required help from everyone in the Kaho house. Elisabeth made some money by weaving cloth at home. Paulus initially worked as a laborer in the harbor under Bubu, then went on to drive trucks through Timor's interior to buy products he could sell in Kupang, and eventually settled on running a succession of market stalls selling foodstuffs in town. All the children contributed in some way. Viktor roamed the city trying to sell packets of rice and pretty stones he found on the beach. He also helped out at the market stall, sometimes spending the night there with some friends so he could wake up early enough to catch some fish for his father to sell. His sister Elsie would mind the stall when their father's failing health prevented him from doing so. Ina would skip school to help out at the

---

important locus of anthropological inquiries into social organization and kinship relations. The importance of houses have certainly been well-documented in eastern Indonesia (Cunningham 1964; Fox 1993; McKinnon 1995; Nordholt 1971; Waterson 1990). When speaking of home in relation to kinship here I am referring less to these traditions, although they undoubtedly continue to resonate in contemporary urban Kupangese' desires to have family homes, and allude more to Janet Carsten's (2004: 31–56) description of the ways in which homes foster a sense of family through its affective spatiality and experiential density.

market. As Ina told me in 2009 while tending to her improvised *kios* down the slope from the family house next to the river, she never really liked school much anyway. She enjoyed working at the market much more than focusing on her lessons. Even after they gave up their market stall, Ina continued to sell small household items such as small sachets of shampoo, laundry detergent, instant noodles and other snacks—first from her home to neighbors, and later by the river to recreationists who would gather to swim.

Ina eventually dropped out of school altogether, the only Kaho sibling to have done so. Despite the economic hardships the family faced, Paulus and Elisabeth placed great importance on their children's education. In contrast to many of their NTT contemporaries, in Savu they had both completed the *Volksschool*, the elementary school originally set up by Dutch missionaries. In Savu, as in the island of Rote, educational systems developed much earlier than in other parts of NTT under Dutch colonial rule (Fox 1977). People from Savu and Rote, therefore, had a relative advantage in taking up employment in the Dutch colonial and subsequent Indonesian administrative and educational apparatus. To this day, Rotenese and Savunese last names are the most dominant ones in Kupang's civil service, fueling suspicions of ethnic favoring (Tidey 2010). Paulus and Elisabeth were thus well aware of education's importance in the path to formal employment and the best opportunity for "becoming a person" in Kupang: through government employment. Although they needed their children's help to get by, they did not want this to interfere with their children's education. And it did not. The two oldest daughters completed high school, and the two youngest even obtained bachelor degrees from a local university, although sadly the youngest daughter passed away. Moreover, the three daughters managed to find employment in Kupang's civil service as low-level administrators and teachers, no doubt to the great satisfaction of their parents.

Viktor's desire to attend university in Java likely exceeded the expectations of his parents. Making such a thing possible, meanwhile, certainly surpassed the kinds of communal responsiveness that came in the quotidian acts of sharing and care that was so pivotal in meeting the needs of everyday life in Kupang. It required appealing to more influential kin. Soon after Viktor told his mother of his goals, she took him to visit two "uncles." Uncle Robert was the provincial head of the Education Department. Uncle Adi was NTT's deputy governor. Viktor confessed to being unsure about the exact nature of their genealogical relation since he could only recall his mother making a visit to her so-called "brothers" once in his life, but when they met this time both uncles greeted his mother with an affectionate Savunese kiss—a light touching of the noses—while addressing her as *susi*, a derivation of the Dutch *zuster* or "sister." She explained to each of them that her son wanted to attend university in Java, and they both expressed their approval of Viktor's plans. Uncle Robert advised her to sell the gold brooch she was wearing to help with the expenses, and then went on to write a letter to a relation of his and Elisabeth's, Joseph, who taught at the very university Viktor wished to attend. When Viktor eventually arrived at the door of his uncle Josef, carrying another letter of support from uncle Robert, he was welcomed with a Savunese kiss and some breakfast—the first breakfast he had ever had. For the duration of his university studies, he would live in a barrack adjacent to the house where uncle Joseph lived with his nuclear family along with as many as sixty other migrants from their "home" region.

"Eastern Character is Like That"

Viktor's extraordinary opportunity was not only facilitated by the excep-tional responsiveness of distant kin, but also made possible because his siblings sacrificed opportunities of their own. This narrative of the Kaho family reveals that not everyone's desires create the same level of ethical demand (Mattingly 2018: 47–48; Schwarz Wentzer 2018a: 213). One hot afternoon as we were sitting idly on the front porch of the Fontein home, Viktor's older sister, Elsie, told me that when she was younger, she had also wanted to go to university, just as her younger brother and two younger sisters would eventually do. In fact, at some point she had already filled out all the necessary paperwork to enroll in the local Nusa Cendana University. She thought she would be able to afford the tui-tion fees and other costs by continuing to help her father at his market stall. She was, however, conflicted because of the needs of her family. Her older sister was already married and could no longer contribute as much to their household and her younger brother and sisters were still in school. Her father was often sick, which impeded his ability to "find money" at the market to feed the family and pay for his children's school-ing. With this in mind, Elsie decided to start the application procedure for job openings at the provincial government. She figured that if she were to get accepted into civil service, she would be in a better position to help her family financially. When, somewhat to her surprise, she was accepted, Elsie decided to join the civil service and, to her regret, put her educational plans on hold.

Elsie thus forewent a university education out of consideration for her parents and younger siblings. The ethical demand to contribute financially to the household she grew up in, outweighed her own desire for educational advancement. This demand would not weigh the same on her brother when he wished to attend university a few years later. The ethical demand to contribute financially to the household also made Elsie decide to postpone marriage and starting a family when she met her future husband at the age of twenty-one in 1976. As she explained:

> I couldn't possibly take care of two families. If I had gotten married so soon my younger brother and sisters would not have had a future. I also would not have money for my own future schooling because I would have to spend it on milk for my children. They [her siblings] would be disadvantaged if I got married. I'd have to take care of a household of my own. Like that.

Mattingly (2018: 47–48) and Schwarz Wentzer (2018a: 213, 215) point to an inescapable asymmetry of ethical demands—demands carry an excess that cannot be adequately met by any specific response. Put differently, when faced with the question of how one ought to live, one responds the best way one can while a perfect response always remains out of reach. For Elsie, facing the demands placed on her as a child and older sister on the one hand, and as a potential wife on the other, her best (if not perfect) response was to postpone marriage and having children, thereby maintaining the ability to contribute financially to her parents' household until her siblings were old enough to do so themselves.

After waiting six years, Elsie finally married in 1982. Her husband held a respectable and, more importantly, steady position at the local branch of *Radio Republik Indonesia*. They welcomed their first child, Sinta, a year later. In 1985, their second child Valentino was born, followed by a third, Yongki, in 1991. The three children grew up in the Fontein house cared for by their unmarried, maternal aunt Ina, while Elsie and her husband worked full-time. While Ina provided childcare, Elsie made sure to contribute to the costs of food, electricity, and water. Elsie never went back to school but, as her parents had done with her and her siblings, made sure her children got the best education she could secure. She sent them to the highest-ranked elementary school in the neighborhood and enrolled them in the best junior and senior high schools available in Kupang. In addition to regular school, she also sent them to extracurricular English courses, because:

I was thinking that even though I didn't go to university, God willing, my children would go. Even though I couldn't learn English because of financial difficulties, my children would be able to learn English. English is the language of the world; you have to know that. For a future, you have to know English first of all.

Elsie thus intended to make sure her children would receive the education she passed up in order to help her parents and younger siblings. For this, she received support from Viktor, whose bright future had been made possible in part because she had foregone a university education years earlier. While Elsie missed out on a university education that Viktor received, Viktor made up for this by attending to the next generation of Kaho children. When Elsie's daughter, Sinta, who had done well in school and had become impressively fluent in English, decided she wanted to study international relations in Java in the early 2000s, Elsie consulted with her brother, who encouraged Elsie to send Sinta to him. Viktor had become firmly established as a university lecturer in the city where Sinta wanted to study, living comfortably with his wife and children. He promised to pay Sinta's tuition and fees, buy her books, and provide other necessities, but still advised Elsie to send Sinta a little bit of money every month, "just so she knows that you care." And so Sinta retraced the footsteps Viktor had made twenty years earlier, traveling to Java to live with an uncle while studying at a university.

When I asked Elsie why she thought Viktor had been so generous, she framed her answer in terms of eastern Indonesian "character" and "family custom":

Eastern character is like that. If I am having a hard time, he is having a hard time. He feels responsibility (*kewajiban*). It is custom (*adat*), a family's custom, to have responsibility to each other. We notice each other when we are in hard times. Back then [when Viktor went to school] he had a hard time and I helped him out. Now he already has it good. Therefore, he helped out.

Indeed, the interdependency between brother and sister and the extraordinary help secured by mothers for their children by soliciting brothers, is a familiar theme in the literature on eastern Indonesian kinship relations and social organization. Danilyn Rutherford (2003: 50), for example, notes that for the Biak of West Papua "the brother-sister pair provides what might be called the 'elementary principle' of Biak kinship." Susan McKinnon (1991: 111) similarly observes in Tanimbar in the South Moluccas that "the prior unity of brother and sister stands at the heart of all kinship relations." We can understand the significance of this brother-sister bond in the context of what Shelly Errington (1989; 1990) calls the "exchange archipelago" character of eastern Indonesia. Societies in this exchange archipelago, which is found in parts of Sumatra and eastern Indonesia, consist of exogamous kin groups that are divided into named patrilineal "houses." The transmission of life flows from mothers to their children via blood (Fox 1980: 12-13). This means that even though women leave their family home in order to get married and provide their husband's house with a source of life, they will forever remain a part of the house of their brothers (McKinnon 1991). Children, who themselves form a part of their paternal houses, similarly remain connected via blood (through this "flow of life") to their maternal uncles (Stasch 2009). The bride-wealth exchanged in return for wives who represent sources of life enables the wife's brother to marry and continue the lineage of his house.

In this schematic, it becomes clear that men are indebted to their sisters and invested in their children. Origin myths throughout eastern Indonesia also tell of a united brother and sister broken apart (Carsten 2004; McKinnon 1991; Rutherford 2003). Against the backdrop of such origin stories, the lifelong flow of bride-wealth makes sense as a way to repair the broken brother-sister unity due to a woman's departure into another's house and the brother's need to marry. The intimacy of brother-sister bonds also becomes clear in a more visceral and affective sense. Rutherford, for instance, professes that the sweet caresses and sentiments of longing exchanged between brothers and sisters in Biak often led her to mistake siblings for lovers (2003: 49–50). Errington considers the long-lasting affective bonds between brothers and sisters to provide the paradigmatic model for the husband-wife relationship (1990: 48). Elsie's "family custom" or what she calls "eastern character" thus marks a more widespread indebtedness and affinity between brothers and sisters, mothers and children, and mother's brother's and sister's children.

Elsie's story of Viktor's educational success in particular and the Kaho family's socioeconomic ascent in general, emphasizes the immediacy of the ethical demands made by family more than it does the cultural schemata of alliance and exchange. Moreover, she highlights the urgency placed on such demands by the experience of hardship. For Elsie, *custom* and *character* come into play when a family member is "having a hard time," for such difficult periods are by definition shared: "If I am having a hard time, he is having a hard time." This is because family members "notice each other." Such recognition of an intimate other's hardship, I contend, marks the "entry of the ethical" (Schwarz Wentzer 2018b: 216; see also Zigon 2007). It marks that point when one faces the necessity of having to decide how to respond to another's hardship. As phenomenologist Bernhard Waldenfels (1994: 37) reminds us, "responding does not begin with talking about something; it does not begin with talking at all, but instead with a looking-at and listening-to which to some extent is inevitable." While inevitably noticing hardship, Elsie could have chosen not to again respond to her family's financial needs and instead pursued a university education paid for with money she earned working at her father's market stall. She chose to forgo higher education and take up a civil service position instead. She could have married and started a family sooner, yet decided to postpone those plans out of consideration for her family.

For Elsie, the only response possible when faced with the ethical demand of family members in need is assistance: "He had a hard time and I helped him out." This response, in turn, is expected to be reciprocated if possible: "Now he already has it good. Therefore, he helped out." Elsie captures this move from "noticing" to "helping out," or from being called to respond to an ethical demand to the final formulation of a response in the form of material and tangible support, with the notion of responsibility: "He feels responsibility. It is custom (*adat*), a family's custom, to have responsibility to each other." Viktor, furthermore, explicitly connects this notion of responsibility that is predicated upon the affective pull of family to the idea of care, when he urged his sister Elsie to send her daughter Sinta some money every month while she lived with him in Java, not out of necessity but "just so she knows that you care." We can thus also understand *family custom* or *eastern character* to point to a kind of caring responsibility that one meets when faced with the hardship of an intimate other—someone whose being is intrinsic to yours. It is this responsibility that I propose we should understand as a kind of care that fuels the *moral engine* that is started by an ethical demand made by those who count as family. This caring responsibility is both predicated upon familial relationality and fundamentally oriented toward, in this case, the continued prosperity of the Kaho family—even if it occurs at the immediate expense of any particular family member.

While Elsie describes an ethics within the context of family, we should keep in mind Dr. Cornelis Lay's earlier words about the social character of kinship ties in Kupang. Such responsibility does not solely occur between people with clear genealogical ties, but also happens between people whose genealogical connection is less clear or absent, such as when *uncles* write introduction letters and take in the children of *sisters*, neighbors send each other food, or when the head of a high school hires *honorer* (as shown in the previous chapter). We can even understand Elsie's attempt to encourage me to find a Dutch sponsor to fund the education of the children of those *honorer* as an example of the caring responsibility one has when faced with the ethical demand of hardship experienced by another. Still, I suggest that it is exactly this association of responsibility with family, and the sense that this responsibility exceeds one's own particular existence, that helps constitute it as a crucial form of care in Kupang.

Additionally, and to return to the possibility of corruption to slip into or be reframed as care, the occurrence of these responses in the specific context of hardship makes them even more convincing moral refutations to potential charges of corruption. In a place where people feel unseen and uncared for by the state, a kind of care that is rooted in family responsibility might offer some much-welcomed support in lieu of state care. However, before being seduced by the redeeming powers of family to offer care and support where it is lacking, we should remember that family can be fickle.

Family Friction

In spite of the efforts of several members of the Kaho family to ensure their collective prosperity through what Elsie calls "taking responsibility" and "helping out," not all family members sacrificed their own desires for the greater good. At the very time Elsie shared with me her perspective on, and her contributions to, Kaho-family success, all was not well between Viktor and Elsie and Sinta. Viktor was angry. In recent phone calls, he had called Elsie a bad mother and refused to ever set foot in Kupang again, much to Elsie's distress. The reason was Sinta's recent marriage to a husband considered unsuitable by the older members of the family. The groom was unemployed and thus showed no promise of securing any of the markers of personhood recognized in Kupang. Aware of her family's disapproval of her long-term boyfriend, Sinta forced their hand by arranging for what youth in Kupang jokingly refer to as an

MBA, or "marriage by accident"—she got pregnant. Her mother had postponed marriage and then postponed motherhood in order to help her family, while Sinta had prioritized her own desires. Instead of meeting her responsibilities in the name of care, she was, in the family's eyes, uncaring, indifferent, or selfish.

Viktor was furious that Sinta might be jeopardizing career opportunities as well as the chance—as an unattached, educated young woman—to enjoy life for a time before settling down. Viktor felt, Elsie said, that Sinta had thrown her life away and with it, perhaps, the accumulated efforts of two Kaho generations that had sacrificed to ensure a better life for all their children. Viktor was so upset that he had refused to attend Sinta's wedding party, an immense slight in Kupang, where family parties form an important part of the creation and confirmation of familial closeness and belonging.

The friction in the family was resolved in time, but Sinta's case serves as a reminder that non-belonging defines family as well. Waldenfels highlights this point, writing:

> On the social level, one encounters the corresponding structure of "belonging in non-belonging": everybody who belongs to a family, people, caste, religious community, or culture never entirely belongs to it. Remoteness, distance, farness, as well as the moments of solitude and being-out-of-place to which phenomenologists often refer to in their analyses of alien experience, do not mean a diminishing of this experience; rather, they belong to it in essence. (1994: 35)

It is this inherent possibility of non-belonging or alterity within the family that I want to turn to in the final section, where I consider these possibilities as they manifest at family parties. If care rooted in family responsibility offers a solution to the lack of state care, we should be attentive to the way in which familial forms of care carry their own powers of exclusion.

Family Parties: Materialities of Alterity and (Non-)Belonging

People in Kupang refer to the dry months between April and September as *musim pesta*, or party season. Ideally, important family events that can be planned, such as wedding celebrations, pre-wedding parties, bridewealth negotiations, and even funeral ceremonies, take place this time of year. These occasions, which recall the life cycle events that others have described in Timor and NTT (Fox 1980; McWilliam 2002: 187), require the attendance of kin from far and wide and could therefore only take place during the dry season when the crops are harvested and the land does not require constant attention. By not having to tend to crops, people actually have the time to travel to events that can even stretch out over days.

During *musim pesta* it is not unusual for people to attend multiple parties a week, or even several a night, although men tend to act on the obligation to attend far less than women do. In Kupang, the agricultural logic behind the party season passes largely unremarked. Most are simply happy there's no rain, as it can ruin festive outfits and mess carefully applied makeup during the often long and bumpy motorcycle rides to the parties. On the whole, these parties for life-cycle events in contemporary Kupang tend to be more modern then traditional and the occasions for them have expanded, now including reasons like sending a child off to university.[10]

All variety of parties tend to fall into the category of *kumpul keluarga*, or family gatherings. They form occasions for everyone who counts as family or, in Elsie's words, "have responsibility" to each other to gather in celebration, mourning, or negotiation. Depending on the size or cause of the party, guests consist of some combination of relatives, neighbors, close acquaintances, school friends, and colleagues. An important goal of these *kumpul keluarga*, besides celebration or mourning, is to amass enough money to pay for whatever served as the impetus for the party, such as covering the costs of a funeral, sending newlyweds off into their new lives together with some extra money, or collecting enough to pay for a child's school tuition. It is often financially impossible for host families to carry the costs of such events alone. Gathering the family, therefore, ensures a significant inflow of money at a time when it is most needed.

If in the ongoing flow of every family life (Fox 1980) the reciprocal acts of family care happen almost inconspicuously, in the more

---

10. As an example of shifts from the traditional, when people of different ethnic, island, or religious backgrounds get married, families can agree to forego the specific artifacts they consider to be crucial to bride wealth exchange (such as the *moko*, or drum, for the Alorese) and instead exchange money. Alternatively, as is increasingly common, bride wealth can be left out of a marriage agreement altogether.

routinized and formalized context of *kumpul keluarga*, the creation and maintenance of caring relationships take a much more marked visible and material form. These materializations of care offer ready sources for speculation about the presence, or absence, of care, as Stasch notes:

> People's understanding of kinship *as* intersubjective belonging and their close reflexive orientation to the making of kinship in practical acts are additional levels at which kinship is a system of otherness. Presence or attenuation of belonging is what makes people's kinship field a 'spectrum of alterity' in the first place. People's attentiveness to the making of kin relations in action means that the alternative possibility of being strangers is a steady presence within the experience of being kin, while people vigilantly monitor material interactions for signs of other's care (2009: 107).

Estrangement, in short, is always a possibility within kin relations and material interactions offer opportunities for examining the state of those relations.

The material aspects of parties, first of all, offer insight regarding the socioeconomic status and prestige of host families, and therefore offer a welcome benchmark for assessing one's own status by comparison. Are invitations sent out via text message or through the mail, and if through the mail, what is the quality of paper and envelope used? What kinds of drinks are served (soft drinks and perhaps some *sopi* for the men, or just water—and if water, is it from the well or store-bought plastic cups of *Aqua*?) What kind of food is served and more importantly in a town where the expression "eating meat" is employed as synonymous with going to a party, how many different meat dishes are offered (just chicken or might there actually be pork)? The material aspects of parties also offer insights into the presumed or desired degree of closeness between hosts and guests. How close do they seem to want us to be and how close do we want them to think we are?

Below are three examples of parties in which the certainty of belonging seems suspect or in question. Through these it becomes clear that the material aspects and practices, which form important parts of family gatherings and are supposed to signal belonging and care, can actually mask an estrangement, distance, and non-belonging. That kinship constitutes a field of otherness (Stasch 2009: 107) is disconcerting in Kupang, where family responsibility often counts as the last vestige of care.

Books of Donations

As we have seen, an important goal of family parties is to collect money. Among the unwritten rules of generalized reciprocity, whenever one is invited to a *kumpul keluarga* organized by a former guest, one is expected to give the same, if not larger, amount than the host provided when they were the guest. The amount people give at family gatherings tend to consist of a couple of rupiah bills in a sealed envelope. On some occasions, such as wedding parties, guests might deposit their envelopes in a nicely decorated cardboard box (with a slot cut into the top) placed on a well-guarded table in a prominent spot. On other occasions, such as smaller *kumpul keluarga* held at people's homes, hosts circulate a book of donations—from an official-looking hardcover, to a schoolchild's notebook, to old booklets on the verge of falling apart—in which guests can write down their names and the amount of their contribution. As Sinta explained to me during a *kumpul keluarga* pre-wedding party held for her friend, these books not only tell the host the amount given by each guest, they remind them of how much to contribute when, in future events, they become the guest.

This party took place outside the house of her friend's parents. Plastic chairs of the kind commonly rented for such occasions were lined up in neat rows around the house. On the little porch in front of the house stood a set of speakers which were connected to a microphone and a CD player playing popular regional songs. Every now and then a member of the bride-to-be's family or a pastor would take the microphone to give a speech or lead us all into prayer. As Sinta and I were sipping from our little *Aqua* cups, only half listening to the speeches and prayers, she asked those around us whether "the book" had already passed. Once we had located the book, I leafed through it and noticed that the contributions ranged from IDR 5,000 ($0.55) and IDR 200,000 ($23), with IDR 20,000 ($2.30) being the most common donation. Sinta said that low contributions suggest that donors might not have much money, are not particularly close to the host family, hold some grudge against them, or are simply too stingy to spend money. High contributions, conversely, suggest wealth, felt or hoped-for closeness, or an intention to show off. Sinta contributed IDR 100,000 ($11.50), which I thought was a fairly high amount. She explained that even though the bride-to-be did not strictly count as "family," she considered her a very good friend, and thus intrinsic to her being, and with a steady job could afford this token of generosity. Furthermore, when she herself would marry she would expect her friend to return a similar amount—provided she would be in a position to afford it.

In a sense, these books of donations offer a visible and legible materialization of care among those who count as family.[11] We could read the amounts listed as indications of (desired) closeness between family members or socioeconomic positions of the guests. As such, they offer a reflection of the "spectrum of alterity" that Isabella Lepri 2005: 710 claims characterizes people's field of relatives: not all relatives are equally close to one another and the donations listed in the books reflect this. However, keeping in mind Webb Keane's (1997) insights that material representational practices are vehicles for risks and tensions within social interactions, merely reading the book of donations in such a manner hides the resentment, manipulation, and friction that can sometimes characterize people's sentiments. As a staff member at a village head office complained, "You can never escape family. If you refuse a family member something, they will remember it. What if you run into them at a party? Or what if you need them at the time of a marriage, a funeral, or when sending your child off to school?"

This resentment shines through the donations of some guests. For example, a department head who consistently contributed relatively large donations at family parties told me that he gave these amounts solely because his family members assumed he could afford to be generous given his prestigious civil service position, while in fact he had a hard time paying his household's monthly bills due to the constant pressure of giving at family parties. He resented the obligation that came with his presumed position as a "big man," and felt taken advantage of by his family members. Viktor and Elsie's younger sister, Mientje, in contrast, consistently contributed the lowest amount of money she could get away with without being disinvited from family parties altogether—a tendency which earned her a reputation that brings to mind Marshall Sahlins's piercing observation that "not all kin are lovable" (2013: 108). A donation does not necessarily confirm closeness or care but can, instead, be a gesture

---

11. Books of donations are not only used at family parties in Kupang to reflect a host family's social capital. Jacqueline Vel (2009) describes a similar book of donations used to record charitable donations for the erection of a Protestant Christian Church on the NTT island of Sumba. As Vel explains, these books ought to be read not only as an indication of donors' Christian charity, but also as a reflection of the strength of the social capital of the project's initiator, who was a prominent Sumbanese politician.

that comes with the desire to escape or an ambivalence about the responsibilities that come with belonging. Signs of care, in other words, cannot be reliably inferred from material interactions themselves, because the material component of these interactions are themselves suspect.

Showing off Gengsi

The unreliability of the visual and material cues, which accompany family parties and which ought to signal belonging, also emerges in other ways. The suspicion that material and visual indications of familial belonging and closeness can be deceptive, for instance, seemed to hang over the Kaho family's participation in an elite and lavish wedding party of a very young couple that took place in 2008. The father of the bride was a high-ranking government official and the father of the groom was a local banker. The reason the couple got married at such a relatively young age became clear upon seeing the bride in profile: another MBA. The wedding invitation was printed on thick, luxurious paper and was received with much excitement in the Kaho family house, especially since the family had also been invited to the pre-wedding party at the bride family's house in one of the most upscale neighborhoods in Kupang. These were prestigious events and we felt honored to be included.

As we walked into Teluk Kupang, an open-air restaurant that served as Kupang's prime location for wedding parties, the venue looked more extravagant than I had ever seen it. Tables stretched far beyond the pillars that supported the roof overhanging the main part of the restaurant. Instead of the usual sealed plastic cups of *Aqua* water, canned soft drinks such as Coca Cola and Fanta *Stroberi* were available on every table. Sinta, clinging to my arm, steered me towards a table set up in the entrance area, deposited her gift envelope in the festively decorated cardboard donation box, and instructed me to write my name down underneath hers in the guest register. When we made our way to an empty table in the back, Mientje grabbed me by the arm and hissed that I was not to talk to anyone else there—I was to sit at their table because I was their *"bule"* (a common, albeit slightly derogatory, term for a White person).

While sipping our soft drinks, Mientje, who always had an eye for those better off than her and keenly felt actual and imagined signs of social inferiority, drew my attention to the layout of the room. She pointed to a slightly elevated area with a few tables and chairs all the way at the front, adjacent to the obligatory cardboard wedding cake that graced every Teluk Kupang wedding and very close to the dinner buffet. "V–I–P," she emphasized with a look of dissatisfaction, "guess who sits there?" I answered that it must be the bride's and groom's immediate family. "No," Mientje said dismissively, "it's for the [government] officials, the big guys," by which she meant higher-up government employees, bank officials, and important politicians. One of the candidates of the gubernatorial elections was sitting in that VIP area. The mayor was rumored to stop by later and indeed ended up giving a politically charged congratulatory speech.

Although Mientje was slightly peeved about not being one of the VIPs, she was noticeably pleased that at least she was in the same room as these very important people. The invitation to the wedding suggested that she belonged in some way to this group of important people. In order to confirm her belonging, she was wearing a new, mail-order outfit and had gotten her hair and makeup done professionally at a local beauty salon. Sitting there, it felt like a little bit of the prestige accumulated in the room rubbed off on us.

Mientje characterized the wedding party as a very *bergengsi* affair.[12] The kind of prestige *gengsi* conveys differs from that afforded by other types of status, such as achievement and seniority. Whereas achievement and seniority point to prestige obtained through individual accomplishment, *gengsi* suggests a kind of prestige that can be shared through association. For example, the daughter of former President Megawati has *gengsi* as the daughter of a former president and the granddaughter of one of Indonesia's founding fathers and its first president, Sukarno, although she has never accomplished anything of note herself. The kind of prestige or status that *gengsi* captures, then, is not solely an abstract indication of individual's hierarchical status or achievement but appears more to be something substantial that can be shared to an extent through relatedness.

Gengsi, in this sense, is not unlike the concept of power that Benedict Anderson (1972) describes in the pre-colonial Javanese Indic state, or the ideas of "potency" that Shelly Errington (1990: 41–44) claims exist throughout the islands of Southeast Asia. Anderson contrasts Western secular ideas of power as an abstract force with Javanese views of power as an invisible, albeit existentially concrete, energy that suffuses all matter organic and nonorganic (1972: 7). Errington reminds us that

---

12. *Gengsi*, according to the second edition of *A Comprehensive Indonesian–English Dictionary*, translates as: 1) prestige, honor, social status, and; 2) descent, relations, relatives. *Bergengsi*, which adds the prefix *ber–* to the noun *gengsi* to create a verb that means having the attribute the prefix is applied to, would translate to "having *gengsi*" or, more simply, "prestigious."

in Indonesia, the visible, tangible realm of human beings intersects with the invisible spirit world (*alam ghaib*). Power or potency is tapped from the invisible spirit realm and demonstrated (rather than exercised) in the tangible world of everyday life. Since potency is invisible, its presence can only be inferred from signs. The wedding party at Teluk Kupang gathered together many of the intangible but existing *gengsi* emanating from the bride and groom's families: the visible display of wealth in the sheer number of tables and guests, offerings of soft drinks, and the presence of VIPs at the front of the room.

An unspoken question that seemed to loom over the evening, nevertheless, was to what extent we belonged—at the party, with the host families, and in the upper middle-class circles they moved in. In other circumstances, all the visual and tangible cues of mutuality common at family gatherings would be accepted without much doubt as signs of inclusion. Having received an invitation to both the wedding and pre-wedding parties, being given food and so forth would confirm and reaffirm belonging and mutuality. At this party, however, visual displays and material offerings seemed less certain. As Errington (1990) explains, the presence of an audience strengthens the suggested existence of power. The audience, then, does not share in the power but merely serves to affirm it as a witness—not unlike the role played by onlookers at the civil service parade presented in the last chapter; they are there to affirm the achievement of desirable personhood by the civil servants on parade. Given the lavish attempts to display *gengsi* at the party, we were uncertain as to whether we shared in the *gengsi*, and thus counted as family, or if we merely served as a supportive audience propping up the *gengsi*.

In this way I understand Mientje's attempt to display *gengsi* of her own through her having her hair done, getting the expensive mail-ordered outfit, and, perhaps, having her *bule* companion. All were ways to performatively suggest belonging to the families of bride and groom, rather than being a mere audience to their prestige. Still, I doubt that she felt confident she could count on any of them for acts of caring responsibility if she were to call on them in a time of need.

Empty Envelopes

These examples of visible and material aspects of family parties that ought to indicate a confirmation of familial belonging and closeness show how the possibility of being strangers is always present, and that even a vigilant monitoring of supposed visualizations and materializations of the caring responsibility that informs family relationality is rife with uncertainty. Those acts that ought to create and confirm familial belonging, such as being invited to a family party, sharing in food and drinks, or jotting down contributions in books of donations, offer no reassurance that what is confirmed is closeness but rather a distance concealed. The material and visual components of these events offer no definitive proof of care but instead offer opportunities for manipulation, posing, and exploitation. This suggests that rather than viewing visible and material suggestions of care in a performative sense, as making kin, we should see them as performances that create the fiction of kin and care.

As a final example of the fickleness and unreliability of visual and material indications of confirmation of belonging, I turn to those donation boxes that often decorate tables at wedding parties. At weddings, as we have seen, guests are supposed to write their names in a guest registry and deposit an envelope with money into the donation box. Most guests will write their name on the envelope to make it known *who* is responsible for giving *what*. However, hosts generally expect to find a number of empty envelopes among all those deposited. Guests can do this for acceptable reasons, such as not having any money but not wanting to lose face in front of others, or for unacceptable ones, like simply being *mean*. While books of donations offer some visible and tangible clues from which to speculate about motivations of the giver and the mutuality between guest and host since the amount given is written next to the name of the donor, empty envelopes slid through the slots in "donation boxes" offer no such clues.

In the previous section on the Kaho family, Elsie made it clear that the caring responsibility between family members does not consist solely in helping, but is predicated on first recognizing another's hardship. Joel Robbins (2003; 2009) reminds us that the exchange of material goods forms a fundamental part of achieving mutual recognition. Recognition both forms the grounding for the possibility of care and is closely tied to material exchange. When tangible offers of mutuality and care, such as envelopes, turn out to be empty, they cast doubt on the existence of care among those who are supposed to count as family and towards whom one might turn in times of hardship.

Treading the Fine Line

This chapter has continued exploring the unintended effects of anti-corruption efforts by attending to the discrepancy in the actions of civil servants in Kupang: enthusiastic endorsement of anti-corruption efforts on the one hand, participation in the perpetuation of everyday petty forms of corruption, especially if they in some way involved family, on the other. In order to make sense of this apparent contradiction, I contrasted understandings of corruption firmly rooted in a rational individualist ontology with one grounded in a relational approach to personhood, and proposed that corruption in Kupang is better understood as a transgression of care rather than as a transgression of public-private boundaries.

A relational understanding of corruption as a transgression of care resonates institutionally and discursively throughout modern Indonesian history. Furthermore, as the analysis of the Kaho family's intergenerational socioeconomic ascent showed, this relational understanding of corruption also reverberates in the daily life of those in Kupang, where it emerges as a moral engine of caring responsibility towards family. As such, a slippage between corruption and care becomes possible in the moral-ethical complexity of everyday life, making it imperative to conceive of corruption not as something severed from larger questions of the political and governmental good but, rather, as intimately connected to larger normative questions.

Viewing corruption in a relational sense, or as a balancing act between acceptable and unacceptable ways of responding to the pull of (familial) relationality, cannot be disconnected from the larger question of how care figures in normative visions of a governmental good. If people, such as Elsie in her search for foreign sponsors, strongly suspect the state does not care for them in spite of the increasingly hollow-sounding promises of democratization and good governance, the reliance on family care starts to look less like corruption and more like survival amidst structural abandonment. Yet, to temper exactly how reliable family as a potential last bastion of care is, we should not forget that family care carries its own forms of uncertainty, unreliability, and possibilities for estrangement. If the state fails to deliver on its promise of a good, and material indications of familial belonging also turn out to be deceptive, where can one turn for care?

In the complex moral-ethical assemblage of post-*reformasi* Kupang, separating corruption from care is a near-impossible task for anyone. However, treading the fine line between these two—when getting it wrong means getting arrested or demoted—makes it a very important one for civil servants.

CHAPTER THREE

Between the Ethical and the Right Thing

A Voluntary Contribution

"Do not show up empty-handed, for hands need to be filled" (*Jangan dengan tangan kosong karena tangan harus diisi*) advised Pater Paulus during a long conversation I had with him in his secluded monastery in Kupang in 2008. As part of a wider teaching about ethical conduct in Kupang, he was telling me about the importance of bringing a small gift to offer my hosts whenever I was invited to someone's home. He recommended, in a perhaps outdated suggestion, that I bring some *siri pinang* and *kapur*, or betel nut, betel leaf, and lime, which, when chewed together would make someone slightly intoxicated. At family parties, a sense of belonging is created and maintained by sharing food and drink and in this case the companionable act of chewing betel, spitting out the telltale red globs of saliva produced by the acidic-bitter flavor combination while sharing a similar state of mild intoxication, which helps to establish the foundation for a possible relationship. Furthermore, bringing *siri pinang* would signal my understanding and respect of local traditions, and allowing myself to experience the *siri* sedation with others would convey a sense of trust as well as perhaps a complicity in rebelling against Indonesian opinions that chewing betel nut is as sign of (eastern) backwardness and intoxication, something to be avoided—especially for women. Pater Paulus did ask me to make sure that, no matter what I chose to bring, I would always bring more than would be consumed during my visit. Hands should still remain filled after I left.

Although Pater Paulus gave his advice while endeavoring to teach me how to act appropriately when visiting people in their homes, he may as well have been advising me how to conduct myself when interacting with civil servants in their offices. If we recall the practices of giving "thank you money" or "bus money" or the frantic reminders Elsie gave her daughter Sinta to make sure to leave some of her salary with the department treasurer, which tended to be glossed as "Kupang custom," the edict not to show up empty-handed seemed similarly suitable in the context of civil service. It is unsurprising then that the anti-corruption messages that littered the offices of Kupang's city-level government in the late 2000s singled out exactly this practice of "filling hands" as a form of corruption that needed to be avoided. As one sticker issued by Indonesia's Corruption Eradication Commission that I found attached to a bathroom door in the mayor's office proclaimed: "Tips are a part of the crime of CORRUPTION! Honey today becomes Poison tomorrow." Another message, which was printed with large letters (all caps) on a sheet of paper taped to a door in the Department of Public Works said: "ATTENTION. DO NOT OFFER/RECEIVE DONATIONS IN ANY FORM."

However, as we have seen, the designation of customary acts of politeness as corruption does not always make sense in a giving city that operates on an ethics of care and exchange. The rigid *public office* understanding of corruption, which informed Indonesia's post-*reformasi* approach to anti-corruption and singles out specific acts such as the offering or receiving of donations in any form as corrupt, could not match the more elastic understanding of corruption in Kupang, where the connection between specific acts and a greater good informed ideas of justice. The need to specify the giving and receiving of tips and donations as forms of corruption in the reminders dispensed by the Corruption Eradication Commission, thus suggests an incommensurability between a rigid legalistic approach to anti-corruption and the more complex moral-ethical assemblage of everyday bureaucratic life in Kupang.[1] For civil servants

---

1. Not everyone will experience this discrepancy between public pronouncements and bureaucratic practice as incommensurable. For example, in what he calls the "Thai regime of images," Peter Jackson (2004) shows how in Thai forms of power what gets said and what happens seem to pertain to two different realms of experience, one discursive, the other practical.

who tried to tread the fine line between corruption and care while continuously feeling threatened by the possibility of legal repercussions, the question of how to navigate the moral-ethical assemblage of post-*reformasi* bureaucracy in Kupang became an increasingly pressing one, yet also one for which it was hard to find a satisfying answer.

That does not mean they did not try, as I learned one late morning while waiting for an appointment with the village head and shooting the proverbial breeze (in lieu of an actual one) with lower-echelon civil servants in their small, sweltering office. The civil servants there had come up with an ingenuous solution to what they viewed as the main problem of corruption in their office, namely clients insisting on offering extra money in exchange for services rendered. As one of the civil servants explained, he completely understood this felt need to offer a token of gratitude in exchange for services. After all, giving something back in exchange for a gift or service in Kupang is *terbiasa*: commonplace, normal. Nevertheless, as the civil servants at the village head's office were all too well aware, accepting money from clients was illegal. Even though propriety prescribed accepting a monetized "thank you," anti-corruption regulations threatened penalties for staff who did so. Pointing at a white cardboard box atop one of the desks they proudly showed the office's elegant solution to this corruption conundrum. On the box the words "*sumbangan sukarela*" (voluntary contribution) were written decoratively in black sharpie. This was a charity box, they explained. If clients really felt compelled to offer some "thank you" or "bus" money, they could post it in the box.

As an answer to the question of how to navigate the post-*reformasi* moral-ethical assemblage of bureaucracy in Kupang, there is much to admire about this charity box response. Rather than refusing the gifts of clients altogether, the charity box ostensibly redirects the route such offerings would take: away from individual civil servants and towards those in need of charity. By recalling the boxes used at wedding parties, the charity box evokes the affective legitimacy of family responsibility. It transforms the potentially corrupt act of accepting money into one of facilitating care. For all intents and purposes, then, the charity box manages to pull off the impressive feat of simultaneously honoring that *terbiasa* custom of offering money and continuing the giving city's charitable ethos of distributing resources to those in need, while also avoiding

---

Without any need for irony or cynicism, these two realms are kept entirely separate and insulated from each other.

the corrupt act of appropriating (public) resources for private gain. Still, mindful of the contradiction that the donation of empty envelopes poses to the affirmation of care and belonging represented by the boxes of donations at weddings, I asked what happened with the money collected in the charity box. "Well," shrugged one of the staff members who had shown me the box, "at the end of the month or so we open it up and divide the money amongst ourselves." An upper-echelon official, who had emerged from his personal office and overheard his subordinate's reply to me, immediately refuted this answer: "No, of course we don't! This money goes to charity, you know, to the poor."

A charitable reader might be inclined to accept the superior's answer. After all, the charity box was only recently installed and perhaps the subordinates were not yet aware of the proper protocol of how to deal with its proceeds. A more cynical reader, in contrast, might be inclined to accept the subordinate's reply, and view the charity box as a mere attempt at giving the ongoing practice of offering and receiving gratuities a veneer of caring legitimacy. What I want to highlight here, however, is that the beauty of the charity box solution inheres in its capacity to contain all of these possibilities: charity, custom, compliance with rules, as well as the continuation of what had come to be defined as corruption. As such, it shows that navigation of the bureaucratic moral-ethical assemblage in post-*reformasi* Kupang is not a matter of simply transitioning from being corrupt to being good, but of a careful maneuvering between many competing, contrasting, conflicting, and overlapping ethical possibilities (Zigon 2009; 2011b).

This careful maneuvering is the central focus of this chapter, in which we will turn to how civil servants navigate the complex moral-ethical assemblage of Kupang's post-*reformasi* bureaucracy. In the previous chapters I showed that this moral-ethical assemblage is constituted not only by the *good* of the good governance approach, but also by understandings of the state as a giving city, and of personhood as embedded in relations of caring responsibility. We have seen repeatedly that the legalistic and public office approach to anti-corruption cannot account for the ethically more complex context of care and corruption in Kupang. We will now attend to the question of how civil servants, who are so often portrayed as the main culprits of corruption, deal with the implementation of anti-corruption efforts in their everyday work. We will focus in particular on young elite civil servants who received their training at specialized civil service preparatory institutes in part because they—more than other civil servants—have been trained in proper civil service conduct in post-*reformasi* Indonesia, but also because as career-focused civil servants with hopes of great professional advancement they stand to lose much if they get it wrong.

I will show that oftentimes anti-corruption efforts do not offer clarity to civil servants as to what counts as corruption. Rather, they only provide more confusion about how to properly navigate their tasks without facing the negative consequences of either corruption allegations or obstructions to career advancement. In order to figure out how to stay upright amongst this confusion, civil servants regularly draw on the familiarity of family responsibility I suggested fuels many moral engines in Kupang. In fact, and perhaps unsurprisingly, responsibility towards family proved to be one of the stickiest ethical points around which coalesced different possibilities for ethical conduct.

It might be tempting to read this persistence of family expectations and obligations within bureaucracy as evidence for Indonesia's failure to transition to liberal democracy and full-fledged Weberian bureaucratic rationality—the rationality that the modernization paradigm-fueled good governance advocates hope for. However, I suggest this would be a misreading of the Indonesian context, where organicist ideas of state formation have offered a modern alternative to liberal democratic ones since the late nineteenth century. Within this organicist ideology, family forms the main organizational principle of the modern Indonesian nation-state, rather than constituting a private contrast to the public realm. Indeed, this primacy of family to the construction of the Indonesian nation-state and state apparatuses allows for possibilities for overlap or slippage between various constructions of what it means to be an ethical civil servant. Such possibilities for slippage pose difficulties for an intervention that is predicated on clear Weberian distinctions between public and private realm, where the only *good* is aligned with bureaucratic rationality.

In short, in what follows we see that questions of proper bureaucratic conduct are not simply a choice between a rational-legal adherence to good governance and the ethical pull of family responsibility. Rather, ethical conduct means negotiating the various ways in which local moral economies, national ideologies of state building, global discourses on the morality of anti-corruption, and a conception of the good that inspires neoliberal ideas of governance overlap. Within this moral-ethical assemblage (Zigon 2011a), not just good or anti-corrupt, but responsible, perfect, right, and ethical all emerge as possible responses to the call of anti-corruption. For civil servants there is then no straightforward or unambiguous way of managing this complexity.

The Bureaucracy, Merit, and KKN

Exactly what KKN entailed was not clear to most civil servants in Kupang. Part of this confusion stemmed from the fact that while Kupangese generally viewed acts of KKN as morally reprehensible, many of the acts that would legally constitute a form of corruption were seen as "commonplace," ethically permissible, or even laudable. KKN was easy to recognize when it concerned faraway people and large-scale cases—the kind presented on daily on the national broadcast channel, Metro TV, with its steady stream of updates on the latest arrests, trials, and suspected cases of corruption by national figures. It was much harder to similarly accept as KKN the cases reported by local newspapers and radio shows.

Whereas national corruption cases provoked near-unanimous contempt and condemnation, local cases did not, since they involved suspects who were well known and operating in contexts that were well understood. There was, for instance, the case of the contractor who went to jail only because he took responsibility for his son's misdoings, as I was told by several neighbors and Department of Public Works. He was not the actual culprit but merely a good father trying to protect his son. Then there was a retired businessman who told me how one of his daughters had been unjustly fired from her civil-service position as sub-district head after an office competitor accused her of an act of KKN she had not committed. In fact, he claimed, she fervently opposed corruption and on several occasions had turned away family members who were asking for preferential treatment because "she wanted to do things right." As these cases showed, anti-corruption efforts were making it increasingly difficult to distinguish corruption as a morally reviled practice from practices that count as "being good" or "doing things right."

More importantly, the existing attempts to clarify what actually constituted KKN—conveyed in stickers and printed messages—did not really offer much elucidation regarding the kinds of corruption civil servants in Kupang actually worried about and thus seemed both ineffective and insufficient. By singling out the tips or donations, they focused only on a small part of the KKN unholy trinity: *korupsi*. This, however, was not the KKN that tended to trouble civil servants most. As we have seen, the act of giving and receiving is often not recognized as corruption but instead as custom, care, or in the case of the charity box, something *commonplace*. At most, *korupsi*, evoked laconic comments among lower-level civil servants regarding how the "higher-ups" now had more money to line their pockets. The second K and the N, *kolusi* and *nepotisme*, which pertain to those relational forms of corruption that can slither between forms of care aimed at helping others *really become somebody*, which as we recall is the manner in which Kupangese refer to people who managed to obtain civil service employment, and acts of self-interested self-aggrandizement, preoccupied civil servants much more. These were the acts that formed the real threats to one's professional advancement in the uncharted territory of post-*reformasi* bureaucracy.

This was particularly so because the post-*reformasi* political devolution that aimed to break up the clientelist character of Indonesian civil service did not entirely manage to eradicate intra-office expectations of loyalty and support of civil servants toward their superiors, especially if these superiors had political ambitions. As we recall, as part of the post-*reformasi* political, fiscal, and administrative reforms, Indonesia had introduced direct district-head elections in 2004. During the New Order, civil servants were prohibited from supporting any political party besides Golkar, an organization that functioned as Suharto's reelection vehicle for three decades (Bourchier 2015: 161–165).

In post-*reformasi* Kupang, civil servants are theoretically free to vote for whichever candidate they wish and, in fact, must refrain from being actively involved in, or supportive of, any political party. Nevertheless, most candidates for district-head positions in state-dependent Kupang have consisted of higher-echelon civil servants who relied on their office subordinates as a base of reliable voters in a continuation of the clientelism associated with the New Order. As civil servants found during Kupang's first-ever direct mayoral elections in 2007, picking sides and rewarding loyalty overrode the supposed neutrality of bureaucracy. One particularly unhappy Department of Public Works employee, who felt he had missed out on a much-deserved promotion, complained to me that he suspected that the new department head, who in his opinion was incompetent, had only received his position in exchange for supporting a mayoral candidate. "Promotions are not based on merit but on KKN!" he exclaimed.

While the tension between merit and KKN in the post-*reformasi* mix of bureaucracy and politics was cause for concern among ordinary lower-level civil servants, it triggered outright anxiety among elite civil servants who were young, ambitious, and trained for fast advancement through the complex layers of administrative ranks. For example, Budi, a 30-something graduate of the prestigious Institute for Domestic Governance (*Institut Pemerintahan Dalam Negeri*, or IPDN) near Bandung, West Java—and head of the village office where civil servants had proudly shown me the charity box—thought advancing in his career would hinge on his ties to appropriate superiors rather than merit. For instance, he told me that he already feared the consequences of the upcoming 2012 mayoral elections, since his career advancement depended partly on the whims of the new mayor and gossip that he, Budi, may be subjected to. His chances of getting promoted would depend not on his professional accomplishments but on whether the new mayor suspected that Budi had supported his candidacy. Failing to support a successful candidate meant that one would have to wait years for a promotion. Budi vividly remembered the punishment that the new mayor Adoe had doled out to his chief opponent, Yonas Salean, after the 2007 mayoral elections: Salean had been made "expert staff," an advisory post outside the formal civil-service hierarchy, and thus effectively excluded from all city-level administrative and political business. This was not a fate Budi was eager to meet early in his career.

Valentino, Elsie's oldest son who had also graduated from the IPDN, shared some of Budi's concerns, but feared much harsher repercussions. After graduating from the IPDN in 2007, Valentino was appointed to the sought-after position of mayoral aide. As an aide, Valentino accompanied the mayor on work trips throughout the Indonesian archipelago, living a cosmopolitan lifestyle few in Kupang enjoyed. Other, less formal, benefits of the position were the tips visitors would slip him in the hope that he would secure them an audience with the mayor. Usually, these tips consisted of cash, but sometimes he would receive a bottle of liquor which he happily shared with his office peers (and guest-sister anthropologist in the mayor's chambers after hours). Valentino estimated that each day he made an average of IDR 200,000 ($15) from such tips, which by payday amounted to almost five times his monthly salary. Besides these financial extras, he also once enjoyed a ten-day holiday in a Bali resort with the mayor, the mayor's wife, and some other local district heads—all paid for by a banker who hoped these district heads would appoint him to the directorship of a local bank.

Valentino was no exception when it came to enjoying the informal perks of working close to the mayor; other civil servants in a comparable situation also received material rewards from those hoping to obtain access to the mayor. During a conversation we had in 2009, Valentino told me that, during the two years he had worked as a civil servant, he had received promotions that would have taken others at least twice as long, simply because he made good use of his closeness to the mayor.

Although this closeness had brought him financial and professional benefits, he feared how it would affect his still-nascent career in Kupang's civil service. Valentino told me about the fate suffered by the previous mayor's aide:

It is impossible for civil servants not to get involved [in elections], not to take sides. I saw what happened to the former aide: he got relegated to a regular staff position. Whereas before he was the hands and feet [*kaki tangan*, generally used pejoratively to mean "assistant"] of the mayor, he was now the one being ordered around to fetch staff cigarettes or lunch in the middle [hottest part] of the day and perform other humiliating tasks in the department.

Valentino feared that his impressive IPDN degree and experience as an aide would never outweigh the fact that he had been the mayor's "hands and feet." Yet, like Budi, he was unsure whether and how his close connection to the mayor might affect his professional future. At the heart of their different ideas on how to prevent the potential disastrous effect of the upcoming mayoral elections on their careers was a basic uncertainty about how to navigate post-Suharto local bureaucracy, where merit and KKN are not easily separated.

This uncertainty resonated across Indonesia where the far-reaching political and administrative changes Indonesia implemented in the post-*reformasi* era yielded uneven effects on the functioning of local bureaucracies and politics. In some places, decentralization seemed to have exacerbated money and vote selling in local politics (Choi 2004). In other places, the recent changes seemed to have made little difference. For example, instead of countering the patrimonialism that so permeated Suharto's New Order regime, institutional changes appeared to have facilitated a continuation of an older form of politics that emanated from Jakarta and spread throughout the country (Hadiz and Robison 2013: 36). Entrenched elites stay in power while aspiring elites employ the logic of patrimonialism to compete in local politics (Choi 2009). In spite of these mostly gloomy analyses that frame the state of Indonesian politics in an age of good governance as a continuation of older, clientelist political practices, Indonesians across the archipelago have also used their newfound political power to vote out known corrupt incumbents (Mietzner 2006). Furthermore, one-dimensional explanations of decentralized Indonesian politics in terms of money politics or entrenched elites, miss the extent to which the political "reshuffling" has actually had multiple effects (Buehler 2007). The only certainty, so it seemed, was uncertainty.

How Budi and Valentino dealt with this uncertainty shows how they thought the cards were stacked in the specific context of Kupang. While both feared potential post-election punishments along the lines of what had happened to the former mayor's aide and the current mayor's competitor, they had different ideas about how to prevent this. Valentino hoped he could count on his established connections with people who were expected to run for office. In his capacity as aide, Valentino felt he had become close enough to one of the candidates, the vice mayor, not to fear any postelection retaliation. A second candidate was a distant relative who would likely look favorably on Valentino. The third candidate was a good friend of one of his uncles, who would probably put in a good word on his behalf.

Unsure of whether counting on various degrees of closeness with potential candidates would keep his career safe, Valentino also devised a strategy to circumvent becoming involved in the coming election turmoil altogether. He would ask the mayor for one last informal favor: to be granted a "learning task," which is a chance to pursue an academic degree sponsored by the local government. Such learning tasks are rare and supposed to be given out only on the basis of merit and not as a favor; this thus arguably constituted a form of KKN. He planned to enroll in a master's program at a prominent university in Java, far away from Kupang. Another uncle held a lecturer position there and could probably help him get accepted into the program. If he started the program at the beginning of the election year, he might avoid election politics and return after the dust had settled; armed with a new degree to complement the one he already had from the IPDN. Maybe this would even earn him a new promotion into managerial ranks so that he could never be demoted.

While Valentino looked upward by strengthening connections with potential candidates, Budi looked downward by strengthening ties with *the people*. As he saw it, the way to advance in post-Suharto administration and politics was by appealing to voters. "These are not the old days when subordinates would actually listen to orders from above," he said. "People can now decide for themselves who they want to vote for." He saw the vice mayor's subtle strategic actions as a good example of career advancement in the present-day Kupang administration. Budi claimed that the vice mayor instructed every village head to notify him of all weddings and funerals held in their sub-districts. On such occasions,

Budi would send a small contribution on the vice mayor's behalf to the celebration: such as sugar, candy, or a pig. People would hopefully remember these gifts long enough to reciprocate with their vote. Budi saw this new unobtrusive way of campaigning as more successful than counting on the obedience of subordinates.

Budi and Valentino's different strategies nonetheless revealed shared perceptions of post-Suharto bureaucracy in Kupang. Both thought favoritism, rather than merit, would help their careers—their promotions depended on supporting the right candidate, not being good at their jobs. Both thought connections were crucial to career advancement. Valentino counted on existing (familial) relationships with seniors both within and outside the governmental bureaucracy, while Budi pinned his hopes on yet-to-be-established relationships with voters. Neither were concerned about corruption. Both flirted with, if not fully engaged in, the kinds of practices the anti-corruption messages tacked to office doors and walls sought to end. Valentino accepted gifts and did not hesitate to ask the mayor for special favors. For Budi, giving gifts to potential voters was a proper means of advancing his career.

For Budi and Valentino, and many others in their position, the post-*reformasi* anti-corruption efforts failed to clearly define corruption while showing how to successfully navigate the bureaucratic maze of career advancement. Rather than decreasing corruption, the move toward good governance merely increased uncertainty of how to stay afloat in local bureaucracy for young, elite civil servants. And in the giving city, these civil servants immediately turn to the idea of reciprocity inherent in relationships, especially family relationships, as an important way to alleviate the stress of that uncertainty.

Between Ethics and the Right Thing

When he hit an unexpected obstacle during his lengthy application process to the prestigious IPDN, Valentino had indeed turned to relationships. The IPDN is a highly selective institute that accepts only a limited number of candidates from each region and the year Valentino got accepted, only one other young man and one young woman from Kupang were accepted besides him. Its selection procedures consist of physical, psychological, and general-knowledge tests, the initial rounds of which take place in the regions where candidates live. The final testing takes place on the IPDN campus near Bandung, West Java. After Valentino made it through the selection rounds in Kupang, he had to travel to Bandung several times for further testing. After the final round of tests, Valentino was happy to find his name on a list of the accepted; a list that had been posted on a campus wall in the middle of the night. Much to his surprise, however, a few hours later his name had disappeared from the list and had been replaced with someone else's. Valentino suspected that one of the other candidates had used connections, influence, or money to gain a place on the list at his expense, so Valentino did the only thing he could think of: ask the help of his uncle, who had a close relationship with the then president of Indonesia, Megawati Sukarnoputri. Within a few hours his name was back on the list.

While family connections were pivotal in Valentino's eventual acceptance into the IPDN, it was unclear to Valentino whether the sudden disappearance of his name from the list was the result of someone's KKN, and equally unclear if his uncle merely rectified a wrongdoing or had to engage in some KKN of his own. It was clear, however, that Valentino had no qualms in calling his influential uncle when he needed help. As we have seen throughout this book, he was not alone in relying unhesitatingly on family connections. Recall that whenever I asked civil servants whether they would pick a family member or an equally skilled unrelated candidate for a position, all said they would pick the family member. The moral engine of a caring responsibility towards those who count as family, especially in times of hardship, can spur those in a position to help to do so whenever they can. As *Pak* Marinus, the head of the local chamber of commerce, explained to me:

> Of course, you have to help out family. The opportunities for employment here are too limited to just say, "Go make it on your own." If at a family party a family member walks up to me and asks me to give their child a project, how can I refuse? I will see them again at the next party.

His reasons for helping family members stemmed from both the inescapability of family demands and the impossibility to refuse someone in need. For both *Pak* Marinus and Valentino, being able to call on family members when in need, or unhesitatingly responding to family members' calls for help, poses no ethical quandary.

For others, in contrast, the question of how to respond to family members' requests for help is answered less easily. Anderius, another IPDN graduate whom I got to know while working in the Department of Governance, continuously struggled with this question. He was born in a small village on the island of Flores, another island in the province of NTT. Although none of his relatives worked in the civil service, his parents, like many other parents in NTT, hoped that he would. They planned to send him to high school in Kupang, where he could receive a better education than was available in Flores. Since this was costly, they followed the practice of collecting small donations from family, neighbors, and friends during a *kumpul keluarga* (family party). Anderius was thus able to attend high school in Kupang and that enabled him to enter the IPDN and ultimately land a highly-prized civil service position.

After he had finished his education and had taken up a position in Kupang's city-level bureaucracy, however, relatives and friends from Flores would occasionally ask Anderius for his help in getting them civil service positions. With them, as he explained to me, he shared "the world of the ethical [*etika*]," which is an ethics that crosses public-private boundaries, blurs distinctions between corruption and care, and follows the reciprocal logic of family parties. He was now, however, also part of what he called the "world of the right thing [*kebenaran*]," which he shared with his university friends and fellow elite civil servants. In this world he felt the obligation to adhere to office rules that differed from, and often contradicted, the ethics of family obligations. In a sense, he thus found himself in what J. P. Olivier de Sardan (1999: 48) calls a "schizophrenic situation," in which the administrative and professional legitimacy of civil servants conflicts with their social legitimacy. By helping family members, he would break office rules, but by adhering to rules he would let down family members. According to him there was no unambiguous distinction between being a good or corrupt civil servant; one was either right and not corrupt or corrupt yet ethical. In between the *etika* of family and the *kebenaran* of professionalism, he felt morally stuck.

This sense of schizophrenia brings to mind the "moral torment" that the newly converted Urapmin of Papua New Guinea experience, which stems from being torn between the two incompatible value spheres of Urapmin relationality and Pentecostal Christian individuality (Robbins 2004; 2007). When Anderius describes himself as being stuck between the ethical and the right thing, he, too, appears to be torn between the two separate value spheres: of Weberian rational-legal bureaucracy on the one hand and a local moral economy characterized by a caring responsibility to family on the other. This was a bind that Valentino and Marinus did not seem to experience. However, while the idea of *moral torment* quite aptly captures Anderius's anguish, this torment does not stem from being pulled by two distinct and incompatible value spheres. Instead such torment comes from experiencing the complications of an already-complex and discombobulating moral-ethical assemblage (Zigon 2009), one in which different institutional and discursive moralities can at times converge and overlap. The anguish does not simply stem from being stuck between two mutually exclusive value spheres but emerges from Anderius' inability to move through the unexpected and temporary alignments of various institutional, discursive, and embodied moralities. The very thing that creates Anderius' torment, while allowing for the unreflective responsiveness to family responsibility of Valentino and Marinus, is the institutional morality of the organicist state, the ideological influence of which has ebbed and waned throughout Indonesia's history (Bourchier 2015). It makes possible an easy elision between the *ethical* and the *right thing* because of the central importance of family to this ideological construction of the Indonesian nation-state. There is no easy distinction between family responsibility and legal-rationality when the modern state apparatus is meant to both embody a family and serve as a model for the modern Indonesian family. When the bureaucratic office is presented as a family, how unethical is it to refuse requests from family members? Anderius' predicament, in other words, does not stem from needing to choose between the two distinct value spheres of the *ethical* and the *right thing*, but from the confusion around the impossibility of separating office from family, public from private, and corruption from care.

Familyism

The idea that the Indonesian state ought to be organized on the basis of a "family principle" (*azas kekeluargaan*, derived from the Indonesian word for family, *keluarga*) has been a fundamental part of what it means to be Indonesian since the very conception of the Indonesian nationalist project in the early twentieth century (Boellstorff 2005; Bourchier 1997; Steedly 2013: 203–207). The family principle is closely aligned with the organicist conceptions of state organization, which have influenced ideas and practices of state formation since the late nineteenth and early twentieth centuries (Bourchier 2015). While organicist thought and influence lessened in popularity during Sukarno's presidency after Indonesian independence in 1945, in part due to its association with the Japanese occupation, it reemerged with renewed force when Suharto rose to power in 1968 and molded his New Order system of governance, drawing heavily on organicist state theory for the ideological and structural organization of his new Indonesian state.

The notion that the state is organized as a family was first articulated and popularized in the 1920s by the national education movement *Taman Siswa* (Shiraishi 1997). Some proponents of this movement envisioned that this principle would offer a model for a new and egalitarian community that contrasted with the Dutch model of colonial rule. Adopting the words for father (*bapak*), mother (*ibu*), and child (*anak*) from Malay, which at that time functioned as a lingua franca throughout the archipelago but had no connection to any particular social structure or location, *Taman Siswa* tried to sociolinguistically unify the vast Indonesian archipelago while providing a model for a new kind of society. From these *Taman Siswa* origins the family principle became enshrined in the 1945 Indonesian constitution and has been central to the organization of schools, the military (McVey 1972), civil service (Suryakusuma 1996), and other examples of modern bureaucratic institutions ever since (McVey 1967: 136–137; Shiraishi 1997: 81–82). Parents, teachers, department heads, and presidents alike would be *Bapak* and *Ibu*, while sons, daughters, pupils, subordinates, and citizens all would be *anak*, so that eventually through the state's use of family ideology "all Indonesians became part of a family in which the Indonesian government was the parent and the student-citizens were the children" (Kuipers 1998: 137).

As Michael Herzfeld points out (2016: 8), it is not uncommon for governments to "co-opt the language of intimacy for its utilitarian ends of commanding loyalty." Even though the family dynamics espoused in the Indonesian family principle emphasize hierarchical relationships between parents and children instead of the more horizontal brother-sister bond central to many eastern Indonesian kinship practices, the adoption of the intimate idiom of family here offers a seductive means to imbue state power and organization with an affective legitimacy. Still, understandings of what this family was and how exactly it would function has shifted over time, for the family principle's notion of the ideal family has never been entirely stable. In nationalist debates that ultimately led to *Taman Siswa's* adoption of the family principle, disagreements already existed concerning what kind of family could provide a suitable model for a future Indonesia. Some advocated a hierarchical family model consisting of a wise father, caring mother, and dutiful, respectful children, commensurate with organicist ideas. Others propagated a so-called democratic republic model in which children did not fear standing up to their parents (Shiraishi 1997: 84–86). While the first model reflects an organicist notion of state organization, the second is more commensurate with a revolutionary nationalist spirit. From its very inception there has thus existed a tension within the family principle between a family dynamic that condones or even encourages the occasional uprisings of children against parents and a more top-down, "father knows best" family dynamic.[2]

Indonesia's first president, Sukarno, fresh out of the anti-colonial struggles against the Dutch, had little affinity for the organicist take on the family principle as advocated by some Indonesian nationalists, and which closely matched ideologies of state organization propagated by the Japanese. His ideas on Indonesian state formation were, instead, at least according to David Bourchier, grounded in modernist and humanist thought influenced by Leninist and Jacobin ideas, and envisioned a "revolutionary and egalitarian collectivism" (Bourchier 2015, 71) more

---

2. This tension has been noted by many scholars of post-independence Indonesian politics and governance. For example, Ruth McVey (1972) describes the institutionalization of *bapakism* in the Indonesian army and notes how during the revolution ensuring the execution of orders depended not on formal authority per se, but rather on the ability of officers to attract loyal soldiers. Initially, shared war experiences gave extra emotional gravity to these father-child (*bapak-anak buah*) bonds in the army. With the passing of time, however, these relationships made way for more instrumental patron-client ties, and for the development of more complex and shifting alliances. The position of *bapaks*, nevertheless, remained an interference with the official chain of commands as, "an officer whose men were strongly loyal to him was obviously in a much better position to act independently than one who had only the general claims of army discipline behind him" (McVey 1972: 154). Donald Fagg (1958), furthermore, mentions the paternalistic responsibility of a *bapak* over his *anak buah* as a consistent feature of the Indonesian bureaucratic system. As he describes, career advancement in civil service was often dependent on closeness to important authority figures. Important to note, nevertheless, is that *bapaks'* authority has to be earned, which Fagg illustrates by describing the continuous efforts made by the *wedono* of Modjokuto's to perform and maintain his paternalistic role. Roelof Oostingh (1970) similarly discusses the importance of personal ties between *bapaks* and *anak buah*, which are not necessarily the same as formal institutional ties, in Indonesian bureaucracy. He also notes the semblance of these personal ties to family ties, characterizing the obligation networks of which the *bapak* forms the center as a, "recasting of the web of kinship."

than a (conservative) organicism, although we might question just how committed Sukarno actually was to the tenets of egalitarianism.[3] In his political reign, known as Guided Democracy, which mixed democracy with autocracy, he and his wife looked over their nation of *anak* as a proud *Bapak* and *Ibu*, while countless other *Bapak* and *Ibu* in homes, classrooms, and bureaucratic offices led their own *anak*/pupils/subordinates as democratic equals rather than authoritarian superiors. Under Suharto's subsequent New Order regime, however, the egalitarian and revolutionary underpinnings of the Indonesian family-cum-state gave way to a more hierarchical conception of family, with a conception of *Bapak* more in line with the organicist hierarchical model. Suharto's leadership style combined strict authoritarianism with a clientelist dispersion of formal and informal favors to loyal subordinates in a way that set the tone for the New Order organization of other state apparatuses, such as the military and civil service (Conkling 1979; Fagg 1958; McVey 1967; Oostingh 1970) .

The New Order interpretation of the family principle did not pertain solely to men's roles. Its state policies, education, and media promoted a strict gender-role division: women as mothers and wives and men as earners of income (Blackwood 2005). Julia I. Suryakusuma (1996) describes the gender ideology that accompanied this version of the family principle as *Bapak Ibuism* (father-motherism). Civil servants played an important part in the New Order entanglement of state, family, and authority. They were a vital source of political support through their required loyalty to Golkar, as well as providing a *perfect* example of Indonesian national personhood. Perfection entailed both loyalty to the Indonesian family-state and an embodiment of its gender and sexual ideologies. Civil servants therefore joined the national Civil Servants Corps of the Republic of Indonesia (*Korps Pegawai Republik Indonesia*, or KORPRI), while their wives joined the female auxiliary *Dharma Wanita* (Women's Association). The New Order family principle required loyal men, caring wives and mothers, and obedient children under the all-seeing, watchful gaze of the ultimate *Bapak*, Father Suharto.

---

3. This was not without difficulty. Fagg (1958) noted the friction civil servants experienced in balancing "traditional" familial ways of interacting based on respect (*hormat*) with new egalitarian principles of independence shortly after Indonesian independence. Oostingh (1970: 33–34), additionally, described similar tensions between family obligations or a "moral code of society" and modern state demands.

It is in this New Order notion of perfection that we can see the possibility for slippage between what Anderius called the ethical and the right thing, since the multiple connotations of family and intra-familial expectations make it difficult to weigh the loyalty to Fathers that characterized New Order perfection against the right thing of office rules and the "ethical" of family obligations. When values regarding bureaucratic conduct borrow their legitimacy from the affective bonds of family— even if this exemplifies a strategic co-option by the state for utilitarian purposes (Herzfeld 2016)—we can wonder how much of a difference there is between responding to demands made by one's *bapak* (the familial father) or *Bapak* (professional superior)? How far apart are the ethical of familial obligations and the correct bureaucratic conduct when the latter lends so much of its legitimacy from the former via the notion of perfection? One is left to face an ever-shifting moral-ethical assemblage where what counts as corruption also counts as ethical, and where the bureaucratic imperative of a loyalty to Fathers encapsulated by the word *perfection* helps to obscure any distinction between them.

In Kupang, the family-cum-state trope resonated in many ways and mostly without much friction. A male employee from the Department of Governance drew on a comparison to family life to explain to me what the office atmosphere was like:

Even if we only know each other through work, we do have the habit of collecting a small contribution (*sumbangan*) when someone has a baby or wedding or something. This also goes for the colleagues that have moved away to other offices. We have very friendly relations at the office, like a family. We give the contribution not because we have to, but because we want to.

Employees of the Department of Governance, furthermore, depicted their department head as a strict yet kind "father" who made sure everything ran correctly. The subdepartment head at the Department of Public Works also portrayed his relationships to coworkers in familial terms. He told me that he viewed the office as a family with the department head as the father and himself as the mother. The department head's job, according to him, was to make sure all the work got done, whereas it was his mothering role to keep all children close to him and take care of them.

This does not necessarily mean a father's wishes are obeyed, especially when his office *children* find them objectionable. The ethical dilemmas faced by civil servants in their everyday bureaucratic practices do not solely consist of demands made by family members (as Anderius faced). Office superiors also attempt to circumvent office rules for personal financial gain. This became evident in a story shared by Christian, a lower-level employee at the Department of Public Works. When he and his coworkers evaluated project proposals, the department head would sometimes enter the room and tell them that so-and-so had to win the project (even if this meant disregarding official tendering rules). Christian said most of his coworkers usually made sure these proposals won, partly because they stood to receive "smoothing" or thank-you money, but also because this is simply what a subordinate does: when the *Bapak* orders something, subordinates obey. Christian himself tried not to listen to such commands from superiors, or at least so he claimed, and instead judged each proposal fairly and honestly, even if by doing this he disobeyed his superior. In terms of navigating the moral-ethical assemblage of bureaucracy, Christian ended up doing what Anderius called the *right thing* but in doing so failed in holding to a perfect loyalty to one's father so prized in the logics of the New Order. Still, as some early *Bapak Siswa* proponents and Sukarno might claim, by standing up to his father, Christian displayed the rebellious spirit required of the children should a democratic and egalitarian Indonesia be safeguarded.

What these examples of moral torment show, is that solving ethical dilemmas is not a straightforward matter, and that the moral-ethical navigation of the post-*reformasi* bureaucratic landscape in Kupang does not consist of choosing between several totalizing moralities or value spheres. The cooptation of the idiom of family into the project of Indonesian nation-building merges contrasting ethical expectations such that several institutional, discursive, and embodied moralities offer, at once, different templates for ethical civil servant conduct. This process substitutes a hierarchical organization of the nuclear family for a more egalitarian organization of extended families common in Kupang where sibling bonds are pivotal to family dynamics. Furthermore, the state-model of an idealized nuclear family offers contradictory moral models of father-child relationality, one in which a father has unwavering authority over his children, and one in which children are encouraged to stand up to their fathers.

The question of how not to be corrupt in contemporary Indonesia, then, takes place in something more akin to a moral assemblage, which consists of "diverse and often contradictory discourses as well as diverse and sometimes incompatible embodied moral dispositions" (Zigon

2013b: 202). This allows people to recognize "more possibilities for resonance that permit individuals to comfortably live, reflect, and ethically
work on themselves" (2013b: 202). In such an assemblage what counts as
corruption at times overlaps with what is *ethical*, *right*, or *perfect*. Given
this existing ethical complexity, how are the young men and women who
are supposed to lead civil service trained for taking up positions in this
uncertain and disorienting bureaucratic landscape?

Training Elite Civil Servants

In order to answer this question, let us return to the elite civil servants who were trained at specialized institutes in the post-*reformasi* era.
As we will see, rather than countering the potential for slippage in the
particular moral-ethical assemblage of post-Suharto Kupangese bureaucracy, it reinforces it.

Recall that the Institute for Domestic Governance (*Institut Pemerintahan Dalam Negeri*) or IPDN is the most prestigious civil service preparatory institute in Indonesia. Located in the city of Bandung in Sume-
dang, West Java, it is situated in a cluster of other institutes for higher
education that prepare cadres for civil service and integrated into the
Institute for Governance (*Institut Ilmu Pemerintahan*) or IIP in Jakarta.
Whereas most universities and other tertiary educational institutions
churn out civil servants to be employed in lower-level bureaucracy with
modest but still-present prospects for promotions, the IPDN trains civil
servants for the elite bureaucracy, where the opportunities for upward
mobility are greater. During their IPDN education, students spend four
years at the secluded campus and are trained in the art of governance,
as well as all the skills—and opportunities—necessary to move up in
regional, provincial, and national bureaucracies.

The IPDN is rumored to be a violent institution. Occasionally, newspapers publish stories about injuries and even deaths among the students. For example, in 2003 several IPDN dropouts discussed the fre-
quent beatings they suffered from their seniors (Tempo 2003), and in
January, 2011 a female student died from internal bleeding after being
beaten in the stomach (Kompas 2011). Although the IPDN alumni in
Kupang's city-level government offices generally remained tight-lipped
about these aspects of their IPDN past, Valentino would occasionally
give in to my relentless inquiries about his training. One afternoon while
we were hanging out on the front porch of the Kaho family home, he

showed me a video shot and edited by a fellow IPDN student that depicted outdoor exercise sessions.[4]

The video started off pleasantly enough with groups of young men and women in exercise outfits jogging, running up and down steps, and doing push-ups and sit-ups. These scenes were followed by others that depicted the same young men in rows, getting kicked or punched in the stomach one-by-one by what appeared to be their superiors, although it was unclear to me whether these superiors were senior students or institute staff. The camera then focused on a row of young men lined up at the top of a long flight of stairs. One superior ran up and forcefully kicked the first student in line, then the second, the third, and so forth. Unable to stay standing, the young men tripped backward and fell down the stairs, gasping and coughing. How did this seem like a suitable way of preparing aspiring civil servants whose most arduous tasks would consist of sitting behind desks and processing documents?

Vigorous physical training has, of course, long formed a part of the IPDN curriculum. This is partly explained by the militaristic style of and close integration of the army in all parts and levels of the Indonesian state apparatus during the New Order regime (Bourchier 2015: 158–160; Suryakusuma 1996). *Pak* Andre, who graduated from the IPDN's forerunner, the STPDN in 1994, recalled that he had to join the army for two years as an "expert lieutenant" after having completed the classroom part of his public administration degree. He told me that during his time, all students from prestigious tertiary educational institutes had to undergo some form of military training: students from Universitas Indonesia and the Bandung Institute of Technology, for example, also had to join the military as part of the proper preparation for their future bureaucratic positions, despite having to do nothing more strenuous than sitting behind a desk, participate in meetings, and check and approve letters. Although the IPDN's current educational system is no longer based on an explicit military ideology, physical training is still a central component. The IPDN's system, as explained on its website in the early 2010s, is based on what it calls the "central trinity" of: *education*, the transfer of knowledge; *training*, the internalization of civil-service values; and *upbringing*, the transfer of motor skills necessary for the execution of civil-service tasks. Civil-servant trainings thus exceed a

---

4.   In April 2007, Indonesia's Metro TV News aired parts of this video. It consequently made its rounds on the internet and attracted a score of outraged comments on YouTube (STPDN, 2007).

classroom exchange or transfer of information and continues to rely to a great extent on disciplining the body.

The importance of this physical discipline becomes clearer if we examine another context in which civil servants are trained: the *Pendidikan dan Pelatihan Prajabatan*, a civil-service course commonly called *diklat*.[5] Newly accepted civil servants who have been working in the offices for a year on a trial basis take this course to become *full* civil servants. Although part of the course consists of classroom learning and lectures on governance, as I found out when I joined a few sessions in Kupang, much of *diklat* training explicitly targets the body. Learning how to march properly or how to hold one's body in a specific manner, for instance, creates a bodily disposition deemed necessary for civil servants. In the documentary, *Performances of Authority*, a drill instructor explains the purpose of these *diklat* marching drills:

> In marching, people have to obey commands. So later in their duty as civil servants, they will also be disciplined. They march in good order, following commands. We are not trying to bring militarism into civil service. In fact, we just take from the UN philosophy to develop discipline and cooperation among the participants. This is not a militarization of civil service.

According to the instructor, learning how to march properly is essential to becoming a well-disciplined and obedient civil servant; for those who can march in rhythm and follow commands will also execute office tasks properly, obediently, and cooperatively.

Another scene from *Performances of Authority*, this one from a *diklat* held in the little western Indonesian island of Bintan, offers further insights into the need for this discipline. The scene shows a trainee struggling, through corrections and scolding on the part of a superior, to lead a roll call by having her fellow trainees repeat, after her, KORPI's code of ethics:

> We the members of the Civil Service Corps of the Republic of Indonesia [*trainees repeat*] are people of faith [*trainees repeat*] and subservient to the one God [*trainees repeat*], loyal and obedient to the

---

5. Indonesian civil service is inundated with acronyms and abbreviations for positions, practices, and procedures. *Diklat* comes from the "dik" in *pendidikan* (education) and the "lat" of *pelatihan* (training).

unified state and government of the Republic of Indonesia [*trainees repeat*], prioritizing the interests of the state [*trainees repeat*] and society [*trainees repeat*] above our personal or group interests [*trainees repeat*].

After the roll call and repetition of the ethics, the instructor steps towards a woman in the assembled row of trainees, one who had been seen lacking the proper posture of attention. He forces her to squat while everyone around her stands. He says:

Please heed this. When there is a command to stay in attention, stay in good attention. When you return to your own duties later, if you ask help from your colleagues, let alone your subordinates, what would you feel if they don't obey you? Especially you, who are educators: if you don't follow my command here, it will also happen to you at work. (Steijlen and Simandjuntak 2011)

Marching, order, rigor, and rigidity at attention all help instill an obedient disposition, part of what Zigon (2011b: 67, 69) calls the "embodied dispositions" of these civil servants. Such dispositions or embodied morality nevertheless appears to be without a clear connection to any particular institutional morality, be that of the *right thing* of Weberian legal-rationality, the *perfection* of the New Order organicist family principle, or the *ethical* of a caring responsibility towards family. What ultimately matters is one's allegiance to a greater good—whether subservience to God or loyalty and obedience to the state—over one's own private or group interests.[6] This training to become a civil servant, in short, emphasizes the importance of loyalty and obedience for the sake of a greater good, but offers no clear escape from the dilemma elite civil servants such as Anderius, Valentino, or Budi face trying to balance the

---

6. The subservience to "the one God" echoes the first of the five pillars (*Pancasila*) that form the founding philosophy of the Indonesian state. Although the vast majority of Indonesians are Muslim, the government also recognizes Hinduism, Catholicism, Protestantism, Buddhism, and Confucianism as part of the first pillar, which is the belief in one God. The IPDN, in line with the secularist basis of the state, does not single out specific religious values in its trainings. It does offer places of worship to students of diverse religious backgrounds, such as Christian students from Kupang. The importance of Indonesia's unity, which is the third pillar, overrides its many internal differences, including religious ones.

expectations of help and support from family members or office superiors, with the demands and legal ramifications of anti-corruption and good governance.

As a kind of extended *diklat* for Indonesia's future bureaucratic elite, the IPDN also succeeds in delivering obedient, loyal civil servants. This, at least, is what Valentino took from his time at the IPDN. He remembered, for instance, the times when senior students would wake him and members of his cohort in the middle of the night and make them run laps. Or when they had to stand in formation for hours in the pouring rain. Or when a senior student had them clean the toilet with a toothbrush when he found the toilet too dirty, and then made them all brush their teeth with it—he could still recall the taste of that rancid toothbrush. He smiled through these stories, never expressing any anger over the harsh or senseless treatment. Instead, he emphasized that although all his cohort members shared feelings of disgust at their communal punishments, they would also laugh together afterward and would cover up for one another's missteps. To him, punishments were about experiencing a sense of togetherness and learning obedience, respect for institutional superiors, and discipline. Punishments such as these, he said, produced strong, long-lasting bonds of loyalty, camaraderie, and solidarity among students and alumni.

While the seemingly pointless and, at times, sadistic training methods employed at the IPDN were thought to successfully produce the valued embodied dispositions of loyalty, subordination, and obedience, there remains an uncertainty over to whom one is loyal. Is it one's office Bapak? One's actual father? Or the strictures of anti-corruption legislation? As a consequence, this successful disciplining into a rule-following disposition disconnected from any specific institutional morality does not offer civil servants any clarity on how to navigate the moral-ethical assemblage of post-*reformasi* Indonesian bureaucracy. Given the complex entanglement of state and family in Kupang's local state apparatus, and the centrality of the family principle in the Indonesian nation-state, civil servants are trapped in a real and persistent ethical dilemma. In other words, in a larger moral-ethical assemblage with overlapping and conflicting discourses and ideologies, the ethical disposition of obedience and loyalty based on the importance of following rules, facilitates the slippage of the *right thing*, the *ethical, perfection*, and *corruption*. It is perhaps no wonder that the latest move against corruption in the civil service—under the auspices of good governance—only adds another opportunity for slippage. Indeed, as we will see, good governance does not clear up the ethical murkiness in which civil servants like Budi and Valentino try to stay afloat. It confuses things even further.

What Does *Good* Mean?

Just as *diklat* trainers attempted to distance themselves from militaristic styles of civil service training by stating their faithful adherence to the UN philosophy, so too did the IPDN signal its move away from New Order governmental ideologies by embracing the post-*reformasi* valuation of good governance. When I was reading the IPDN website in 2014, it dedicated a special section to the principles of good governance, in which it claimed these principles to be an important part of the IPDN's institutional aims. The section could have been translated directly from a World Bank publication, covering general topics such as public participation, upholding the rule of law, transparency, accountability, effectiveness, and efficiency.[7] It also included an Indonesia-specific agenda to "realize good government," which depicted Indonesia in a state of political, economic, and social turmoil all traced to a "less democratic" past. It argued that the way forward was through political, economic, and legal reforms "adapted to the real conditions of the nation at this time." Indeed, according to the IPDN, good governance had become an integral part of public discourse in post-Suharto Indonesia:

> Since the fall of the New Order and its replacement with the *reformasi* movement, the term *Good governance* has become so popular. On almost every occasion or important event related to governance, this term is not left out. Even in speeches, government officials use the above-mentioned words. In short, *Good governance* has become an increasingly popular discourse in society.

Whereas similar neoliberal catchwords such as *transparency, efficiency,* and *accountability* have been borrowed from English and phonologically adapted (*transparansi, efisiensi, akuntabilitas*), "good governance" remained untranslated. The text therefore strove to define it: "Even though the words *Good governance* are often mentioned . . . at various events and by various groups, the meaning of *Good governance* can differ

---

7. These good-governance principles were on the IPDN's website as of August 1, 2014 but are no longer accessible.

from one [person, institution] to the next." Among the various possible definitions, however, it specifically showcased the World Bank's stress on responsibility, market efficiency, principles of democracy, prevention of corruption, and legal and political stimulation of business activity. From this it attempted a final, concise definition: *"Good governance* is . . . 'the management of government that is good.'" If such a tautology were not enough, it further ventured: "The word 'good' here is intended as following certain rules in accordance with the principles of *Good governance.*" At this point it is probably unnecessary to point out that this equation of *good* with following rules is more than familiar to IPDN students and civil servants in general, and highlights again the nucleus of the dilemma. Following rules is, after all, what civil servants are taught to do, and matches the embodied dispositions of loyalty and obedience that civil service education so painstakingly develops. As a result, the idea of the good that neoliberal good governance ideology offers does not, in this case, lead to an unequivocal moral victory over corruption. Instead, it becomes incorporated into the entanglements of *perfection*, the *ethical*, and the *right thing*, which conflict and overlap in the wider moral-ethical bureaucratic assemblage that Kupang's civil servants so anxiously try to navigate.[8]

---

8. Daromir Rudnyckyj (2010) demonstrates such moral-ethical entanglements and neoliberalism's capacity to co-opt and transform existing values, in his analysis of how seemingly incompatible discourses of neoliberal capitalist ethics and Islam converge in trainings aimed at morally reforming Indonesian factory workers.

CHAPTER FOUR

Poetics and Poiesis

Public Secrets and Intimate Knowledge

One hot afternoon in early October, 2009, I found myself on the front porch of the Kaho family house with *Tante* Elsie. I was happy to have some time alone with her. Elsie had not been spending a lot of time in the house after her youngest son, Yongki, had graduated from high school and she no longer needed to get him up each morning for classes. She now spent most of her nights at the house she and her husband built in a nearby neighborhood. Elsie was frail looking and soft-spoken. Unlike her sisters, she hardly ever raised her voice or engaged in the quarrels that occasionally erupted in the house. She tended to keep her grievances to herself and rarely spoke about matters that troubled her. This afternoon, however, she wanted to talk. She wanted to talk about Yongki. After graduating high school, he had not started pursuing any higher education and his uncertain future weighed heavily on her.

Finding steady employment in Kupang, Elsie reminded me, is no easy feat. It is even harder for those without a degree of some kind. Certainly, there are no job opportunities that come with the kind of financial certainty and perks (e.g., health insurance, a monthly rice allowance, and the possibility of credit) to be had with a position in the civil service. Elsie felt relieved that her two older children had managed to find steady jobs in the city-level and provincial civil service. Her daughter, Sinta, had recently started a post in the town of Nagakeo on the island of Flores, and her eldest son, Valentino, had been working as the mayor's aide for almost two years already.

Still, examples of well-educated others who had not been this lucky abounded in the neighborhood. For instance, her daughter's husband had been unable to find any kind of permanent position for years despite having a bachelor's degree, which partly explained why Sinta's uncles and aunts deemed him to be an undesirable husband. Prospects were even worse for those without any kind of university degree or diploma. Niko, for example, a twenty-something high school graduate, who lived down the road and often visited the house, had been trying to get a job for years but had not found anything permanent and was left taking odd jobs. With a permanent job, he would say, maybe his family could have some vegetables or meat instead eating plain rice with *sambal* for nights on end. Moreover, maybe his girlfriend's mother would allow them to get married.

Elsie herself was getting older and often thought about her children's futures without her; she desperately wanted them in secure jobs with financial stability. She wanted them *to be somebody* before she passed on. For his part, Yongki wanted to enroll in the local police academy, as evidenced by his enthusiastic exclamations while watching the civil servants in Kupang's anniversary parade. Instead of focusing on the work, he mostly he fantasized about the perks—getting to ride motorcycles, wearing custom-made uniforms that would certainly attract the gaze of the town's young women, and finding possibilities for illicit moneymaking. Elsie was more concerned with the task of actually getting him accepted into the academy. A big impediment to that, as she explained to me, was that getting him into the academy "clean" seemed impossible.

It was a public secret (*rahasia umum*) that, as with other schools, you had to pay to get into the police academy. It was a public secret insofar it fit the definition of "that which is generally known but cannot be spoken" (Taussig 1999: 50) and pertained to "knowing what not to know, where not to look, what not to see" (Jusionyte 2015: 129). According to Elsie, the current "entrance fee" was IDR 50 million ($4000). This fantastic sum was equivalent to the amount Elsie's younger sister hoped to save for a once-in-a-lifetime, two-week holiday to Europe for her, her husband, and their daughter. It was exorbitant. Getting into the academy used to cost less, Elsie informed me. When her eldest son, Valentino, graduated from senior high school a few years earlier, the going rate had been only IDR 15 million ($1200). Without questioning the truth of the public secret or the ethics of paying an informal entrance fee, Elsie tried to figure out how to compile such a large amount of money. As a civil servant, she could easily get a loan at the bank. She had done this before, for instance when building the house that she and her husband lived in and also when buying Yongki's flashy Honda Tiger motorcycle. However, because she was only two years away from retirement, it was unlikely a bank would agree to a large enough loan. Perhaps, she mused, the police would accept Yongki's motorcycle, which was worth at least IDR 25 million ($2000) and take the rest in cash.

She knew there were risks to such transactions. Even if she could get the police to agree to this deal, there was always the possibility that they would accept the money but still not accept Yongki into the academy. A few years earlier, a friend of hers had paid a similar amount of money to an official at the local prosecutor's office in order to get her daughter a position there, but the friend's daughter never got in and the money was lost. I asked Elsie how she planned to prevent this from happening and she told me she would not pay anything in advance. Even if she handed over a mere IDR 5 million ($400) and lost it, she said, money is still money. Instead, she planned to give the *promise* of payment and then give them the cash only when Yongki was indeed accepted. She finally added, if it did not work, Yongki could always go to nursing school—after all, there are always sick people.

The assumption that entrance fees are necessary in order to gain access to Indonesia's civil service or other governmental or educational institutions is not new (Kristiansen and Ramli 2006). In a sense, the public secret of entrance fees is tied to the larger "distrust of official forms of veracity" that Indonesians feel, as well as their general suspicion they have regarding "the fundamental opacity of state authority" (Bubandt 2009: 561, 575). To be sure, to some extent such opacity and secrecy is imperative to the successful functioning of the state. For instance, an intimate sociability, inside knowledge, familiarity, and informality, can smooth over the rusty workings of bureaucracy (Herzfeld 2016: 64), help stave off the worst potential effects of high modernist state planning (Scott 1998), and grease a successful functioning of bureaucratic organizations (Shore 2005). Dominic Boyer (2000) even goes so far as to suggest that the German Democratic Republic's demise was because restrictions placed on this illicit zone of familiarity undid the smooth functioning of state apparatuses.

Put another way, public secrets, according to Michael Taussig (1999), combine the clarity of an existence in clear view with the opacity of concealment. This is what posed a particular problem for Elsie. In order to avoid, like her friend, paying money for access that was not forthcoming, she needed to *see what ought not to be seen*, look at what should not be looked at, and acquire the know-how needed to navigate what is not truly known. Lacking that intimate knowledge necessary to confidently pay police officials so as to get Yongki into their academy, Elsie was adrift in the opaque space between public secret and intimate knowledge.

In this chapter, we will attend to this opaque zone of familiarity and cultural intimacy. In particular, I want to address its (social) poetics, a concept I loosely borrow from Michael Herzfeld (2016) in order to name how civil servants and citizens both bend, brave, and manipulate understood social rules in interactions with each other. I then look at its productive capacity, or poiesis. By drawing on ethnographic cases of interactions between civil servants and citizens, I will tease out some aspects of the cultural intimacies, performative competencies, and mutual complicity that characterize the intimate knowledge necessary for a successful navigation of this realm. It will become clear that the navigational poetics described not only bring into being novel forms of corruption, they also irrevocably taint perceptions of bureaucratic machinations in Kupang. In doing so, they reinforce the power of the public secret without ever necessitating the question as to whether there is any actual veracity to the secret.

In the previous chapter, we examined the complexity of navigating the moral-ethical assemblage of post-*reformasi* bureaucracy in Kupang from the vantage point of civil servants. This chapter shifts its view to the perspective of citizens, who are often portrayed as victims of unscrupulous civil servants. While not entirely contradicting this portrait, we will see how the post-*reformasi* bureaucratic landscape poses challenges for the people of Kupang and civil servants alike. In that way it becomes a space of collaboration, or a mutual *muddling through*. Additionally, we will move from an emphasis on experiences to appearances, and contrast the opaque character of public secrets with the emphasis on transparency that has become so central to the project of anti-corruption. We ask how successful efforts that depend on transparency can be when public secrets thrive on the deceptiveness of appearances? How can Kupang ever seem *clean* when the public secret would seem to render it perpetually *dirty*? How can transparency clear up opacity in the space between public secrets and intimate knowledge, when that space is forever and irredeemably tainted?

Perceptions of Corruption

In Kupang, definitions of corruption centered on the *public office* model do not account for the complex entanglements of relationality, gift-giving, and an ethics of care and exchange that make it hard to pinpoint what exactly counts as corruption. In spite of this uncertainty, suspicions that Kupang was rife with corruption, especially when dealing with the many different parts and branches of the state apparatus, were widespread. Everybody in Kupang knew that KKN was part of dealing with civil servants in particular and the government generally. To the degree that KKN was a public secret, it was less secret than it was public, which is something I became aware of well before commencing my own fieldwork in Kupang.

Before my first visit to Kupang, I had learned that it was necessary to approach offices of the Indonesian government with some apprehension. In language classes in Yogyakarta, Java, I translated newspaper articles about corruption in the Indonesian police, judiciary, and even the most prominent anti-corruption body, the KPK. Reading about the Suharto family taught me about graft, collusion, and nepotism on an unimaginable scale. Documentary films showed me the pervasiveness of KKN in everyday dealings with the state, state representatives, and others in positions of authority. When I finally arrived in Kupang, knowing outsiders almost never had success dealing with local bureaucracies—which I nonetheless had to do for reasons related to my research—I soaked up the advice, insights, and common knowledge of locals about how to deal with bureaucrats.

For example, instead of taking the official driver's test to get a local driver's license, I was told to give some money and a passport-size photo to one of the young policemen who played cards on the front porch of the Kaho family house. Some of that money would be used to pay the required fee, some of it would go to the civil servant in charge of preparing my license, some more would go to higher ups, and what was left the young policeman would keep. However, when I went to get my motorcycle ownership papers—with the help of a savvy broker who helped clients at the Department of Motor Vehicles obtain the necessary paperwork—my *Tante* Ina, who had accompanied me, expressly forbade me from offering him any thank-you money. This broker, she told me, was like family. It would be insulting to give him something extra. Then, when it was time to proudly ride my moped through Kupang, people told me I should be sure to carry around extra cash on those days at the end of the month known as *tanggal tua* ("old dates") when, several times a year, police officers who were bound to have already spent most of their monthly paycheck would set up ad hoc checkpoints in order to check all vehicles for proper registration—if anything was out of order, there could be a fine, or perhaps, money given directly to the officer. Those first months in Kupang were an education in the nuances of exchange and degrees of familiarity understood as necessary to work through the public secret of KKN.

Interestingly, in all this, the truth of the public secret of KKN was never questioned. Why question it, after all, when Transparency International bestowed the unenviable title of "Indonesia's Most Corrupt City" on Kupang (Melayu 2009) in 2008, the year during which I did the bulk of my research? Existing critiques of Transparency International's corruption indices gives us reason to be at least somewhat suspicious of those things everyone knows but refrains from speaking about. One of Transparency International's better-known indices is the *Corruption Perceptions Index*. However, as various anthropologists have pointed out (Harrison 2006: 674; Parry 2000: 53), *perceptions* of corruption do not necessarily correspond to the actual incidence of corruption and can, in fact, give a vastly incorrect and exaggerated impression of existing practices. In a place like Kupang, the publication of the index merely worked to strengthen rather than interrogate the public secret of KKN. The only questions it likely provokes are those of a practical nature, such as the one Elsie was mulling over: how does one approach and handle bureaucratic gatekeepers in such a way that one gets what one wants without being taken advantage of?

Poetics

These practical questions go beyond giving bribes as a blunt economic transaction but point to the "performative competence" (Gupta 1995: 381) one needs to navigate between a public secret and intimate knowledge; or, to borrow an expression from Deborah Reed-Danahay (1993: 224), they point to the necessary skills of *débrouiller*. By *débrouiller* or *débrouillardise*, she refers to the cunning ability of French villagers in dealing with the state. *Brouillard* means fog, hence *débrouiller* means "getting out of the fog," or what Reed-Danahay defines as shrewdly *making out* or *making do*. Rooted in the local social valuation of protecting insiders, such as family and friends, and exploiting outsiders (most notably the state and its representatives), this shrewdness comes out in efforts to manipulate insider-outsider boundaries for one's own gain. Such performative competence requires skill, creativity, and an ability to improvise according to context. For the on-the-ground kaleidoscopic reality of what Akhil Gupta (2012) characterizes as a "refracted" state, people's intimate knowledge of how to "make out" when dealing with a local government office or the Department for Motor Vehicles might be insufficient when dealing with other departments, bodies, and offices.

For example, the Immigration Office where I had to apply for a visa extension each month was a place where no one could offer me advice on how to *get out of the fog*. The office held a particularly disreputable position in a local bureaucratic landscape described by degrees of wetness— "wet places" (*tempat basah*) were departments known for higher levels of KKN. *Wet places* are often departments, such as Public Works or Social Services, where large amounts of money circulate and where there is ample opportunity for the personal enrichment of the civil servants. The Immigration Office's notorious reputation came from people who were both inexperienced in getting through the fog, and particularly vulnerable to exploitation.

Those who must contend with the Immigration Office are vulnerable because it is the only place to obtain the formal documents necessary for a range of crucial, legal statuses, from maintaining legal residency, undertaking international travel, or working abroad as a domestic servant. However, as my coworkers at the mayor's warned me when it came time to renew my visa the first time, getting one's documents required an investment of time and money. I was told to bring plenty of cash. Someone scribbled down the phone number of an influential uncle who might be able to help me out when in need. So, certain about the veracity of the public secret of needing to rely on KKN but lacking any intimate knowledge beyond the general usefulness of acquaintances and money, I headed over to the Immigration Office to extend my visa for the first time.

A friend who acted as my local sponsor accompanied me.[1] There were initial difficulties raised by a low-level official, which I chalked

---

1. Daniel Jordan Smith (2018) offers an important account of the ways in which our writings about corruption can adversely affect our interlocutors, who are so often incredibly generous with their time and assistance. To safeguard the anonymity of a dear friend in my recounting of this adventure, I prefer to use them/they pronouns and simply refer to them as "my friend."

up to their attempt to make some extra money off our interaction—an interpretation which was undoubtedly prejudiced by all the warnings I had received about this *wet place*. When my friend discovered that their former neighbor, who was "like family" to them, worked in the department, everything became much smoother. Each month thereafter we'd give him my passport and he returned it to us with the requisite stamps and signatures a few hours later. As I had learned from my interactions with the middleman at the Department of Motor Vehicles, since our friend at Immigration was *like family*, I did not need to pay any extra money. A bottle of Black Label Jack Daniels bought in Bali sufficed as a thank you.

This routine worked smoothly for three months. During the fourth extension I ran into unexpected difficulties. After having given my visa extension forms and sponsor's letter of support to their former neighbor as usual, we left the office to get some lunch, confident that we would once again be able to pick up my passport with a new stamp afterwards. During lunch, however, my friend got a phone call from that former neighbor. An office superior had noticed that the institution that initially sponsored my visa was not the sponsor for my extensions. We had to come to the office immediately. Once at the office, a stern young official, whose darker colored uniform indicated her upper-echelon status, came out of her office somewhere behind the row of ticket windows to tell us there was a problem with my visa. She told us to sit on the wooden benches in the waiting area while they tried to sort it out. It was around noon and getting uncomfortably hot. Then, as happened regularly in Kupang, the electricity went off. The temperature in the stifling office went up and the clock kept ticking. My friend and I grew increasingly anxious. Was there really something wrong or was this a ploy to extract some money? Were they keeping us waiting this long on purpose to heighten our anxiety and increase our willingness to comply with whatever potentially illicit scheme they were planning? Should I call my coworker's uncle, whose phone number I had stashed away somewhere? Did I have enough cash on hand for whatever might be asked of me?

After waiting for over an hour, the immigration official called us into a small room in the back where a handful of civil servants were working on piles of files and documents that were spread out across a few wooden desks. She informed us curtly that we both potentially faced time in prison since we were guilty of trying to extend a visa under false pretenses. Perhaps feeling me tense up, my friend whispered to

me that I should stay quiet and polite and let them do the talking. I let
them talk. They explained, offered pleas, cajoled. They told the official
that I did not mean any harm and that because the visa procedure is so
hard to understand, especially for foreigners, it was an innocent mistake.
My friend seemed to sway the stern young woman, because she asked
me for passport photos and my fingerprints and said that perhaps they
could work something out with the office in Jakarta. We should come
back tomorrow. When we got up to leave, a male civil servant—a low-
level one judging from the khaki color of his uniform—leaned over to
my friend and whispered something in their ear. My friend stopped,
looked around hesitatingly and pulled me aside: "I think they want
some money." My friend later told me the civil servant had not explicitly asked for money but merely hinted that a thank you would be ap-
preciated. I replied, "All right, but how much?" My friend leaned over to
the civil servant and whispered "how much?" They did not get an answer
they understood. They asked it a few more times but the civil servant,
instead of answering, looked away and gave no indication that he had
heard anything. Asking directly, apparently, is not part of a performance
that includes that which should not be mentioned. Public secrets might
be hinted at, approached obliquely, or mentioned in euphemistic terms.
Finally, my friend pulled out a pen, wrote something on the inside of
their hand and held their palm up to the civil servant. The man nod-
ded. My friend had written down: IDR 100,000. "*Tanggal tua*," they
mouthed apologetically to me. The immigration official told us to come
back the next day.

When we returned to the office, the upper-echelon official's demea-
nor had reversed. Where the day before she had been strict, authoritative,
and far from polite, she was now helpful, accommodating, ingratiating,
especially to my friend. She chatted, touched their arm, giggled, and was
extremely friendly. My friend easily reciprocated the smiles and flattery
and behaved with markedly more confidence around her. She invited us
back into the small room in the back. There she asked us to please sit
down and offered us coffee, which she herself would get for us. Did we
want milk? Sugar? What a difference a day made.

What had happened? While the official had left the office to get us
coffee, my friend explained to me that after our ordeal on the previous
day, the official had found out that my friend was her senior in GMNI
(*Gerakan Mahasiswa Nasional Indonesia*, the Indonesian National Student Movement). She had called my friend the night before and said she
felt *tidak enak* (not right/good) about her treatment of a GMNI senior.

What had apparently transpired was that the official had been unaware of the existing relationship of mutuality between herself and my friend and the seniority they had over her in that relationship. Instead of "muddling along" as two insiders in mutually complicit and illicit familiarity, she mistook my friend for an outsider to cunningly exploit by using her official position and the real threat of legal repercussions. Realizing now that the insider-outsider boundaries had shifted, that she and my friend had been on the same side all along and that, in fact, she owed them loyalty due to their junior-senior relationship in GMNI, she now vowed to help conceal from higher-level exposure what turned out the be a serious legal problem with my visa.

As she explained, I had obtained my visa with a sponsorship from an Indonesian university. Officially, this university had to provide me with sponsor letters with every visa extension. Instead, and not knowing we did something wrong, my friend wrote these sponsor letters for me. Officially, an immigration official would have noticed this discrepancy in sponsorship at my very first extension appointment and alerted me to this mistake. The immigration official handling my case, however, was *like family* to my friend and smoothed over the inconsistencies. After all, helping out family members is customary. Whether his superior, who initially intervened, was simply fulfilling her professional duties or seeing an opportunity for enrichment on a *tanggal tua*, or both, she notified us of the problem while at least pretending to be able to keep it hidden from legal repercussions from a higher level—for a small token of appreciation negotiated in that sweaty backroom of the Immigration Office. When she found out that my friend was her GMNI senior, however, she did her best to cover up the visible discrepancies in sponsorship on my passport as well as the extension forms. Unfortunately, later that day she told us that she could not cover up the sponsorship discrepancy because all visa extension information is computerized, stored in national databases, and subject to occasional checks from higher-ups. If she would continue, she said, she might be liable for official misconduct. The only stamp I received in my passport that day was one that stated I had seven days to leave Indonesia.

This experience in social poetics, or *débrouillardise*, shows the shifting character of the insider-outsider boundaries in this space between the public secret and the intimate knowledge necessary to understand the process fully. Within this space, civil servants and clients are not necessarily positioned on opposite sides of boundaries. Instead, these boundaries, and who counts as insider or outsider, can shift as various bonds of mutuality and exchange potentially rearrange dynamics of complicity and collaboration.[2] Furthermore, the poetics necessary to make it out of the fog are at their most effective as long as they stay within the administrative confines of Kupang. Once exposed to the glare of higher-level scrutiny, the fogginess so conducive to play and manipulation dissolves. Any illicit cover-ups at the local level leave traces in national databases that could cost civil servants if their actions are discovered. Public secrets lose their locally productive, opaque ambiguity when exposed to the certainty of the public record.

Yet, the fact that the law caught up with what amounted to an illicit visa extension process, with which bureaucratic insiders cooperated, did not diminish the persuasiveness of the public secret that KKN is necessary to get things done. When I told coworkers and Kaho family members about my predicament, they were quick to weave my experience into the existing discursive tapestry of KKN and the typical exploitations of civil servants. The civil servants took my money and then kicked me out of the country. The civil servants failed to do their jobs because they wanted to take advantage of somebody. No one pointed out that a reliance on the informal ethics of care and exchange had actually kept me in the country for far longer than was legally permitted, if unbeknownst to me and my friend. No one dwelled on the fact that my deportation could, in fact, be considered as a victory of the rule of law over KKN. The public character of the public secret, that everybody knows what ought not to be known, ensures that no one doubts its veracity. Doubts only come into play when figuring out how to navigate the public secret and intimate knowledge, adding the use of dates, money, and connections on the inside to one's repertoire of performance. Even when legality catches up with illegality, such as happened in the case of my visa, the persuasiveness of the public secret colors people's interpretation of events, so that even a potential story of the victory of the rule of law becomes yet another example of the irrevocably murky space between civil servants

2. Michael Herzfeld (2005) notes this when he critiques James C. Scott's (1998) analysis of high-modernist planning and the failure to grasp that bureaucrats are eager to "muddle along with their clients" (Herzfeld 2005: 372). If, for Scott, bureaucrats remain representative and executors of the state's high-modernist visions, and for Reed-Danahay (1996) they remain outsiders to be cunningly exploited, for Herzfeld they are complicit in continuing the dirty secret of the state that it needs some degree of illicit familiarity to function.

and citizens. In this forever tainted space, how can one ever prove or perform cleanliness?

Performing Cleanliness

Given all of this, getting in "clean," as Elsie called it, is a near impossibility, and she did not mind doing what was necessary to help Yongki get into the police academy. Working on the widespread assumptions built into the public secret—that one needs to engage in KKN to gain access to government offices, institutions, and services—she figured that everyone got at least a little dirty when trying to secure their children's futures. This acceptance of taking part in bribery and collusion on behalf of Yongki contrasted, however, with her devotion to the appearance of cleanliness when it came to her daughter, Sinta, who had applied for a job a year or so earlier.

Shortly after obtaining her bachelor's degree in international relations in Yogyakarta, Sinta was anxiously looking for steady employment. Unbeknownst to her parents, Sinta had therefore applied for a job at the local branch of the national radio station Radio Republik Indonesia (RRI) where, coincidentally, her father had been working for many years. When Elsie found out, she worried about the possibility of Sinta getting accepted. Would people think she got in by using her connections? If people suspected that Sinta had used family to get the position would she be tainted? Even in a context where everyone knows it's impossible to get in clean, some ways of getting dirty are apparently more acceptable than others. We thus anxiously followed Sinta's progression over the various hurdles of the application process, unable to know definitively what, if anything, beyond her qualifications was helping her advance toward a job with the RRI.

Sinta had previously told me about her intention to apply for the position at RRI when we were catching up on each other's days before going to sleep in the bed we shared. When the station advertised positions for broadcasters, Sinta had applied. She was one of eighty-nine who applied for six positions. She explained the steps of the application process. First, an administrative selection would take place, during which candidates who lacked the appropriate educational background and degrees would be dismissed. After this first culling of the applicant pool, those still being considered had to take both a general knowledge and an English language test. Those with the highest test scores would be invited for an interview. Finally, RRI's head would decide who to hire. Sinta doubted whether those with the highest test scores would get the job. Drawing an unfavorable comparison with the supposed cleaner hiring procedures in Java, she said:

> In Kupang, we never see the test scores on the lists with names of those who get in. In Java, you always read the applicant's number, name, and test score. Here it is just the number and name. That, Silvy, is KKN, never putting in the test score because if "stupid" gets picked it is clear that there is KKN. If you don't see the test score no one can complain.

Sinta mostly relied on hearsay and on what friends and acquaintances had told her about hiring procedures. In other words, she relied on the veracity of the public secret. While Sinta had only recently joined the ranks of highly educated job-seekers, many of her friends had more experience with the disappointing drudgery of applying for elusive civil service positions. Along with hundreds of other eager applicants, they had repeatedly submitted their applications whenever an office, agency, or department advertised a handful of vacancies in local newspapers or on the radio. They told Sinta about the behind-the-scenes procedures in Kupang that created those acceptance lists without test scores. The Kupang habit of not including the test scores alongside the names of the new hires, which Sinta assured me did not happen in Java, suggested to them that informal means, rather than formal rules, decided outcomes. For how else could they explain *stupid* being selected over them with their qualifications, again and again?

The civil servants involved in hiring give a different account of how formal procedures and informal means shape the process. Few contested that some forms of informal favoring happen within the offices: being close to influential people might help one get transferred more easily or speed up access to a *kartu istri/suami* (the identification card that entitles spouses of civil servants to health insurance and pension). Then there was the post-election practice of rewarding one's political supporters in the civil service with plum positions in the bureaucracy. Most civil servants I spoke with, however, doubted it was possible to bypass formal testing results during hiring, especially since the implementation of the Civil Service Testing Procedure. Furthermore, a hiring procedure for new civil servants in 2008 displayed no trace of the separation of test scores and names that Sinta found so suspicious in Kupang. In fact, the department posted a list containing both names and test scores to the outside door for applicants to see who was hired. Sinta simply shrugged in response to this information. She was not convinced by my attempt to question her presumption of hidden KKN in hiring practices, just as it would probably fail to convince other perpetually disappointed job-seekers. Indeed, lists with test scores do little to dispel the persuasiveness of the public secret. Stories of money lost on failed attempts to buy access into the police academy or prosecutor's office similarly do not tear at the persuasiveness of the public secret.

Sinta's assessment of her chances of getting the RRI job was that, regardless of how well or poorly one did on the tests, it was ultimately the boss' decision and she wondered how her father's relationship with his boss might influence her chances of getting the position. This was her mother's fear. Her father and his boss had been friendly for years. They exchanged news about their children and occasionally attended each other's family parties. Unfortunately, as Sinta found out when meeting her fellow applicants while signing up, the parents of several other applicants also worked at RRI. Perhaps, her connections would not give her as much of an advantage as she had hoped. She therefore proposed to her parents that they offer the boss some money. Her father vehemently opposed this suggestion.

Sinta eventually agreed that this was probably for the best. Relaying the same incident her mother would tell me about a year later, she told me of a friend's mother who had failed in attempting to pay an official in the prosecutor's office for her daughter's acceptance. And about another friend who did get a position there without paying at all. Not knowing what to make of this and feeling ill at home in the opaque space between public secret and intimate knowledge, where the supposed certainties of money and connections suddenly seemed less reliable, Sinta endeavored to prepare for the tests. We both spent the following afternoons and nights brushing up on our knowledge of Indonesian history; former heads of state, province, and city, as well as practicing potential interview questions in English.

A few weeks later, as we were getting ready for a family party, Sinta told me she had passed all the RRI tests and was accepted as a broadcaster. Out of the initial eighty-nine applicants, four young women had been accepted as broadcasters and two young men as operators. A list with the names of applicants and their test scores had been made public. Sinta had passed the final test with the highest score. Not quite convinced that the published test scores reflected actual test scores, she initially thought that her father had, after all, put in a good word with his boss despite his initial objections. He assured her he had not. Perhaps, Sinta speculated, connections on the inside had not mattered that much in this case. Another applicant's failure to pass the tests even though her mother held a high position at RRI supported Sinta's supposition. What all new hires seemed to have in common was a fairly good grasp of English. Some of them had studied in Australia and others simply spoke English quite well. Because of Elsie's insistence that Sinta and her brothers take private English lessons, as we read about in the previous chapter, Sinta herself was also remarkably fluent in English. She also thought the hours spent practicing answers to potential interview questions had prepared her well for the interview. As far as Sinta could tell, and contrary to the seductive persuasiveness of the public secret that demands all access to civil service requires getting somewhat dirty in some way, she had gotten in clean.

Still, when Elsie overheard our conversation and Sinta's surprising conclusion that she must have gotten her job on her own, she urged me to visit Sinta at her new job: "Speak English with Sinta, so her work friends can see that she got accepted because of her English, not because of her father." Elsie worried that even though Sinta was now convinced of her cleanliness, others might still suspect dirty dealings. In order to refute such suspicions and prove her fair acceptance, Sinta should put some effort in performing her cleanliness by demonstrating her English fluency in conversations with me.

The pervasiveness of corruption discourses and the certainty of the public secret means that no civil servant is exempt from suspicions of being corrupt. Even when legality seems to win over informal familiarity, as with the example of my visa example; or when disclosure counters assertions of concealment, as when lists report test scores along with names; or when merit seems to facilitate access more than connections, as in Sinta's RRI position—the public secret does not lose power or conviction. What one sees might always turn out to be deceptive. As we saw in previous chapters with the donation books at family parties, donation envelopes at weddings, and the charity box in the village-head office, performing cleanliness is an impossible task. As we will see, however, this irrevocable murkiness also opens the possibility for new forms of corruption and is, therefore, unexpectedly productive.

Camouflage

Recall that Elsie was certain of the public secret of needing to pay for Yongki's acceptance into the police academy. She was also uncertain about how to do it. This created constant worry. For others, in contrast, the certainty of the public secret of necessary KKN and people's unfamiliarity with the intimate knowledge needed to successfully engage in it offered opportunities. During the months I spent there, the Department of Human Resources was going through the process of hiring new staff members and some civil servants told me about a scheme they had managed to pull off a few times when city-level government had accepted new hires. The Department of Human Resources is responsible, among other things, for entering the names of the newly accepted civil servants into the database that contains the names and background information of all temporary and full civil servants.

One day, I was talking with some staff members who were tasked with the fairly tedious chores of typing out a list with the names and background information of the new hires so they could be uploaded into a database, and composing letters informing the new hires that they had been accepted into the civil service as trainees. Such clerical tasks are typically performed by those at the lowest rungs of the office hierarchy. Indeed, the handful of young men clustered around the office computer working on the list and letters wore the tell-tale khaki of lower-level employment. Although they did not have any kind of influence over hiring decisions, they were in possession of the contact information of all new hires. During previous rounds of hiring they had, therefore, waited until everyone else in the office had gone home and then made phone calls to the newly accepted civil servants. They would tell them, or their parents, that they were very close to being hired and that, in fact, their names could be entered into the database if only they would be willing to give some money to a certain person at a certain time at a certain location. To their great hilarity, the applicants or parents never questioned the validity of the claim that they held any power and invariably paid.

These civil servants were able to pull off this scheme by drawing on the accepted veracity of the public secret, the desirability of the jobs, and most people's lack of performative competence on how to successfully navigate the murky space between public secret and intimate knowledge. In other words, they exploited bureaucratic outsiders by making (false) claims of possessing state authority, creatively sampling from a wide array of moral, legal, aesthetic, and performative realms. What these civil servants, in effect, did was deploy the cultural logics of camouflage.

Ieva Jusionyte (2015) introduces the notion of camouflage to capture a mode of statecraft that is deeply intertwined morally, aesthetically, and pragmatically with criminality in the tri-border area of Brazil, Argentina, and Paraguay. In this area, some retired Argentinian firefighters had been trafficking narcotics by concealing them in a counterfeit ambulance containing a fake patient while pretending to respond to emergencies. Their success depended on a simulation of state-sanctioned action. The ability to cover up their illegal activities, then, depended on the idea of camouflage, or on "the use of one symbolic and material order to protect another one from being recognized by blurring the boundaries between the two" (Jusionyte 2015: 115).

The civil servants at the Department of Human Resources similarly blurred the boundaries between the realms of law and criminality by donning the political authority of the state in order to solicit bribes. Still, there are important differences between Jusionyte's firefighters, who out on the mask of state authority to facilitate their trafficking operation, and the Kupang civil servants, who are actual state agents. The civil servants camouflage their true position by cloaking themselves in official authority, a disguise greatly bolstered by the certainty of the public secret. They cunningly operated within the opaque realm between public secret and intimate knowledge. They did not so much use the symbolic and material means of one order to protect another from being detected—say that of the state to protect KKN—as they used the already accepted and known fact that these realms are intertwined (Bubandt 2009). Although the new hires did not have to pay to enter the database, and KKN was completely unnecessary, the strength of the public secret ensured that KKN would occur. As we will see in the next chapter, such creative possibilities for new forms of KKN abound because of the new good governance ideals and demands for transparency.

Transparency, Truth, and the Play of Unconcealment and Concealment

Let us return to the question that no one in Kupang seemed to ask: how much truth is there to the public secret that KKN is necessary for access to institutions? Do you have to pay to get your child into college? Do you have to know people on the inside to get a civil service position? Martin Heidegger (1998) offers a concept of truth that is relevant here, one he traces from the Greek *alethia* and then translates as *unconcealment*. In this definition, truth is a play of presence from absence, of disclosure from enclosure, and hence, of unconcealment from concealment. Truth-as-unconcealment has less to do with correspondence to a state of affairs and more with what *emerges* from opacity. In the context of Kupang, it is what emerges from the opaque and foggy space between public secret and intimate knowledge. In a similar vein, when it comes to unconceal-ment in relation to public secrets, Taussig, drawing on Walter Benjamin, distinguishes *revelation*, which points to the slow unmasking of what is hidden at the heart of the public secret, thereby strengthening it, from exposure which threatens to destroy that secret (Taussig 1999: 2–3). The task and life force of the public secret is "to maintain that verge where the secret is not destroyed through exposure, but subject to a quite dif-ferent sort of revelation that does justice to it" (1999: 3).

This threshold is very strong in Kupang, where the great preoccupa-tion with uncovering the secret of the secret—the know-how needed to successfully navigate that which is known but cannot be spoken of—overshadows any imaginable exposure of the possibility that there might be nothing to the public secret. Therefore, the legality of my eviction from Indonesia, the attachment of names to test scores, or the lack of reciprocation after offering an entrance fee, fail to break the spell of the public secret. Instead, these give even more power to and perpetuate the public secret by revealing that, indeed, money, connections, and *tanggal tua* are what really matter. In this constant oscillation between exposure and revelation, what emerges from the fog as truth is ever-changing.

This unstable understanding of truth as a balance between conceal-ment and unconcealment complicates anti-corruption efforts. The good governance version of unconcealment is captured by its focus on trans-parency, which assumes an uncomplicated convergence between visibil-ity and proof. However, the promotion of transparency in international development and financial institutions has not been free from suspicion and conspiracy. As Todd Sanders and Harry G. West (2003) argue, the post-Cold War rise in the popularity and use of the concept of trans-parency went hand-in-hand with a proliferation of conspiracy theories and occult cosmologies.[3] Proclamations of openness, transparency, and

---

3. Examples of this are the increased skepticism of globalism and elites in the United States, including the invigoration of the militia movement

holding power accountable left many people around the world suspicious of the workings of power. This is certainly true in Indonesia, where the exertion of power is often shrouded and the political imaginary is infused with fantasies of unidentifiable enemies within the body politic (Siegel 1998). Specters of ghosts, unseen threats, and an accompanying "hyperhermeneutic" need to unravel and interpret invisible power dynamics were part and parcel of Suharto's New Order (Spyer 2002). Indeed, post-*reformasi* democratization has been accompanied by an emergence of sorcery and the occult in informal politics (Bubandt 2006; Strassler 2010).

Transparency and its assumptions of clear and causal connections between appearances and the good make even less sense in Kupang, where what is seen can turn out to be deceptive, and what is *clean* perceived as irredeemably *tainted*. This does not mean that what emerges as truth in the opaque space between public secret and intimate knowledge cannot coincide with the truth as understood in transparency, but simply there are many other possible truths as well. As we will see in the next chapter, civil servants in post-*reformasi* Kupang regularly face the important task of ensuring that the truth that emerges from their bureaucratic practices is one that proves their compliance with anti-corruption regulations.

---

throughout the country (Sanders and West 2003: 2–3); the rebirth of spirit mediumship in South Korea (Kendall 2003); and the suspicion among the Nigerian poor that the discourse of transparency is used to cover over the hidden unsavory, supernatural, and exploitative acts that distribute economic prosperity unevenly and incomprehensibly (Bastian 2003).

CHAPTER FIVE

Reading the Bidding Books

Adherence to Form in the Age of Transparency

In the fall of 2008, the Department of Public Works in Kupang held a public auction for construction contracts, an elaborate process known as a tender. When I interviewed contractors who were planning to submit bids and thus compete for city business, they lamented the discrepancy between what the project committees *ought* to consider when judging their proposals—experience, financial backing, personnel, etc.—and the small administrative mistakes that would be used to reject many proposals. One said:

> Because they [Public Works committee] think we have mistakes [in our administrative package], we cannot enter the tender. Because of matters that are actually small. Even though we have good experience in the field, we have the financial ability, and we have the personnel, we cannot enter. They prioritize the documentation more. We might as well throw our good proposal out the window since surely we will lose.

This contractor wanted the actual content of his proposal to take priority in the consideration of his bid. Yet it appeared to him that the technical details of his application, its mere form, weighed heavier on the minds of the committee. While this preoccupation with adherence to form characterized the bidding processes during the 2008 tender more generally, the overt focus on the form of rules, regulations, and procedures did not mean these were necessarily the basis of the contracts awarded. Despite an apparent adherence to rules and regulations, it was, rather, good relations, lobbying, and commitment that ultimately mattered more when it came to whose bids were selected.

The contractor's complaint repeats what by this point is a familiar refrain: in the post-*reformasi* era of good governance, corruption continued to proliferate in Kupang. It also brings to mind the suspicions voiced by the young elite civil servants from chapter three, Budi and Valentino, who understood that professional success was determined more by relations than merit. There is, however, something new in the contractor's concerns about the state of their documents—namely the problematic role played by visual and material proof in ascertaining the presence or absence of corruption. While the previous chapters offered ethical and experiential analyses of the unintended and sometimes contradictory effects of anti-corruption efforts in the complex and opaque moral-ethical assemblic context of Kupang, we now turn to the question of how civil servants and other Kupangese attempt to get out of this ethical and experiential limbo, and manage to live with the project of anti-corruption in ways that might, nevertheless, contradict its aims. We will focus on how they engage with the governmental virtue of transparency, which forms a central part of anti-corruption efforts inspired by the ideals of good governance. In doing so, the project of anti-corruption itself offers the very tools for its failure via the naïve trust it asks one to place in *transparency*.

Along with buzzwords like *accountability* and *efficiency*, the goal of transparency has become an indissoluble corollary of—if not a term synonymous with—*good governance* (Sanders and West 2003: 1). As Karen Strassler (2020) beautifully demonstrates, the "dream of transparency" and its promise of political freedom captured the post-*reformasi* Indonesian popular imaginary as it assumes a certain uncomplicated ease and fidelity to the truth of perception. For governments to be transparent, or to appear as such, their machinations ought to be available to public scrutiny. That way the corruption that would have been rampant with conditions of obscurity become easy to perceive, prosecute, and punish, or so the logic runs. However, this idea of transparency assumes a steadfast connection between representation and reality without accounting for the possibilities of manipulated information (Fenster 2015; Hetherington 2012; Tidey 2016), asking questions about "whose version of reality is being represented" (Hetherington 2008: 47), or understanding its potential for reinforcing state opacity (Sharma 2013).

The reliance on transparency in anti-corruption efforts indeed requires a trust in the clarity of the visual field. As phenomenology teaches (e.g., Husserl 1970; Merleau-Ponty 2013), however, while perception discloses worlds to us, points-of-view and orientations matter in what worlds can be disclosed and how they come to be disclosed. These perspectives are not "views from nowhere" (Nagel 1986) but always biased and partial; they require some inferential imaginative work. In this sense, the inference of corruption as present or absent based on the existence of material proof within a document is not the result of straightforward transparency, or a clear appearance of illuminated truth. Rather, the appearance of corruption is an inference facilitated by the reductionist and legalistic *perspective* according to which, for example, proper documentation suggests an absence of corruption during the process of a tender, even though corruption seems rampant. Such a strict trust in the "scopic regime" (Jay 1994) appears to be central for good governance and anti-corruption efforts, but such an approach brings a certain amount of *not seeing* and leaving things obscured.

This paradox certainly played out in how the rules, regulations, and laws for reducing corruption in Indonesia's construction sector affected that 2008 tender for construction projects in Kupang. Anti-corruption efforts in the construction sector indeed enabled new opportunities for corruption, and it was the emphasis on transparency that facilitated those opportunities. In order to avoid suspicions of corrupt behavior, contractors and officials strictly adhered to the stated rules and regulations for obtaining a government contract and proved that adherence by making sure all aspects of the tender that could be seen, read, and checked by auditors. As long as what was visible and tangible in the documentation was in line with the rules, then there was no evidence to support an anti-corruption investigation.

Again, it was the documents that served as the bureaucratic artifacts from which corruption could be discovered, for they facilitated the kind of transparency that anti-corruption programs advocate. At the same time, these documents also enabled a continuation of the ethics of exchange that we have seen form an important part of everyday life in Kupang, and by doing so help enable new forms of corruption precisely because of their visible adherence to the new rules and regulations. In short, these documents performed the paradox of strengthening anti-corruption discourse while subverting it, thereby showing us how the project of anti-corruption itself inadvertently offers the tools for its own failure.

In the current conjuncture of increasingly influential international anti-corruption programs and their potentially contradictory local effects, this attention to documents—"the most despised of all ethnographic subjects" (Latour 1988: 54)—and what they do is particularly interesting. Carrying deceptively convincing Weberian associations as a dominant emblem of bureaucracy on which "the management of the modern office is based" (Weber 1968: 67), documents are often considered to be the "neutral purveyors of discourse" (Hull 2012a: 253) that indicate the influence of recent anti-corruption legislation throughout national and regional bureaucracies. However, as we have seen in previous chapters with the deceptive properties of charity boxes and empty envelopes, Kupangese know very well that what you see is not necessarily what you get. Similarly, as the growing body of literature on documents as ethnographic artifacts shows (Das 2004; Hull 2012b; Poole 2004; Riles 2001; Scherz 2011), documents are not merely the material outputs of bureaucratic programs. Instead they are laced with discrepancies between official and other possible readings (Tarlo 2001: 77); provide opportunities for state functionaries to pursue their own private interests (Hull 2003: 510–511); enable forms of cognition that contrast with bureaucratic reasoning (Riles 2006: 10). In short, documents do not always do what they say they do.

There were many different kinds of documents that circulated during the 2008 tender. Of particular interest, however, are the simple and grimy "bidding books" that the Department of Public Works keeps in a manila folder and then makes available for every available project. In these books, prospective contractors indicate their interest in projects. They write down the name of their company and its owner, and complete it with a representative's signature and the mark of a company stamp. On the surface, the bidding books exemplify exactly those objectives stressed in the anti-corruption discourse for they seem to offer a clear and transparent record of a stage of the tendering process and an outline of the competition between contractors. A closer reading, however, reveals certain discrepancies that contradict this discourse. For the tremendous importance put on the adherence to the form of this discourse not only allows for a continuation of certain corrupt practices, but also enables novel forms of corruption that are inextricably linked to efforts to make the books *look good.*

Anti-Corruption, Fear, and Form

Certain offices and departments in Kupang are known as *wet*, which means they are seen as particularly corrupt, and that to enter them was to be drenched in their practices. Within a bureaucratic landscape described according to degrees of murky water, the Department of Public Works was described in terms befitting a monsoon downpour. On the front porch of the Kaho family home, one former department head who lived close by and was counted as family, half-jokingly said that Public Works was so wet that it was as if the department was a flood zone.

Such an association between the construction sector and corruption is not unique to Kupang or to Indonesia. On a global scale, the construction sector appears especially prone to corruption (Stansbury 2005: 36), repeatedly listed as the most corrupt in Transparency International's measurements (2008). Construction companies, for which the state is the main client, moreover, report particularly high levels of corruption in both non-Western (Davis 2004; Ding 2001) and Western contexts (Van Klinken and Aspinall 2011). Corrupt practices in government-funded construction projects, nevertheless, seem to be particularly marked in Indonesia, where an estimated thirty percent of the national procurement budget is said to be lost annually to corruption (Transparency International 2009: 263), and eighty percent of the building contractors are dependent on government projects (World Bank 2001: 29).[1] Therefore, according to measurements of corruption as a quantifiable and clearly defined concept, Indonesia—and its construction sector in particular—is indeed very corrupt.

Since the late 1990s Indonesia has taken serious steps to curb this corruption in its construction sector as part of its wider post-*reformasi* legal and administrative reforms.[2] It has strengthened the weak legal basis underlying the construction business, standardizing all regulations pertaining to the procurement of goods and services.[3] It removed some

---

1. While in Jakarta, the capital, and tourist hotspots such as Bali this percentage can be expected to be lower, the vast majority of contractors in the regencies and provinces outside Java and Bali rely on government funding.
2. The legal revisions that particularly aimed to do this were articulated in Presidential Decree 80/2003.
3. The legal backing for these changes was provided among others by the ratification of Act 31/1999 on the eradication of corruption by the first post-Suharto president Habibie (later amended in Law 31/1999 by his

of the loopholes thought to facilitate corruption and promote a more open, transparent, and competitive tender process. Additionally, it established two governmental bodies to audit the procurement of goods and services in the Development and Finance Surveillance Agency (BPKP) and the Supreme Audit Board (BPK). In spite of these efforts, corruption remains prevalent in the construction sector, a persistence that has generated much scholarship (Kurniasih and Yuwono 2004; Purwanto and Van Klinken 2010; Van Klinken and Aspinall 2011).

Unsurprisingly, the reductive and legalistic shape of these measures were not well matched to the moral-ethical assemblic complexity of Kupang. For instance, when Rudi, an experienced contractor in his forties who owns four construction companies, listed all the investigation agencies related to the construction business he was not acknowledging them as obstacles of corruption but naming those trying to get in on the action:

We have to be very careful because there are so many investigators that can be involved in investigating a project. There are internal investigation bodies on both the province and regency level. There are also internal investigations straight from the center. For investigation agencies there are BPK; BPKP; Justice Department; police; army; KPK. KPK and the police are like lizards and crocodiles. The KPK is the smaller version, and the police the big, hungry version. It is not just businessmen that are involved. It is a world surrounded by Satan. What the investigations do is they add more people who want to share in the pie.

Rudi's statement supports the finding of scholars who have shown that restructuring the tendering process and the establishment of anti-corruption agencies have not reduced corrupt practices but instead merely added to what he vividly evokes as *a world surrounded by Satan*. The layers of good governance did not necessarily alter illicit exchange practices, the work of informal fees, or the importance of "good

---

successor Wahid); the issuing of Presidential Regulation 19/2000 on a joint team to combat corruption and Presidential Regulation 71/2000 on public participation to eradicate corruption by Wahid; the ratification by former president Megawati of Law 30/2002 that enabled the formation of the anticorruption commission KPK; and current president Susilo Bambang Yudhoyono's consequent issuing of Presidential Instruction 5/2004 on accelerating the eradication of corruption.

relations," all of which scholars have noticed in Indonesia's procurement sector since at least the 1980s (Van Klinken and Aspinall 2011: 140; Sannen 1983: 9). However, since these new parties do have the authority to start corruption investigations and expose corrupt actors, they represent a powerful new interest in bidding practices. Under their influence, the structurally weak can be investigated and judged by the structurally powerful. Thus, rather than decreasing corruption, these anti-corruption initiatives only added new parties eager to share in the wealth.

Consequently, anti-corruption measures increased fear among those involved in the construction sector. Some civil servants under suspicion of corruption have become so afraid of possible investigation that they have even committed suicide (Purwanto and Van Klinken 2010: 7). This fear of anti-corruption investigations was also tangible in Kupang. One contractor claimed that since President Yudhoyono promised to clamp down hard on corruption, there had been a steep rise in investigations: "Everybody who wants to win a tender can be reported these days. If there is an investigation, we can get arrested." In 2008, local contractor Cosmas Lay, who was well known and respected, was convicted and sent to prison for corruption in an unfinished infrastructure project in 2008 (*Pos Kupang* 2010). The contractors I spoke with all stated that in just a few years they had become more worried about ending up in jail.

In this context, contractors and officials at the Department of Public Works alike became increasingly preoccupied with avoiding anything that might generate suspicions of malfeasance and began strict adherence to the rules. For instance, the head of Public Works expressed his concern with the avoidance of irregularities and the importance of sticking to tendering regulations. He showed annoyance with various contractors who made a habit of visiting him at his house at the time of a tender. For their part, contractors tended to think such a personal approach of establishing or maintaining direct relations with the head would increase their chances of winning the tender. The head himself, however, claimed to tell these contractors off and to send them to the office to enlist at the proper place because "now we have to play by the official rules."

The 2008 tender, which I followed from beginning to end, showed just how heavily invested Public Works officials were in acting in accordance with the new rules. Throughout the tender, discussions on how to interpret the multiple, and sometimes contradictory, and often unclear, regulations on tendering erupted regularly at the water sub-department. Desks were cluttered with the kind of law books commonly found in Indonesian bookstores, where they occupy entire sections, and many employees made serious attempts to understand them. Leo, an ambitious Public Works employee in his thirties, said that he had recently purchased a booklet version of Presidential Decree 80/2003 so as to learn everything he could about the new framework for tendering, since being young and still a fairly new employee, he found the process difficult to understand. He was not alone. Even the very experienced in the department struggled to the process, so Leo brought the booklet to the office for them all to reference. In this atmosphere, civil servants in the department repeatedly treated me to extended elaborations on all steps involved in a tender, explanations often aided by diagrams or references they created from their engagement with these law books.

Following the dictates of the decree, after publicly announcing the upcoming tender via local newspapers, the department invited interested contractors to list themselves in the bidding books and submit their association certificate, as well as lists of personnel and machinery. After this, the department organized a session to give prospective contractors more in-depth information regarding the respective projects. The contractors still willing to compete, were then given the opportunity to submit an official project proposal consisting of a time schedule and proposed project value, and an administrative package containing the contractor's identification card, educational and occupational background information, and official company documentation. A special departmental committee then carefully reviewed submitted proposals and scored them according to a system that awarded points for lower costs and promised completion dates. Committees also reviewed the administrative packages and weeded out those that were incomplete or not in line with national guidelines. As I spent more time at the Department of Public Works, talking with employees and contractors, and reading the bidding books accompanying the projects, I found that the form of tendering rules and regulations were, indeed, passionately followed. However, in a giving city where envelopes that supposedly convey care can turn out to be empty and corruption may (or may not) continue under the guise of charity boxes, we would do well to view such visible and material suggestions of transparency with some skepticism, and wonder whether to view the bidding books as a performance of transparency that together created a fiction of anti-corruption.

What Documents Do

The anthropology of Indonesia has for a long time stressed the importance of form as an expression of, and performance of, authority (Geertz 1981; Pemberton 1994; Siegel 1998). The importance of form in bureaucratic settings, however, is not unique to Indonesia. Don Handelman (1981) already characterized bureaucracy as a sociality organized by form. Michael Herzfeld (1992), furthermore, stresses that the use of a consistent form permits the perpetration of widely divergent bureaucratic practices. Uncovering the "symbolic roots of Western bureaucracy," he describes how the deployment of the rhetoric of kinship can achieve the seemingly opposing goals of providing an "easily understood model for the loyalty and collective responsibility that citizens must feel towards the state" as well as serving "more sinister aims" of bureaucratic inclusion and exclusion based on blood or race. The idea that the state rhetoric of kinship is merely symbolic obscures both the multiplicity of meanings symbols can engender and the role actors play in shaping symbolic meaning (1992: 10–16, 65–70). As he so poignantly states, "rhetoric is never simply the pure art of classification. It is the practice of symbolic action—a process in which a fixed form is often not only the mask, but even the enabling condition, for labile meaning" (1992: 69).

To a certain extent, the claim here is similar: the adherence to the form of anti-corruption rhetoric both repeats and reconstitutes bureaucratic classifications of what counts as corruption and enables novel practices that undermine this very discourse. However, I take a different approach to analyzing discrepancies and the interplay between *form* and *content*. Although a focus on the multiplicity of meaning that symbols can engender offers a good analytic tool to look at why documents *do not do what they say they do*, this symbolic or interpretive approach nevertheless holds open the possibility that if all surrounding conditions allow it, there can be an indexical relation between symbols and their meaning that would ultimately ground this relationship. In contrast, instead of focusing on this possible indexical relationship, let us consider the ever-present possibility that documents become unanchored from anti-corruption discourse. To understand how this becomes possible, it is important to see how adherence to form emerges from the current constellation of anti-corruption, fear, and threats of investigation in Kupang. Adherence to form reflects the importance of visibility and transparency necessary to avoid anti-corruption investigations.

In her insightful study of intimacy and corruption in Thailand, Rosalind Morris (2004) describes how the idiom of transparency has been applied to a range of social and economic ills. The idiom's wide range of uses comes from the fact that it would seem related to an "ethics of sincerity" (2004: 226) and suggests a certain honesty—at least from an IMF or World Bank perspective. When political processes are therefore rendered visible and transparent, surely, so the assumption runs, they must be honest and sincere. But Morris shows that visibility, transparency, and ethics need not align and visibility can be produced for its own sake. As Morris writes:

> The law works in the realm of appearances, of what can be seen and what can be hidden. What matters now in Thailand is that everything be visible, and more: that the processes of making visible, of moving things from the domain of the secret into that of the public, themselves be revealed, unfurled in the brilliant light of the media's perpetual day. (2004: 233–234)

This need for neoliberal transparency as in Thailand plays out in Kupang as well. If the construction company's tender is submitted and appraised in a transparent manner, it is said to be honest and free from corruption. If what can be seen, read, and proved is in accordance with the letter of the law, there is no corruption. Hence visibility, or the adherence to form, becomes paramount such that the department head insists that contractors appear at his office instead of his house and officials strive to determine the correct interpretation of confusing and contradictory rules. The importance of adhering to form becomes particularly clear in the most visible and tangible objects that circulate in a tender: documents.

The looming threat of investigations make it important for officials from the Department of Public Works to strictly follow the regulations during a tender and for contractors to present an immaculate set of documents. The contractors know that failure to adhere to the proper form of the administrative package can lead to disqualification from the bidding process. Because of this vulnerability, some officials in the Department of Public Works rent out their expertise in tendering to contractors developing proposals. For example, one night over dinner I was interviewing Leo, the Public Works employee who had bought the Presidential Decree 80/2003 booklet. We were repeatedly interrupted by incoming phone calls. Speaking quietly into his phone in an attempt to remain out of earshot, Leo at last gave the person on the line directions to the restaurant where we were eating. After a short while, a man entered the dining room and Leo took him to a corner table. They chatted for a few minutes, after which Leo saw the man out and returned. Smiling brightly, Leo exclaimed that this was a case of KKN! It turns out that the man was a contractor seeking Leo's help in making sure his documentation was in order for the tender. Leo accepted this request as, apparently, he had been lending his expertise to a few other contractors as well for the lucrative fee of IDR $500,000 ($55, about half of a starting civil servant's monthly salary) per contractor.

The heightened preoccupation with an *appearance of adherence* to regulations could be seen in the department head's urging of contractors to enlist at the proper location and mirrored in the treatment of documents involved in the tendering process. After all, documents could constitute material proof of wrongdoings should there be an investigation into corrupt practices. Leo was therefore paid to make sure there were no visible digressions from the letter of the law in the contractor's documents. Yet, the fact that Leo accepted payments from contractors to draft the documents he and his coworkers would later evaluate in the tender contradicts the stipulations of the legal reforms laid down in Presidential Decree 80/2003. The efforts Leo undertook to get acquainted with all aspects of the decree actually enabled him to engage in new ways of making money that directly countered the spirit of transparency, fair competition, and the anti-corruption stance underlying the decree. As with Morris' example of Thailand, the visibility displayed in these tender documents, therefore, does not necessarily convey the kind of transparency, sincerity, and honesty favored in good governance programs. Such tender documents could at once adhere to the law's letter while offering Leo a way to make some extra money on the side. They visibly carry out compliance with the anti-corruption discourse but enable a new form of corruption in their very production.

In addition to offering officials in the Department of Public Works a new way to make money, documents also serve to legitimize an informally won bid. Michael, a contractor with years of experience in the construction business, explains that even when you know your proposal is more competitive than that of a rival contractor favored to win, the project committee can always find problems in your submitted administration package: a stamp that was forgotten or a signature that was omitted. Failure to adhere to the proper form of documents—proper punctuation and required signatures and stamps—indeed served as a legitimate reason to disqualify contractors. Sometimes things go further. When Michael's proposal ought to have formally won based on the merits according to the point system of evaluating bidding documents and yet another contractor was promised the project, someone from the Department of Public Works went looking for trivial mistakes in his documents, and then even resorted to removing some necessary forms to disqualify his bid. Rudi, a contractor, referred to the minor administrative errors within documents as "lice." Counter to Michael's experience, however, when those mistakes were found in his document, a civil servant from Public Works would alert him so he had the chance to clean up his proposal. Because Rudi's documents display adherence to the proper format, concealed from view is the informal process through which he had actually won the contract.

These contractor experiences illustrate how adherence to form has become a means through which to formalize informal actions. The increased role of proper documentation under the guise of transparency creates a visible and tangible layer of legitimization for hidden acts of KKN. At the same time, by adhering to the form of anti-corruption discourse, they nevertheless perform a taxonomic act of bureaucratic logic (Handelman 1990) because they reinforce what counts as corruption. The consequence of such repeated performances is ambiguous and contradictory, and often leads to new and unanticipated possibilities (cf. Yurchak 2006). For on the one hand, documents reproduce and maintain the dominant anti-corruption discourse codified in the letter of the law; on the other hand, they mask and enable practices that contradict and subvert this discourse.

Recent anthropological studies of documents disclose how form, iterability, and the possibility of rupture are essential characteristics. Annelise Riles, for example, demonstrates that the drafting of the 1992 Pacific Platform for Action document—in particular, filling the not-yet-decided-on content of the "brackets"—involved mainly the production of "properly patterned language" (2001: 80). This document, therefore, represents a carefully selected and negotiated reiteration of countless preceding documents in which aesthetic conventions regarding layering and patterning mattered more than the actual meaning of the words used. In another example, Marilyn Strathern considers university mission statements in the United Kingdom as "utterances of a specific kind, namely a turn-of-the-century language of good governance" (2006: 194). Here Strathern too shows that the replication of a species of utterance ensures that content remains subordinate to form and that the actual form of those statements in fact opposes the task of education. Additionally, Veena Das (2004: 244–245), when asking how the state can claim legitimacy in the face of obvious forgery and corruption, claims that in their reproducibility, documents are open to forgeries and infelicitous use beyond a proper context. This iterability, however, does not signal vulnerability, but rather, in a sense, a multiplying of state power even when carried out infelicitously without the signature of the state. For Das, the reproduction of state authority in documents—even in the case of forgery—adds to state legitimacy. In short, documents can indeed emphasize form over content, contradict the intentions of a discourse that the documents supposedly represent, and legitimize illegitimate claims.

The effects of the project proposals and administrative packages in Kupang are, therefore, not shocking bureaucratic anomalies or deviations from the anti-corruption discourse. They exemplify the ever-present possibility of documents becoming unanchored from their initial context and intended meaning. Such unmooring is made possible by the iterability of an anti-corruption discourse that is layered throughout the process: in the layout of the project proposals and administrative packages; in the Presidential Decree 80/2003, which circulated throughout the Department of Public Works; the vision and mission statements of the newly founded auditing bodies; and in statements on good governance as promulgated by NGOs such as Transparency International. The concern with form during a tender process, therefore, exceeds a certain "aesthetics of bureaucratic practices" (Riles 2001: 16). Adherence to form may ensure the compliance with the anti-corruption discourse, but also a break from it. It is thus simultaneously a performative and performance.

Let us now turn to the bidding books to see how this adherence to form of the anti-corruption discourse enabled what from the perspective of this discourse would be considered corrupt practices, while still serving as adherence to the rules in the event of an investigation.

Reading the Bidding Books

The fall 2008 tender enlivened everyday routines at the Department of Public Works. The civil servants who sometimes confessed being bored at the office were busily engaged in tender preparations. Bidding books were drafted to note how many contractors signed up for a given project, how many consequently handed in a proposal, and, finally, who won.

Clarification sessions were organized so interested contractors could find out more about the various projects offered. The tender process also gave officials and contractors, many of whom see each other at every tender and at various formal occasions in Kupang's fairly limited social circles, an opportunity to reconnect and catch up. After the public announcement of projects in a local newspaper in late August, a steady stream of contractors and representatives from local construction companies stopped by to enlist, join clarification sessions, and submit proposals. Many contractors lingered to inquire about family members or to sit down, smoke cigarettes together, and chat. These amiable interactions continued into the clarification sessions, in which contractors and officials engaged in a constant good-natured bantering back and forth. This pleasant sociability was indeed part of the competition for profitable construction projects and the social component left its trace, if hardly perceptible, in the bidding books.

On the surface, the bidding books that the Department of Public Works made available for the thirty-five projects it advertised certainly suggested a thriving market-oriented competition between a number of construction companies—all in line with Presidential Decree 80/2003. Intending to compile an up-to-date list of construction companies in Kupang, I set out to check all bidding books and to write down the names of the companies and their owners. Assembling such a list was a daunting task that took days of copying down the names of all the companies that had enlisted for each project. Staring at the books during the long and tedious task of manually copying the entries of the 227 companies listed for the 35 projects revealed certain inconsistencies.

While it was not surprising that I found that some companies had enlisted for more than one project, it was notable that in several bidding books clusters of entries were written in the same handwriting, even though the companies enlisted had different names, different owners, and a unique stamp. Furthermore, when comparing the names of the companies that had enlisted in the bidding book with those that had handed in an actual project proposal during a later stage in the bidding process, it became clear that some companies had enlisted many times but had never handed in a proposal. The company Amin, for instance, had enlisted seven times without handing in a single proposal. Hiasan Cahaya had enlisted nineteen times yet also never handed in a proposal. In contrast, Pengharapan Perkembangan had enlisted for only one project, handed in one proposal, and consequently won the tender.

These inconsistencies are not proof of foul play per se, and this is the strength of the bidding books as a materialized performance of adherence to the rules of the tender process. Perhaps the similarity in handwriting of multiple entries was the result of some helpful employee helping several companies waiting in line to enlist in the bidding books, but if so, why did the signatures put in by a representative of the company still look so similar? Perhaps Hiasan Cahaya lost its courage after the clarification phase of all nineteen projects it signed up for and decided to withdraw from all of them. Perhaps Pengharapan Perkembangan decided to place all bets on one horse and won because of the effort put into that single proposal. I discussed these inconsistencies with Christian, a low-level employee at the department:

Sylvia: There are some companies that enlisted in the bidding book, yet never handed in a proposal?
Christian: Oh yeah. These probably enlist to make it look as if there is a competition, a strong enough competition. So, if we just look at the list, it will look like, "wow, so open! Everybody can enter." But in fact, it will just go to one person. One person enlists and invites some friends to enlist as well. But this is just in order to make it look crowded.
Sylvia: So, there are some that only enlist to make the list look good, they never want to hand in a proposal?
Christian: They are just used to liven [the list] up. That is not good.
Sylvia: Then there are companies that were enlisted in the same handwriting. Why is that?
Christian: The same reason. To fill the list and make it seem as if there is competition. To make it look fair. While actually, the competition is between only three contractors. So, these just invite their friends to enlist.

Christian claimed that the entries in the same handwriting and companies enlisting while not handing in a project proposal were part of strategies meant to ensure the *appearance* of competition and fairness. A few examples from interviews with contractors and officials in the Department of Public Works provide some insights into the mechanisms of the informal process that was underlying the formal competition registered in the bidding books.

According to some contractors, the actual contest for a bid takes place long before a tender is opened. The competition for a project begins, they explained, around the central government allocation of funds to the Department of Public Works. Contractors therefore attempt to influence the allocation of those funds. According to Rudi:

Rudi: With regards to lobbying, we can go to the center. This is lobbying for the budget, meaning the budget for the upcoming year at national parliament.
Sylvia: What are you lobbying for then?
Rudi: That is lobbying for state budget.
Sylvia: That is lobbying in the center so the funds for the region are bigger? Have you ever done that?
Rudi: Yeah, the lobbying in the center is carried out so the allocation of funds is bigger. For instance, once I have gotten a project worth [IDR 17 billion (approximately $2 million)] that was going to be sent down [from center to region] like this. We had to prepare five percent of that amount, so a friend and I had to pay about [IDR 750 million (almost $8,500)].
Sylvia: In which way did you give an amount that big? Via a bank account?
Rudi: We brought cash, not a check, so it could not be verified. So, while [members of the national parliament] were still [in Kupang] that money was given directly, because if it would have been given in Jakarta we could have been arrested. And as long as they were here, we would pay for their enjoyable stay, for their hotel and so forth.

Through this kind of lobbying, Rudi had once managed to get a large project worth IDR 17 billion ($12 million) allocated to the region. By offering around five percent of the total project value to these parliament members, he secured his company the right to execute the project.

The bidding book for this project could hide the lobbying process that resulted in its existence and also gave a false impression of competition because other contractors who had signed up for this project stood no chance of winning. Furthermore, Rudi showed some concern about getting caught, which is why he paid in cash and ensuring the transaction took place in the familiar surroundings of Kupang. In other words, in the realm of appearances there was no visible, tangible, provable trace of corruption. All that was rendered visible was his submitted documentation—the project proposal and his administrative package, which no doubt displayed adherence to form and therefore suggested transparency. The bidding book in this case similarly portrayed an open and fair competition among several contractors without traces of manipulation. As such, it legitimized Rudi's informal lobbying with members of national parliament.

Rudi's example contrasts nicely with Joshua Barker's (2005) description of the strategies that the state-owned electronics enterprise, Lembaga Elektronika Nasional (LEN), employed to sell its earth stations after the launching of Indonesia's own satellite. In that case, LEN lobbied regional government officials and the military to accept the stations by promising the benefits of showing off national development at the local level (Barker 2005: 718). In Kupang, the lobbying was initiated by local agents in such a way as to keep things local. The Public Works officials and contractors I interviewed tended to prefer keeping government projects close by having them executed by local contractors as opposed to bringing in larger outfits from Jakarta or Surabaya. The reason for this, according to one official I interviewed, is that when it came to the larger companies from outside Kupang, "their manner of *pergaulan* (fraternization) is unknown to us, so we don't know how to *suap-menyuap* (engage in bribery) with them. At least the people here know how it works."

Alfred, a contractor, explained the importance of having acquaintances or "good relations" with those one is lobbying for projects. He explained that while his proposal was being considered by the tender committee, he needs to engage them. He said that if he were to give money to the committee head it would trickle down to all the committee members and help bring a favorable judgment of his proposal. Nevertheless, he preferred to spend his time and money on all the committee members individually. Such a process was aided by establishing relations with one or more committee members who, he said, might feel obliged to help and even count the relationship as a reason for rendering a favorable judgment of his proposal.

While Alfred preferred to give money to all members of the tender committee for the sake of good relations, both contractors lobbying from below and those lobbying from above might give money directly to the committee head. Leo confirmed that from his perspective both strategies had potential for success. He had seen influential and wealthy contractors contact the head of the department, who had supposedly urged contractors to stay away from his house and *play by the rules* while nonetheless shaping the judgements of the committee.

Another important aspect of effective lobbying for projects is having proper financial backing. Officially, a contractor's bid is judged on the amount of time and money needed to execute the project: the contractor that offers to finish the project fastest and cheapest wins. This contractor then gets (an advance of) the total project value from the Department of Public Works to fund the project. Unofficially, however, as explained to me by various contractors, bids are judged on the percentage of the total project value that the contractor promises to return to the tender committee as an informal fee, euphemistically labeled "commitment." As one contractor explained:

> Ok, it's like this. We want to get a project. For that we have to show a certain commitment. This can be 5 percent, 7.5 percent, 10 percent, 12.5 percent or 15 percent … If our commitment is hesitant, another contractor with a bigger commitment will get it. This is not yet a guarantee that we'll get it. They can give it to someone else. They can find mistakes in our administration.

Interestingly, this contractor notes how the focus on form, which seeks out "mistakes in our administration," can be used to delegitimize a bid when another contractor has offered a larger "commitment," suggesting again that visible adherence to the form of the anti-corruption discourse that matters. Even after having been allocated a project, the money flow to Public Works officials doesn't stop. He explained it this way:

> There is also "returning-a-favor money," this is given throughout the project, not at the beginning. It can happen that he [committee member] wants to go somewhere. He then asks us for a ticket. That is "answering back." And if we don't give this money, sometime in the future they will discredit us. So, they will refuse us other projects, so they refuse us in a very polite way.

Money does not just flow from contractors to officials, it also circulates among contractors. As I flipped through the bidding books for all thirty-five projects of the 2008 tender, and saw list after list with names of companies, names of owners, and stamps, one final discrepancy caught my attention. Recall that 227 companies enlisted for those 35 projects in a town where most contractors are dependent on government projects. Because adherence to form demands all documents in a tender be fully in line with stated rules and regulations, only contractors who could provide the proper administrative package would eventually be considered. How could so many construction companies survive in Kupang? Were these real companies? If so, why would so many only enlist but never hand in an actual bid? Why bother enlisting when lacking the financial backing or lobbying skills to engage in informal competition?

Most, if not all, of the companies entered in the bidding books are at least a member of one of the established construction associations and, therefore have the status required to enter tendering process. Yet, as re-search on the construction sector in other parts of Indonesia has found, many companies entering a tender nonetheless lack an office, machinery, and employees (Van Klinken and Aspinall 2011: 154). They are indeed fictive competitors and enter the bidding for various reasons. One reason is to lend the appearance of competition for an actual contractor. At the time of signing up, that contractor adds the names of fictive companies to, as was said, "make the list look good." This explains why some of the entries in the bidding book are in the same handwriting. As a thank you for lending their names and stamps, a small fee or even percentage of the project value, often referred to as "withdrawal money," may be given.

Another reason many fictive companies sign up is to collect fees for, in the end, backing out. A retired entrepreneur who plays tennis with a few young owners of such fictive construction companies explained to me that many companies do not have the ambition to ever hand in a project proposal. They are merely *fee seekers* in it for that withdrawal money that the real, functioning companies offer them. In the meantime, these informal fee seekers and receivers of thank-you money do add to the adherence to the form of the anti-corruption discourse displayed in the bidding books by making the competition look real and in line with official regulations.

It might be tempting to view the bidding for contracts in Kupang as a way for the involved parties to seek rents and, in Rudi's words, "share in the pie." However, the circulation of money in the tendering process cannot merely be understood in terms of economic gain, for those mon-ey flows intimately follow social ties and the reciprocal obligations im-plied therein. What counts as "corruption" under the letter of the law was framed as proper behavior during the tender, invoking the moral weight of the caring responsibility that structures proper ethical responses to-wards others in Kupang. To illustrate this, John, the head of Kupang's Chamber of Commerce, described the situation this way:

When asked at a family party to give a project to a family mem-ber, one cannot really refuse. Projects in Kupang are small, and there aren't many. When lucky, a contractor might get one project a year.

The profits contractors get from a project are not very big, so what would happen if the relative does not get a new project? How will he live? How will he eat?

The obligation of care felt toward the relative in this example at times motivates John to give projects to family members when solicited. As officials told me during informal chats, the commitment contractors give "from above" trickles down to the lower echelons of the department. This is not just to make sure no employee will talk but also because it is the ethical thing to do. Similarly, one contractor, Niko, gave me another example of inter-contractor loyalty. After he won three projects during one tender he decided to subcontract two of those to other contractors so they could profit as well. Although he still expected to receive a percentage of the project value as a return for his generosity, he framed his actions to me in terms of a caring responsibility, as a matter of "returning a favor." Such practices not only help ensure that "we can all get something," as one contractor put it to me, but more importantly for our purposes, it is an indication of the responsiveness that is central to a Kupangese ethics of care and exchange.

It is important to emphasize that the bidding book processes are embedded, and only make sense, within such an ethics. As such, although that combination of fraternization and bribery—*pergaulan* and *suap-menyuap*—may be perceived as corrupt from the perspective of a good governance model of anti-corruption, from the perspective of many of my Kupangese interlocutors they are clearly the ethical thing to do. Consequently, "fairness" in the tendering process does not entail a neoliberal, market-oriented competition, as anti-corruption efforts tried to produce, but rather sharing the pie in such a way that "we all get something." These locally considered ethical practices of sharing, therefore, did not take place outside of anti-corruption efforts and the good governance model, but are inextricably linked to and, in fact, made possible by them. That is, the adherence to the proper form of anti-corruption transparency efforts enables continuation of an already existing ethics of care and exchange—a continuation helped along by new practices of corruption.

Corruption or Care

The 2008 tender at the Department of Public Works in Kupang demonstrates how initiatives aimed at curbing corruption in the construction sector helped produce effects that undermined those initiatives. In light of some high-profile national and local corruption investigations, they did produce a fear of possible investigations among contractors and Public Works officials. To avoid suspicions of corrupt behavior, therefore, contractors and officials focused on adherence to the form of the anti-corruption discourse, as exemplified by the department head's urging of contractors to enlist at the proper place, officials' obsession with figuring out the tender rules and conducting the steps of the tender in line with Presidential Decree 80/2003, and contractors paying of officials to draft their (proper) documentation. This adherence to form became particularly visible in office documents, those bureaucratic artifacts in which corruption can be read and proved most easily. However, although the various documents that circulated during the tender visibly adhered to the anti-corruption discourse, they, nevertheless, also enabled a continuation of informal (and illegal) practices and provided new opportunities for what anti-corruption initiatives would consider as corruption, but what many of my Kupangese interlocutors would call the ethical thing to do.

The entanglement of documents in the continuation of existing and enabling of new forms of corruption, problematizes transparency's self-evident connection between reality and representation, or between that which is given in perception and how this is interpreted. What emerges in Kupang at the current conjuncture of anti-corruption discourse, threats, fear, and a neoliberal need for transparency is the importance of visibility, tangibility, and provability. If what is visible, tangible, and provable in Kupang shows adherence to the anti-corruption discourse, then surely there is no corruption. However, as any Kupangese auntie could tell us, trusting representations to converge with the realities they purportedly represent—be it envelopes with care or proper documentation with good governance—would be incredibly naïve.

The contestation that the adherence to form displayed by the documents involved in the 2008 tender so elegantly covered up, ultimately revolves around questions concerning what comes to count as the governmental good in the aftermath of good governance inspired anti-corruption efforts. The governmental virtue of transparency offered civil servants and others in Kupang a space in which to perform the fiction of anti-corruption and in doing so avoid the threat of arrests, while enabling a continuation of the kinds of practices that straddle the fine line between corruption and care. It is this connection between corruption and care that forms the most important starting point for imagining what might come to count as a governmental good. Given the failure of the existing project of anti-corruption to reach its goals of decreasing corruption and achieving its own version of good governance, it is worth returning to the question of what a governmental good might look like when it is rooted in conceptions of corruption as a transgression of care.

The Return of the *Bapak*

As he served the two-and-a-half-year prison sentence for his corruption conviction, Daniel Adoe had plenty of time for reflection and, possibly, regret. There was little doubt he had not been as starry-eyed about the break with the political past and democratic progress as the voters who elected him in 2007, for he was then a seasoned, if often sidelined, career bureaucrat. Surely his proclaimed anti-corruption and pro-democracy stances were the product of political expediency more than ideological conviction. Still, he probably did not anticipate the abrupt nosedive his popularity would take during his years at the city's helm. That it was Yonas Salean—known to be corrupt and his long-time nemesis—who won Kupang's second-ever direct mayoral elections in 2012, and opened an investigation into the suspected corruption of his predecessor must have left a bitter taste in his mouth.

That Kupang voted Salean mayor despite his aura of corruption forms a fitting coda to a book that addressed the contradictory effects of anti-corruption efforts on civil servants and their behavior in an eastern Indonesian bureaucracy. In its study that roughly coincided with Adoe's mayoral reign from 2007–2012, this book sought to understand transformations of local governance during a period in which Indonesian ideologies and practices of governance were in flux. It was only in 1998 that the authoritarian Suharto had stepped down after three decades in power, a shift that initiated a period of thorough administrative and governmental adjustment, the era of *reformasi*. The political changes that came were heavily influenced by ideas from the world of international development and the efforts of financial institutions seeking to promote the advancement of liberal democracy around the world. Under the umbrella of such ideas of good governance, anti-corruption figured prominently. Initially the administrative adjustments implemented in Indonesia prompted a surge of democratic optimism among citizens, scholars, and policy makers. After a few years, however, little remained of this optimism about the conjoined projects of democratization, good governance, and anti-corruption. Corruption had followed the decentralization of power, moving from the national center to the regional governments; massive corruption scandals plagued even those organizations erected to combat corruption; and trust in public officials and civil servants reached new lows. In short, the push for anti-corruption did not make Indonesia less corrupt. If anything, good governance initiatives seemed to have made governance worse.

This book set out to discover what effects anti-corruption efforts had if not a decrease in corruption. It looked for answers in how civil servants in the eastern Indonesian city of Kupang—named Indonesia's most corrupt city during the time I conducted field research for this project in the late 2000s—responded to the anti-corruption efforts that came to shape and influence their work. It traces the gradual change that occurred among civil servants during this period: from an initial excitement about promises of progress to a profound disillusionment with actual possibilities for betterment. In this way, the book offers a detailed, in-depth, and intimate intersubjective study of the experiential-ethical navigation of an altered, uncertain, and opaque bureaucratic landscape. It shows that there exist plenty of reasons for skepticism regarding good governance's ability to ensure a *good* in governance or secure possibilities for human flourishing.

The first two chapters focused on the difficulty of distinguishing corruption from care in Kupang. Chapter one proposed that the neoliberal models of governance cannot account for what the state is and means in Kupang, which is better thought of as a "giving city." It is embedded in larger webs of sovereignty and suzerainty and the state is therefore connected to its citizens through an ethics of care and exchange. Consequently, what comes to count as corruption according to the expectations of the neoliberal state can be viewed as care within the dynamics of the giving city. Chapter two demonstrated the limitations of legalistic, *public office* approaches to corruption in post-*reformasi* Kupang. It argued that in order to understand acts of corruption in a giving city, we need to emplace them within a relational context; a context where ideas of corruption are connected to larger ideas of a common good; where a caring responsibility towards intimate others is an important ethical drive; and where contestations about corruption do not inhere in the act itself, but in decisions on where to draw a line between acceptable and unacceptable ways of responding to expectations from and obligations to others. Corruption in the giving city is thus best understood not as a transgression of public-private boundaries, but as a transgression of care.

Having outlined key elements of this relational context, the next two chapters turned to the ethical and practical difficulties that both civil servants and citizens experience in their navigation of bureaucratic obstacles. Chapter three focused on young career civil servants who were uncertain of the proper conduct needed for their advancement when different institutional, discursive, and embodied moralities conflicted and overlapped. The idiom of family proved to be central. It reverberated within the caring responsibility of intimate family life *and* the inherently ambiguous family principle so central to ideological construction of the Indonesian nation-state. Given this confusion, ideas of proper bureaucratic conduct did little to clarify or combat corruption. It only added to the ethical bewilderment of civil servants.

Chapter four looked at how clients and other outsiders to the bureaucratic process navigate the opaque space between the sense that corruption is necessary and the intimate knowledge required to successfully get what one needs. A significant finding was the seeming impossibility of ever disproving the public secret of corruption, even in the face of counterexamples. This was because Kupangese, who routinely expect to receive empty envelopes as donations from supposedly close relations, know that appearances are often deceptive and performative. Visible and tangible indications of fair play (i.e., transparency) are thus viewed with suspicion and not as an absence of corruption. The notion that *what you see is not what you get* as related to the civil servants of Kupang was taken up in the final chapter by focusing on the interactions of the city's construction sector and the Department of Public Works. In that context, civil servants understood that the project of anti-corruption and its emphasis on transparency meant that corruption had to be present on the surface of documents in order to be proven. What mattered, then, was form and appearance. This insight gave them a great deal of control over how things looked, which helped alleviate worries about investigations. It enabled the continuation of existing informal business arrangements, and even offered enterprising civil servants new illicit opportunities for enrichment.

Ultimately this book argues that by articulating the governmental good in liberal economic terms and translating that idea into one-size-fits-all policies via legalistic and technocratic measures, anti-corruption efforts in this period were unfit for the moral-ethical complexities of Kupang. They left many civil servants, in the words of one of them, "stuck between the ethical and the right thing." These civil servants could not determine where the boundaries of corruption were and thus how to lead one's professional life in an ethical manner. In order to lessen the anxiety of what effectively constitutes a moral breakdown (Zigon 2007) in their everyday lives, they resorted to an adherence to the form of anti-corruption measures, supported by the good governance valuation of transparency. Such adherence to form, however, enabled a continuation of existing practices that would count as corruption under legal definitions while creating even greater opportunity for novel forms of corruption to emerge. This is how the project of good governance creates the very means for its contradiction. Good governance becomes intimately implicated in corruption's production and continuation.

At a more fundamental level, this book addresses the tension between modes of governance and the possibilities they afford for human flourishing. Good governance appears to severely diminish such possibilities. While we have seen examples of people's malicious intent, manipulation, and self-aggrandizement, what we mostly encounter is their profound ethical confusion and sincere attempts at forging worthwhile lives for themselves and those for whom they bear responsibility. The impression left by this study is not one of rent-seeking individuals out to exploit the public, but of governing imperatives experienced as harsh and uncaring. It is not about bad apples, but about bad ideology. At their heart, anti-corruption efforts fail to account for the centrality of care within a governmental good. This is an argument that extends well beyond Kupang or Indonesia, as it increasingly appears to be a shared shortcoming of late-liberal democratic modes of governance. People living under the austerity that followed the Great Recession in the UK and Greece might well recognize the feeling of being uncared for. Voters in the US, Brazil, and Hungary, who also elected strongmen with corrupt tendencies may very well understand the attraction Salean holds to voters in Kupang. It is therefore worth entertaining the thought that someone known for corruption might be considered to offer the best governmental arrangement to secure some semblance of human flourishing.

A Governmental Good Grounded in Care

The attractiveness of a corrupt leader in a climate of anti-corruption sentiment might sound counterintuitive. For those who express their hopes of political progress through the teleological narrative of good governance—a narrative in which clientelism gives way to democracy—the election of Salean, a New Order standard bearer and understood as corrupt, only underscores the view that Indonesian democracy is still in transition. His election also supports the nagging suspicions of geographical disparity that Kupangese sometimes entertain when they state that they are lagging behind the West. However, from a perspective that stresses the centrality of care to the governmental good, this is not at all such a strange proposition.

After all, we have seen how in Kupang, a caring responsibility toward intimate others is a moral engine that drives ethical behavior. This is especially true in times of precarity. *Tante* Elsie succinctly explained that caring responsibility is both "noticing" and "helping out," or recognition tied to reciprocity. Offering of material or non-material goods, such as help, food, shelter, employment, only counts as care when it follows a recognition of someone's hardship and for reasons of selfless munificence rather than self-aggrandizement. In this way, care is distinguished from corruption. In the realm of governance, the school head's illicit hiring of *honorer* was an example of care, whereas the former mayor's promise of opening hundreds of *honorer* positions if his protégé would emerge as the victor of the 2007 elections was an example of corruption. On a larger scale, Suharto's corruption was acceptable as long as the Indonesian people thought they also profited from the nation's riches, but became insupportable when Indonesia hit dire economic straits. If care, as an ethically driven response to the needs of others, is an element of governance so too is a foundational, relational understanding of personhood.

Such an emphasis on relationality and connected morality is suspect in the liberal ideology of good governance. Central to liberal political ideas of good democratic practice is, indeed, a disavowal of relationality, which contradicts liberalism's crucial values of egalitarianism, disinterestedness, impersonality, and individualism. However, this emphasis on individualism and impersonality belies the fact that, as Piliavsky (2014: 27–33) observes, ultimately, all politics imply some kind of relational morality. Any ideological or institutional arrangement contains conceptions of the ways in which those who govern and those who are governed ought to relate to one another, as well as the larger societal good this relatedness serves. In a system of representative democracy, relational logic comes to the fore in the relationship between voters and their representatives, but also in the supposition that voters cast their vote out of a selfless dedication to a larger ideal of a societal good. Such expectations of selfless dedication on the part of supposedly disinterested voters points to a paradox inherent in liberal democracy as a governing ideology: that expectations of a great social investment exist alongside an apparent denial of sociality.

Despite this paradox, the dominant model for good governance holds on to the pretense of abstraction, impersonality, and asociality (Piliavsky 2014). It thus leaves analyses of evident relationality in politics and electoral processes—such as the patronage politics that is the focus of much contemporary scholarship on Indonesian politics and governance—stuck with the sterile, cold, and incomplete language of clientelism. In such rational-choice-tinged analyses, *gifts* with all their possible moral connotations of affirmation and maintenance of mutuality and intimacy can only ever be read as *bribes*. Similarly, hierarchical political relationships can only ever be understood as exploitative and transactional. Against these restricted and partial analyses, the recent literature on patronage and hierarchy (e.g. Ansell 2010; Haynes and Hickel 2016; Keeler 2017; Peacock 2015; Piliavsky 2021) poses a welcome challenge to the dominant models of good governance by emphasizing the moral logic inherent in many hierarchical political arrangements, and by showing that patronage, for many, actually serves as a model of good society.

This brings us, again, back to Salean. During the first few years of experimentation with the newly installed system of direct district-head elections, voters in Kupang were very eager to participate in the representational logic of liberal democracy. Proclaiming themselves to be "citizens of NTT" or Indonesia with the right to vote, they cast themselves as vote-bearing "possessive individuals" (Macpherson 1962; see also Ansell 2018) who deserved to be seen and cared about as citizens rather than treated as members of clientelist cliques. They wanted affordable tuition, accessible healthcare, and no inflation on the prices of household necessities. In contrast to suspicions that they were "still stupid" or "not yet ready," voters in Kupang showed themselves to be more than ready for liberal democracy and its promise of progress.

But this progress never materialized. Tuition and healthcare remained expensive for most, and the prices of essential food stuffs and gas only went up. Politicians failed to represent the interests of their constituencies, and newly elected district heads seemed to forget about their campaign promises as soon as the elections were over (Tidey 2018). In short, the recognition and reciprocity so foundational to care in Kupang were nowhere to be found. To make matters worse, the only kind of care that people in Kupang had been able to reliably count on, the giving city's steady expansion of civil service as a part of the national government's regular redistribution of resources to ensure state coherence, was now threatened. The notion of the good in good governance, after all, was informed by an economic liberal impetus that prioritized efficiency and lean states. In short, under the new institutional arrangement of liberal democracy, people felt unseen and uncared for. In many ways, they appeared to have gotten the worst of all worlds: they missed out on the liberal democratic promise of care as well as the caring responsibility of the giving city.

Against this background, the renewed appeal of someone like Salean becomes more understandable. Already in the late 2000s, a nostalgia for Suharto's New Order was steadily growing among Indonesians. In Kupang, this longing for a strong *Bapak* was only strengthened when Adoe failed to embody possibilities for democratic change, but also proved an unsuccessful *Bapak* in the organicist family-oriented tradition of the New Order. Salean in contrast offered an approach to governing reminiscent of a father-figure from the New Order, one willing to quell any infighting among competing political factions while drawing on the caring responsibility of Kupangese fatherhood to remind him of the importance to respond to those in need. He also had years of experience navigating the opaque landscape of Kupangese bureaucracy. In other words, he offered competence *and* care.

It would be wrong to claim Salean's mayoral win indicated that voters were unprepared for the democratic process, or to frame it in clientelist terms of cold transactional logic. In a political context devoid of care and relational morality, a vote for Salean might well have constituted a vote for care. In 2007, he lost because of his well-known transgression of the balance between care and corruption: he unapologetically pursued self-aggrandizement instead of displaying the selfless munificence befitting patrons and demonstrating the caring responsibility towards others that turns potentially corrupt acts into ones of care. His election in 2012 suggests that people expected his defeat and ensuing political humiliation to have taught him how to better perform this balancing act. He might still be inclined to look out for himself, but if he fails to look out for his constituents, they are likely vote him out again.

Kupang's embrace of Salean is best understood as choosing the possibility of attaining a good life under an ideology of governance that lacked the inextricable necessity of care. In other words, Salean's victory was not an endorsement of corruption, but an attempt to escape a lack of care created by good governance. As late liberal democracies increasingly betray a core moral principle that elected officials act on behalf of citizens through a recognition of their needs and the proper reciprocation to ensure those needs are met, citizens no doubt feel evermore betrayed. To dissatisfied voters who feel uncared for and excluded from even the most basic of benefits, the liberal democratic governance with an emphasis on economic efficiency seems like one that might function all the better if it did not have to deal with the existence of actual people: a democratic system in which the demos itself presents a problem to democracy.

For those who consider political progress in terms of crafting a kind of political care that is founded in recognition—in feeling as though one is seen—Kupangese do not appear to be all that different from similarly positioned citizens in what are called Western democracies, where we could also frame the contemporary appeal of leftist or rightist reformers in terms of a desire on the part of voters to be seen when political care is lacking. Furthermore, just as voters in provincial urban Kupang are willing to put up with a candidate who is known for his corruption, it is increasingly apparent that voters elsewhere are similarly willing to accept a certain degree of corruption, collusion, or nepotism as long as they feel recognized and cared for.

Discerning Alternative Visions of a Governmental Good

Amidst this ostensible failure of the project of good governance, where is the alternative vision of a governmental good? I propose we chart our search for such alternatives around three questions.

First, we need to attend to the fraught question of legitimacy in the ethically complex reality into which anti-corruption efforts were inserted, a reality which I have portrayed throughout this book in terms of a moral-ethical assemblage (Zigon 2011). Here, I want to recall Pardo's (2013) insight about the ever-present possibility for a discrepancy between legality and morality, by which he means that what is legal is not necessarily popularly perceived as moral and vice versa. Laws and regulations, in other words, derive their legitimacy not solely from their legal status but also, and more importantly, from the extent to which they are considered to be moral. The legalistic shape that anti-corruption efforts took failed to secure their legitimacy by neglecting morality. Just as Weber had long ago observed about the rational-legal nature of modernity, these anti-corruption efforts failed precisely because they continued modernity's conceit that legality and legitimacy can be equated (D'Entréves 1963).

In this book, I outlined an alternative vision of the governmental good by attending to this neglected dimension of morality. Starting from Kupang as a particularly situated sedimentation of a much larger moral-ethical assemblage—one of different, sometimes contrasting, and sometimes overlapping institutional, discursive, and embodied moralities—I presented an image of a governmental good rooted in an ethos of care and exchange. In contrast to the ethos of leanness proposed by liberal good governance that finds but a few feeble points of resonance within this moral-ethical assemblage, and virtually no grounding in Kupang at all, this ethos of care and exchange resonates across the assemblage, adding to its legitimacy. We can trace it from the intra-familial moral engine of a caring responsibility to the Indonesian state ideology of *Pancasila*; from the now-outdated anti-corruption legislation that emphasized public interest over public office to the ideology of familyism in both its revolutionary and New Order organicist guises. This alternative governmental good, then, is one rooted in relationality and care, in which corruption becomes not a transgression of public-private boundaries but a transgression of the fine balance between acceptable and unacceptable ways of responding to the pull of relationality—a transgression of care.

To be sure, I am not claiming that this outline of an alternative image of a governmental good is the only one we can trace from the complex moral-ethical assemblage in which good governance arrived in Indonesia. Religion offers powerful institutional, discursive, and embodied moralities for the many Muslim, Protestant, Catholic, and Hindu Indonesians in ways that I do not fully do justice to here. For example, Islamic political theories of state formation and organicism have presented persuasive institutional moral contrast to liberal democracy since the very conception of Indonesian nationalism in the late nineteenth century and continue to do so today (Bourchier 2015). Marxist ideas of the governmental good, while effectively having lost political standing after the New Order communist purges, continue to haunt political debates if only as a specter against which to protect the body politic. While I do not exhaust all possible ways in which we can trace connections between the many nodes in this moral-ethical assemblage and imagine alternative images of a governmental good, the existence of these possibilities only reinforces the need for attending to the situated moral complexity in which the legitimation of anti-corruption efforts take shape.

Second, we need to keep in view questions of substantive justice. By favoring legalistic understandings of corruption, the current *public office* approach to corruption tends to forgo more substantive questions of what counts as good, just, or fair (Philp 1997). For example, when civil servants are preoccupied with adherence to the form of anti-corruption in the documents of in a state construction-project tender, the current battle of anti-corruption is one primarily waged in the realm of appearances and has as its prize the production and reproduction of boundaries between public and private. In doing so, it safeguards what Peter Bratsis (2003) refers to as the public realm's illusion of purity, while excluding from political ontology more substantive questions of what ought to be or what might be conceived of as political goods. As we have seen, plenty of people in Kupang are well aware that public realm purity is a fiction and not at all surprised that private interests may influence one's professional conduct. This is not considered to be problematic and does not rise to the charge of corruption as long as a sense of the common good is kept in view. The adulteration of the public-private distinction is not the main concern people have with corruption. Instead, as Rika, a civil servant we met in Chapter two, said: "the important thing is that there has to be a balance."

Connected to this question of substantive justice is the question of the redistribution of resources, especially to relatively poor regions where "hungry season" is still an expected regular occurrence. I have posited here that care is grounded in recognition and substantive reciprocity. The occasional expansion of the state apparatus that Van Klinken described as a form of "state socialism" (2014: 10), and which has facilitated Kupang's tenuous incorporation into the fragile fabric of the nation-state, as well as its position as the provider of locally worthy personhood, appears to be but a poor substitute for real recognition and, by extension, care. This state expansion may have proven to be an effective strategy for quieting regional rebellions and dissatisfaction since the founding of the Indonesian nation-state but it does not engender long-term relationships of trust and belonging. As with gubernatorial candidates who think casually handing out rupiah bills to market vendors would suffice to ensure their loyalty on election day (Tidey 2018), it does not evoke a sense of being seen or taken seriously. As *Tante* Mientje's family members will confirm, by giving the absolute bare minimum required for a performance of recognition one conveys only the bare minimum of care. When the idea of Jakarta is viewed with suspicion by Kupangese, who prefer to keep things local, and openly rebelled against by separatist movements from Indonesia's westernmost to easternmost regions, the question of care, and along with it, of recognition and substantive reciprocity, should be central to discussions of how to ensure Indonesian national cohesion and belonging.

Finally, a third point to consider when contemplating alternative visions of a governmental good pertains to the question of who gets to decide on which visions of such a good to pursue. While politicians can make persuasive cases for particular versions of a governmental good and scholars can offer critical contextualization of such views and perhaps offer some of their own, I propose we leave the decision-making power to those sometimes described as "not yet ready" and "still stupid." Voters may elect a known corruptor to the position of mayor, or president, after previously having elected a candidate who represented liberal democratic progress but in doing so may also display a more astute understanding of the potential emptiness of promises of progress. Instead of finding hope for good governance in the teleological temporality of the liberal progress narrative, we might, instead, appreciate the rhythmic temporality of regular election cycles. Knowing one can vote for a new mayor, governor, or president at regular intervals is perhaps the most comforting source of hope for a governmental good that many of us have.

References

Abrams, Philip. 1988. "Notes on the Difficulty of Studying the State (1977)." *Journal of Historical Sociology* 1 (1): 58–89.

Althusser, Louis. 1971. "Ideology and Ideological State Apparatuses (Notes towards an Investigation)." In *Lenin and Philosophy and Other Essays*, translated by Ben Brewster, 127–86. New York: Monthly Review Press.

Anders, Gerhard, and Monique Nuijten. 2007. "Corruption and the Secret of Law: An Introduction." In *Corruption and the Secret of Law: A Legal Anthropological Perspective*, edited by Monique Nuijten and Gerhard Anders, 1–24. London: Routledge.

Anderson, Benedict and Richard O'Gorman. 1972. *The Idea of Power in Javanese Culture*. Ithaca, NY: Cornell University Press.

Ansell, Aaron. 2010. "Auctioning Patronage in Northeast Brazil: The Political Value of Money in a Ritual Market." *American Anthropologist* 112 (2): 283–94.

———. 2014. *Zero Hunger: Political Culture and Antipoverty Policy in Northeast Brazil*. Chapel Hill, NC: University of North Carolina Press.

———. 2018. "Clientelism, Elections, and the Dialectic of Numerical People in Northeast Brazil." *Current Anthropology* 59 (18): S128–37.

Antlöv, Hans. 2003. "Civic Engagement in Local Government Renewal in Indonesia." In *Logolink SEA: Citizen Participation in Local Governance: Experiences from Thailand, Indonesia, and the Philippines*, 139–71. Manila: Institute for Popular Democracy.

Arendt, Hannah. 1958. *The Human Condition*. Chicago: University of Chicago Press.

Aretxaga, Begoña. 2003. "Maddening States." *Annual Review of Anthropology* 32 (1): 393–410.

Armstrong, Neil, and Peter Agulnik. 2020. "'I Was at the Right Place at the Right Time' The Neglected Role of Happenstance in the Lives of People and Institutions." *HAU: Journal of Ethnographic Theory* 10 (3): 890-905.

Asad, Talal. 2003. *Formations of the Secular: Christianity, Islam, Modernity.* Stanford, CA: Stanford University Press.

Aspinall, Edward, and Ward Berenschot. 2019. *Democracy for Sale: Elections, Clientelism, and the State in Indonesia.* Ithaca, NY: Cornell University Press.

Aspinall, Edward, Diego Fossati, Burhanuddin Muhtadi, and Eve Warburton. 2020. "Elites, Masses, and Democratic Decline in Indonesia." *Democratization* 27 (4): 505–26.

Aspinall, Edward, and Marcus Mietzner. 2019. "Indonesia's Democratic Paradox: Competitive Elections amidst Rising Illiberalism." *Bulletin of Indonesian Economic Studies* 55 (3): 295–317.

Barker, Joshua. 2005. "Engineers and Political Dreams—Indonesia in the Satellite Age." *Current Anthropology* 46 (5): 703–28.

Barker, Joshua, and Gerry van Klinken. 2009. "Reflections on the State in Indonesia." In *State of Authority*, edited by Joshua Barker and Gerry van Klinken, 17–46. State in Society in Indonesia. Ithaca, NY: Cornell University Press.

Barlow, Colin, Alex Bellis, and Kate Andrews. 1991. "Nusa Tenggara Timur: The Challenges of Development." In *Political and Social Change Monograph No. 12.* Canberra: Australian National University.

Bastian, Misty L. 2003. "'Diabolic Realities': Narratives of Conspiracy, Transparency, and 'Ritual Murder' in the Nigerian Popular Print Media." In *Transparency and Conspiracy: Ethnographies of Suspicion in the New World Order*, edited by Harry G. West and Todd Sanders, 65–91. Durham, NC: Duke University Press.

Bayart, Jean-Francois. 1993. *The State in Africa: The Politics of the Belly.* London: Longman.

Becker, Gary S. 1994. "To Root Out Corruption, Boot Out Big Government." *Bloomberg.Com*, January 31, 1994. https://www.bloomberg.com/news/articles/1994-01-30/to-root-out-corruption-boot-out-big-government.

———. 1995. "If You Want to Cut Corruption, Cut Government." *Bloomberg.Com*, December 11, 1995. https://www.bloomberg.com/news/articles/1995-12-10/if-you-want-to-cut-corruption-cut-government.

Benstead, Lindsay J., Lonna Rae Atkeson, and Muhammad Adnan Shahid. 2020. "Does Wasta Undermine Support for Democracy? Corruption, Clientelism, and Attitudes Toward Political Regimes." In *Corruption and Informal Practices in the Middle East and North Africa*, edited by Ina Knubbe and Aiyisha Varraich, 77–90. London: Routledge.

Berenschot, Ward, and Edward Aspinall. 2019. "How Clientelism Varies: Comparing Patronage Democracies." *Democratization* 27 (1): 1–19.

Blackwood, Evelyn. 2005. "Transnational Sexualities in One Place: Indonesian Readings." *Gender and Society* 19 (2): 221–42.

Blundo, Giorgio and Jean-Pierre Olivier de Sardan, eds. 2006. *Everyday Corruption and the State: Citizens and Public Officials in Africa*, translated by Susan Cox. London: Zed Books.

Blundo, Giorgio, and Jean-Pierre Olivier de Sardan. 2006a. "Everyday Corruption in West Africa." In *Everyday Corruption and the State: Citizens and Public Officials in Africa*, edited by Giorgio Blundo and Jean-Pierre Olivier de Sardan and translated by Susan Cox, 69–109. London: Zed Books.

———. 2006b. "Why Should We Study Everyday Corruption and How Should We Go About It?" In *Everyday Corruption and the State: Citizens and Public Officials in Africa*, edited by Giorgio Blundo and Jean-Pierre Olivier de Sardan and translated by Susan Cox, 3–14. London: Zed Books.

Boellstorff, Tom. 2005. *The Gay Archipelago: Sexuality and the Nation in Indonesia*. Princeton, NJ: Princeton University Press.

Bourchier, David. 1997. "Totalitarianism and the 'National Personality': Recent Controversy about the Philosophical Basis for the Indonesian State." In *Imagining Indonesia: Cultural Politics and Political Culture*, edited by Jim Schiller and Barbara Martin-Schiller, 157–85. Athens, OH: Ohio University Press.

———. 2015. *Illiberal Democracy in Indonesia: The Ideology of the Family State*. London: Routledge.

Boxer, Charles R. 1947. *The Topasses of Timor*. Amsterdam: Indisch Instituut.

Boyer, Dominic C. 2000. "On the Sedimentation and Accreditation of Social Knowledges of Difference: Mass Media, Journalism, and the

Reproduction of East/West Alterities in Unified Germany." *Cultural Anthropology* 15 (4): 459–92.

BPS. 2008. "Kota Kupang dalam angka 2008 [Kupang municipality in figures 2008]." Kupang: Budan Pusat Statistik.

Bratsis, Peter. 2003. "The Construction of Corruption, or Rules of Separation and Illusions of Purity in Bourgeois Societies." *Social Text* 21 (4): 9–33.

Brown, Ed, and Jonathan Cloke. 2004. "Neoliberal Reform, Governance and Corruption in the South: Assessing the International Anti-Corruption Crusade." *Antipode* 36 (2): 272–94.

Brown, Wendy. 2001. *Politics Out of History.* Princeton, NJ: Princeton University Press.

Bubandt, Nils. 2006. "Sorcery, Corruption, and the Dangers of Democracy in Indonesia." *The Journal of the Royal Anthropological Institute* 12 (2): 413–32.

———. 2009. "From the Enemy's Point of View: Violence, Empathy, and the Ethnography of Fakes." *Cultural Anthropology* 24 (3): 553–88.

Buchan, Bruce, and Lisa Hill. 2014. *An Intellectual History of Political Corruption.* Houndmills, UK: Palgrave Macmillan.

Buehler, Michael. 2007. "Local Elite Reconfiguration in Post-New Order Indonesia: The 2005 Election of District Government Heads in South Sulawesi." *Review of Indonesian and Malaysian Affairs* 41 (1): 119–47.

Bukovansky, Mlada. 2006. "The Hollowness of Anti-Corruption Discourse." *Review of International Political Economy* 13 (2): 181–209.

Bünte, Marco. 2009. "Indonesia's Protracted Decentralization: Contested Reforms and Their Unintended Consequences." In *Democratization in New Order Indonesia*, edited by Marco Bünte and Andreas Ufen, 102–23. London: Routledge.

Bünte, Marco, and Andreas Ufen. 2009. "The New Order and Its Legacy: Reflections on Democratization in Indonesia." In *Democratization in New Order Indonesia*, edited by Marco Bünte and Andreas Ufen, 3–29. London: Routledge.

Butt, Simon. 2012a. "A Wolf in Sheep's Clothing." *Inside Indonesia*, April 2, 2012.

———. 2012b. *Corruption and Law in Indonesia.* London: Routledge.

Carsten, Janet. 2004. *After Kinship.* Cambridge: Cambridge University Press.

Choi, Nangkyung. 2004. "Local Elections and Party Politics in Post-Reformasi Indonesia: A View from Yogyakarta." *Contemporary Southeast Asia* 26 (2): 280–301.

———. 2009. "Democracy and Patrimonial Politics in Local Indonesia." *Indonesia* 88: 131–64.

Collier, Stephen J. 2005. "Budgets and Biopolitics." In *Global Assemblages: Technology, Politics, and Ethics as Anthropological Problems*, edited by Aihwa Ong and Stephen J. Collier, 373–90. London: Blackwell.

Conkling, Robert. 1979. "Authority and Change in the Indonesian Bureaucracy." *American Ethnologist* 6 (3): 543–54.

Corrigan, Philip, and Derek Sayer. 1985. *The Great Arch: English State Formation as Cultural Revolution*. Oxford: Blackwell.

Crouch, Harold. 1979. "Patrimonialism and Military Rule in Indonesia." *World Politics* 31 (4): 571–87.

Crouch, Melissa. 2008. "Indonesia's National and Local Ombudsman Reforms: Salvaging a Failed Experiment?" In *Indonesia: Law and Society*, edited by Tim Lindsey, 382–406. Sydney: The Federation Press.

Cunningham, Clark. 1962. "People of the Dry Land: A Study of Social Organization of an Indonesian People," Ph.D diss, Oxford University.

———. 1964. "Order in the Atoni House." *Bijdragen Tot de Taal-, Land- En Volkenkunde* 120: 34–68.

Das, Veena. 2004. "The Signature of the State." In *Anthropology in the Margins of the State*, edited by Veena Das and Deborah Poole, 225–52. Santa Fe: School of American Research Press.

Davis, Jennifer. 2004. "Corruption in Public Service Delivery: Experiences from South Asia's Water and Sanitation Sector." *World Development* 32 (1): 53–71.

Deeb, Hadi Nicholas, and George E. Marcus. 2011. "In the Green Room: An Experiment in Ethnographic Method at the WTO." *PoLAR: Political and Legal Anthropology Review* 34 (1): 51–76.

D'Entréves, Alexander P. 1963. "Legality and Legitimacy." *Review of Metaphysics* 16 (4): 687–702.

Ding, Xueliang. 2001. "The Quasi Criminalization of a Business Sector in China; Deconstructing the Construction-Sector Syndrome." *Crime, Law and Social Change* 35: 177–201.

Diprose, Rachael, Dave McRae, and Vedi R. Hadiz. 2019. "Two Decades of Reformasi in Indonesia: Its Illiberal Turn." *Journal of Contemporary Asia* 49 (5): 691–712.

Edelman, Lee. 2004. *No Future: Queer Theory and the Death Drive*. Durham, NC: Duke University Press.

Errington, Shelly. 1989. *Meaning and Power in a Southeast Asia Realm*. Princeton, NJ: Princeton University Press.

———. 1990. "Recasting Sex, Gender and Power: A Theoretical and Regional Overview." In *Power and Difference: Gender in Island Southeast Asia*, edited by Jane Monning Atkinson and Shelly Errington, 1–58. Stanford, CA: Stanford University Press.

Fagg, Donald R. 1958. "Authority and Social Structure: A Study in Javanese Bureaucracy," Ph.D diss, Harvard University.

Farram, Steven. 2010. *A Political History of West Timor: 1901-1967*. Cologne: Lambert Academic Publishing.

Feldman, Ilana. 2008. *Governing Gaza: Bureaucracy, Authority, and the Work of Rule, 1917-1967*. Durham, NC: Duke University Press.

———. 2019. *Life Lived in Relief: Humanitarian Predicaments and Palestinian Refugee Politics*. Berkeley: University of California Press.

Fenster, Mark. 2015. "Transparency in Search of a Theory." *European Journal of Social Theory* 18 (2): 150–68.

Ferguson, James, and Akhil Gupta. 2002. "Spatializing States: Toward an Ethnography of Neoliberal Governmentality." *American Ethnologist* 29 (4): 981–1002.

Fox, James J. 1977. *Harvest of the Palm. Ecological Change in Eastern Indonesia*. Cambridge, MA: Harvard University Press.

———. 1980. "Introduction." In *The Flow of Life: Essays on Eastern Indonesia*, edited by James J. Fox, 1–18. Cambridge, MA: Harvard University Press.

———, ed. 1993. *Inside Austronesian Houses: Perspectives on Domestic Designs for Living*. Canberra: Australian National University.

Garcia, Angela. 2010. *The Pastoral Clinic: Addiction and Dispossession Along the Rio Grande*. Berkeley: University of California Press.

Geertz, Clifford. 1981. *Negara: The Theater State in 19th Century Bali*. Princeton, NJ: Princeton University Press.

Guilhot, Nicolas. 2005. *The Democracy Makers*. New York: Columbia University Press.

Gupta, Akhil. 1995. "Blurred Boundaries: The Discourse of Corruption, the Culture of Politics, and the Imagined State." *American Ethnologist* 22 (2): 375–402.

————. 2012. *Red Tape: Bureaucracy, Structural Violence, and Poverty in India*. Durham, NC: Duke University Press.

Habermas, Jürgen. 1991. *The Structural Transformation of the Public Sphere: An Inquiry into a Category of Bourgeois Society*. Translated by Thomas Burger. Cambridge, MA: MIT Press.

Hadiz, Vedi. 2008. "How Far to a Meaningful Democracy–1." *Inside Indonesia*, April 20, 2008.

Hadiz, Vedi, and Richard Robison. 2013. "The Political Economy of Oligarchy and the Reorganization of Power in Indonesia." *Indonesia* 96: 35–57.

Handelman, Don. 1981. "The Idea of Bureaucratic Organization." *Social Analysis* 9: 5–23.

————. 1990. *Models and Mirrors: Towards an Anthropology of Public Events*. Cambridge: Cambridge University Press.

Harrison, Elizabeth. 2006. "Unpacking the Anti-Corruption Agenda: Dilemmas for Anthropologists." *Oxford Development Studies* 34 (1): 15–29.

Hasty, Jennifer. 2005. "Sympathetic Magic/Contagious Corruption: Sociality, Democracy, and the Press in Ghana." *Public Culture* 17 (3): 339–70.

Haynes, Naomi, and Jason Hickel. 2016. "Introduction: Hierarchy, Value, and the Value of Hierarchy." *Social Analysis* 60 (4): 1–20.

Hazan, Haim, and Esther Hertzog. 2011. *Serendipity in Anthropological Research: The Nomadic Turn*. Farnham, UK: Ashgate.

Heidegger, Martin. 1998. *Parmenides*, translated by Andrè Schuwer and Richard Rojcewicz. Bloomington: Indiana University Press.

————. 2008. *Being and Time*. Translated by John Macquarrie and Edward Robinson. New York: Harper Perennial.

Herzfeld, Michael. 1992. *The Social Production of Indifference: Exploring the Symbolic Roots of Western Bureaucracy*. Chicago: University of Chicago Press.

————. 2005. "Political Optics and the Occlusion of Intimate Knowledge." *American Anthropologist* 107 (3): 369–76.

————. 2016. *Cultural Intimacy: Social Poetics and the Real Life of States, Societies, and Institutions*. 3rd edition. London: Routledge.

Hetherington, Kregg. 2008. "Populist Transparency: The Documentation of Reality in Rural Paraguay." *Journal of Legal Anthropology* 1 (1): 45–69.

————. 2011. *Guerilla Auditors: The Politics of Transparency in Neoliberal Paraguay*. Durham, NC: Duke University Press.

————. 2012. "Agency, Scale, and the Ethnography of Transparency." *Political and Legal Anthropology Review* 35 (2): 242–47.

————. 2018. "Peasants, Experts, Clients, and Soybeans: The Fixing of Paraguay's Civil Service." *Current Anthropology* 59 (18): S171–81.

Hofman, Bert, and Kai Kaiser. 2004. "The Making of the Big Bang and Its Aftermath: A Political Economy Perspective." In *Reforming Intergovernmental Fiscal Relations and the Rebuilding of Indonesia. The "Big Bang" Program and Its Consequences*, edited by James Alm, Jorge Martinez-Vazquez, and Sri Mulyani Indrawati, 15–46. Cheltenham, UK: Edward Elgar.

Hornberger, Julia. 2018. "A Ritual of Corruption: How Young Middle-Class South Africans Get Their Driver's Licenses." *Current Anthropology* 59 (S18): S138–48.

Hough, Dan. 2013. *Corruption, Anti-Corruption, and Governance*. Houndmills, UK: Palgrave Macmillan.

Hull, Matthew S. 2003. "The File: Agency, Authority, and Autography in an Islamabad Bureaucracy." *Language and Communication* 23 (3): 287–315.

————. 2012a. "Documents and Bureaucracy. Annual Review of Anthropology." *Annual Review of Anthropology* 41: 251–67.

————. 2012b. *Government of Paper: The Materiality of Bureaucracy in Urban Pakistan*. Berkeley: University of California Press.

Huntington, Samuel, P. 1991. *The Third Wave: Democratization in the Late 20th Century*. Norman: University of Oklahoma Press.

Husserl, Edmund. 1970. *Logical Investigations*, translated by J. N. Findlay. London: Routledge & Kegan Paul, Ltd.

Jackson, Peter A. 2004. "The Thai Regime of Images." *Sojourn: Journal of Social Issues in Southeast Asia* 19 (2): 181–218.

Jauregui, Beatrice. 2014. "Provisional Agency in India: Jugaad and Legitimation of Corruption." *American Ethnologist* 41 (1): 76–91.

Jay, Martin. 1994. *Downcast Eyes: The Denigration of Vision in Twentieth-Century French Thought*. Berkeley: University of California Press.

Joseph, Gilbert M., and David Nugent, eds. 1994. *Everyday Forms of State Formation: Revolution and the Renegotiation of Rule in Rural Mexico*. Durham, NC: Duke University Press.

Joseph, Richard. 1987. *Democracy and Prebendal Politics in Nigeria: The Rise and Fall of the Second Republic*. Cambridge: Cambridge University Press.

Jusionyte, Ieva. 2015. "States of Camouflage." *Cultural Anthropology* 30 (1): 113–39.

Kantorowicz, Ernst H. 1958. *The King's Two Bodies: A Study in Medieval Political Theology*. Princeton, NJ: Princeton University Press.

Kaufmann, Daniel. 2009. "Aid Effectiveness and Governance: The Good, the Bad and the Ugly." *Developmental Outreach* 11 (1): 26–9.

Keane, Webb. 1997. *Signs of Recognition: Powers and Hazards of Representation in an Indonesian Society*. Berkeley, CA: University of California Press.

———. 2016. *Ethical Life: Its Natural and Social Histories*. Princeton, NJ: Princeton University Press.

Keeler, Ward. 2017. *The Traffic in Hierarchy: Masculinity and Its Others in Buddhist Burma*. Honolulu: University of Hawai'i Press.

Kendall, Laurie. 2003. "Gods, Markets, and the IMF in the Korean Spirit World." In *Transparency and Conspiracy: Ethnographies of Suspicion in the New World Order*, edited by Harry G. West and Todd Sanders, 38–64. Durham, NC: Duke University Press.

Kompas. 2011. "Gubernur Sulsel tak akan tuntut IPDN [Governor of South Sulawesi will not prosecute IPDN]," January 31, 2011.

Kota Kupang. 2021. "Sejarah Kota Kupang [History of Kupang City]" *Resmi Pemerintah Kota Kupang*. Accessed August 1, 2021. https://kupang-kota.go.id/2021/03/31/sejarah-kota-kupang/

Kristiansen, Stein, and Muhid Ramli. 2006. "Buying an Income: The Market for Civil Service Positions in Indonesia." *Contemporary Southeast Asia* 28 (2): 207–33.

Kuipers, Joel C. 1998. *Language, Identity, and Marginality in Indonesia: The Changing Nature of Ritual Speech on the Island of Sumba*. Studies in the Social and Cultural Foundations of Language. Cambridge: Cambridge University Press.

Kupang News. 2011. "Pejabat instansi vertikal tak pernah berkoordinasi" [Officials from vertical institutions never coordinate]." *Pos Kupang*, July 15, 2011. https://kupang.tribunnews.com/amp/2011/07/15/pejabat-instansi-vertikal-tak-pernah-berkoordinasi

Kurniasih, Elysabeth Dwi, and Prapto Yuwono. 2004. "The Illegal Retribution Faced by the Construction Business: A Case Study in Salatiga." *KRITIS Jurnal Studi Pembangunan Interdisiplin* 16 (1): 1–23.

Latour, Bruno. 1988. "Drawing Things Together." In *Representation in Scientific Practice*, edited by Michael Lynch and Steve Woolgar, 19–68. Cambridge, MA: MIT Press.

Lay, Cornelis, and Gerry van Klinken. 2014. "Growing up in Kupang." *In Search of Middle Indonesia*, edited by Gerry van Klinken and Ward Berenschot, 145–69. Leiden: Brill.

Ledeneva, Alena V. 1998. *Russia's Economy of Favors: Blat, Networking, and Informal Exchange*. Cambridge: Cambridge University Press.

Lee, Doreen. 2016. *Activist Archives: Youth Culture and the Political Past in Indonesia*. Durham, NC: Duke University Press.

Lepri, Isabella. 2005. "The Meanings of Kinship Among the Ese Ejja of Northern Bolivia." *The Journal of the Royal Anthropological Institute* 11 (4): 703–24.

Lévi-Strauss, Claude. 1983. *The Way of the Masks*, translated by Sylvia Modelski. London: Jonathan Cape.

Levitsky, Steven, and Daniel Zieblatt. 2018. *How Democracies Die*. New York: Crown.

Lewanmeru, Oby. 2014. "Anak mantan walikota Kupang disebut terima Rp 600 juta [Son of former mayor of Kupang is said to receive IDR 600 million]" *Pos Kupang*, April 24, 2014. https://kupang.tribunnews.com/2014/04/24/anak-mantan-walikota-kupang-disebut-terima-rp-600-juta.

Li, Tanya Murray. 2007. *Will to Improve: Governmentality, Development, and the Practice of Politics*. Durham, NC: Duke University Press.

MacLennan, Carol. 2005. "Corruption in Corporate America: Enron—Before and After." In *Corruption: Anthropological Perspectives*, edited by Dieter Haller and Cris Shore, 156–70. London: Pluto Press.

MacPherson, C.B. 1962. *The Political Theory of Possessive Individualism: Hobbes to Locke*. Oxford: Clarendon.

Malley, Michael. 2000. "Beyond Democratic Elections: Indonesia Embarks on a Protracted Transition." *Democratization* 7 (3): 153–80.

Mani, Lata. 1990. "Multiple Mediations: Feminist Scholarship in the Age of Multinational Reception." *Feminist Review* 35 (1): 24-41.

Marx, Karl. 1978. "The German Ideology: Part I." In *The Marx-Engels Reader*, edited by Robert C. Tucker, 2nd ed., 146–200. New York: Norton.

Mattingly, Cheryl. 2018. "Ethics, Immanent Transcendence, and the Experimental Narrative Self." In *Moral Engines: Exploring the Ethical Drives in*

Human Life, 39–60, edited by Cheryl Mattingly, Rasmus Dyring, Maria Louw, and Thomas Schwarz Wentzer. New York: Berghahn Books.

Mattingly, Cheryl, Rasmus Dyring, Maria Louw, and Thomas Schwarz Wentzer, eds. 2018. *Moral Engines: Exploring the Ethical Drives in Human Life*. New York: Berghahn Books.

McKinnon, Susan. 1991. *From a Shattered Sun: Hierarchy, Gender, and Alliance in the Tanimbar Islands*. Madison, WI: University of Wisconsin Press.

———. 1995. "Houses and Hierarchy: The View from a South Moluccan Society." In *About the House: Lévi-Strauss and Beyond*, edited by Janet Carsten and S. Hugh Jones, 170–88. Cambridge: Cambridge University Press.

McVey, Ruth T. 1967. "Taman Siswa and the Indonesian National Awakening." *Indonesia* 4: 128–49.

———. 1972. "The Post-Revolutionary Transformation of the Indonesian Army: Part II." *Indonesia* 13: 147–81.

McWilliam, Andrew. 2002. *Paths of Origin, Gates of Life: A Study of Place and Precedence in Southwest Timor*. Leiden: Brill.

Melayu Online. 2009. "Research: Kupang Most Indonesian Corrupt City," January 22, 2009.

Merleau-Ponty, Maurice. 2013. *Phenomenology of Perception*. Translated by Donald A. Landes. London: Routledge.

Mietzner, Marcus. 2006. "The 2005 Local Elections—Empowerment of the Electorate or Entrenchment of the New Order Oligarchy?" In *Soeharto's New Order and Its Legacy: Essays in Honour of Harold Crouch*, edited by Edward Aspinall and Greg Fealy, 173–90. Canberra: Australian National University E Press.

———. 2009. "Indonesia and the Pitfalls of Low-Quality Democracy: A Case Study of the Gubernatorial Election in North Sulawesi." In *Democratization in New Order Indonesia*, edited by Marco Bünte and Andreas Ufen, 124–48. London: Routledge.

Mitchell, Timothy. 1991. "The Limits of the State: Beyond Statist Approaches and Their Critics." *The American Political Science Review* 85 (1): 77–96.

Morris, Rosalind. 2004. "Intimacy and Corruption in Thailand's Age of Transparency." In *Off Stage/On Display: Intimacy and Ethnography in the Age of Public Culture*, edited by Andrew Shyrock, 225–43. Stanford, CA: Stanford University Press.

Moyn, Samuel. 2010. *The Last Utopia: Human Rights in History*. Cambridge, MA: Harvard University Press.

Muehlebach, Andrea. 2012. *The Moral Neoliberal: Welfare and Citizenship in Italy*. Chicago: University of Chicago Press.

Muir, Sarah, and Akhil Gupta. 2018. "Rethinking the Anthropology of Corruption. An Introduction to Supplement 18." *Current Anthropology (Supplement)* 59 (18): S4–15.

Musaraj, Smoki. 2020. *Tales from Albarado: Ponzi Logic of Accumulation in Postsocialist Albania*. Ithaca, NY: Cornell University Press.

Nagel, Thomas. 1986. *The View from Nowhere*. Oxford: Oxford University Press.

Navaro-Yashin, Yael. 2002. *Faces of the State: Secularism and Public Life in Turkey*. Princeton, NJ: Princeton University Press.

Nordholt, H. G. Schulte. 1971. *The Political System of the Atoni of Timor*. Leiden: Brill.

Nugent, David. 1994. "Building the State, Making the Nation: The Bases and Limits of State Centralization in 'Modern' Peru." *American Anthropologist* 96 (2): 333–69.

———. 2018. "Corruption Now and Then: Managing Threats to the Nation in Twentieth-Century Peru." *Current Anthropology* 59 (S18): S28–36.

Nuijten, Monique, and Gerhard Anders, eds. 2007. *Corruption and the Secret of Law: A Legal Anthropological Perspective*. London: Routledge.

Olivier de Sardan, Jean-Pierre. 1999. "A Moral Economy of Corruption in Africa?" *Journal of Modern Africa Studies* 36 (1): 25–52.

Ong, Aihwa. 2000. "Graduated Sovereignty in South-East Asia." *Theory, Culture & Society* 17 (4): 55-75.

Oostingh, Roelof van Zeeveld. 1970. "The Pegawai Negeri of Bandung: Structure and Process in Indonesia" Ph.D diss, University of Virginia.

Ormeling, Ferdinand Jan. 1956. *The Timor Problem: A Geographical Interpretation of an Underdeveloped Island*. The Hague: Martinus Nijhoff.

Osburg, John. 2013. *Anxious Wealth: Money and Morality Among China's New Rich*. Stanford, CA: Stanford University Press.

Pardo, Italo. 2000. *Morals of Legitimacy: Between Agency and the System*. Oxford: Berghahn Books.

———. 2013. "Who Is Corrupt? Anthropological Reflections on the Moral, the Criminal and the Borderline." *Human Affairs* 23 (2): 124–47.

————. 2018. "Corrupt, Abusive, and Legal: Italian Breaches of the Democratic Contract." *Current Anthropology* 59 (S18): S60–71.

Parry, Jonathan. 2000. "The Crisis of Corruption and the Idea of India—a Worm's Eye View." In *Morals of Legitimacy: Between Agency and System*, edited by Italo Pardo, 27–56. Oxford: Berghahn Books.

Peacock, Vita. 2015. "The Negation of Hierarchy and Its Consequences." *Anthropological Theory* 15 (1): 3–21.

Pemberton, John. 1994. *On the Subject of "Java"*. Ithaca, NY: Cornell University Press.

Philp, Mark. 1997. "Defining Political Corruption." *Political Studies* 45 (3): 43–62.

Pierce, Steven. 2016. *Moral Economies of Corruption: State Formation and Political Culture in Nigeria*. Durham, NC: Duke University Press.

Piliavsky, Anastasia. 2014. "Introduction." In *Patronage as Politics in South Asia*, edited by Anastasia Piliavsky, 1–36. Cambridge: Cambridge University Press.

————. 2021. *Nobody's People: South Asia in Motion, Hierarchy as Hope in a Society of Thieves*. Stanford, CA: Stanford University Press.

Polanyi, Karl. 1944. *The Great Transformation: The Political and Economic Origins of Our Time*. Boston: Beacon.

Poole, Deborah. 2004. "Between Threat and Guarantee: Justice and Community in the Margins of the State." In *Anthropology at the Margins of the State*, edited by Veena Das and Deborah Poole, 35–66. Santa Fe: School of American Research Press.

Pos Kupang. 2010. "*Fredrik Alo didenda rp 50 juta* [Fredrik Alo fined IDR 50 million]," *Pos Kupang.com*, May 5, 2010. https://kupang.tribunnews.com/2010/05/05/fredrik-alo-didenda-rp-50-juta

————. 2013. "Topik: Dugaan korupsi pengadaan buku [Alleged corruption around the procurement of books]." Accessed July 22 2020. http://kupang.tribunnews.com/topic/dugaan-korupsi-pengadaan-buku.

Povinelli, Elizabeth A. 2011. *Economies of Abandonment: Social Belonging and Endurance in Late Liberalism*. Durham, NC: Duke University Press.

Przeworski, Adam. 2019. *Crises of Democracy*. Cambridge: Cambridge University Press.

Purwanto, Erwan, and Gerry van Klinken. 2010. "Eluding Laws and Regulations: Case Study of the Practices of KKN among Indonesian Local

Bureaucrats in Districts." *In Search of Middle Indonesia Conference, September 27-29, 2010.* Leiden.

Reed-Danahay, Deborah. 1993. "Talking about Resistance: Ethnography and Theory in Rural France." *Anthropological Quarterly* 66 (4): 221–30.

Ricklefs, M. C. 2008. *A History of Modern Indonesia Since C. 1200.* Houndmills, UK: Palgrave Macmillan.

Riles, Annelise. 2001. *The Network Inside Out.* Ann Arbor: University of Michigan Press.

———. 2006. *Documents: Artifacts of Modern Knowledge.* Ann Arbor: University of Michigan Press.

Rivkin-Fish, Michelle. 2005. "Bribes, Gifts, and Unofficial Payments: Rethinking Corruption in Post-Soviet Russian Healthcare." In *Corruption: Anthropological Perspectives*, edited by Dieter Haller and Cris Shore, 47–64. London: Pluto Press.

Rivoal, Isabelle, and Noel B. Salazar. 2013. "Contemporary Ethnographic Practice and the Value of Serendipity." *Social Anthropology/Anthropologie Sociale* 21 (2): 178–85.

Robbins, Joel. 2003. "Properties of Nature, Properties of Culture: Possession, Recognition, and the Substance of Politics in a Papua New Guinea Society." *Journal of the Finnish Anthropological Society* 28 (1): 9–28.

———. 2004. *Becoming Sinners: Christianity and Moral Torment in a Papua New Guinea Society.* Berkeley: University of California Press.

———. 2007. "Between Reproduction and Freedom: Morality, Value, and Radical Cultural Change." *Ethnos: Journal of Anthropology* 72 (3): 293-314.

———. 2009. "Rethinking Gifts and Commodities: Reciprocity, Recognition, and the Morality of Exchange." In *Economy and Morality: Anthropological Approaches*, edited by Katherine Browne and B. Lynne Milgram, 43–58. Lanham, MD: Altamira Press.

Robertson-Snape, Fiona. 1999. "Corruption, Collusion and Nepotism in Indonesia." *Third World Quarterly* 20 (3): 598-602.

Robinson, Mary. 2003. "Human Rights and Ethical Globalization." Tanner Lectures on Human Values, Stanford, CA, February 13. https://tanner-lectures.utah.edu/_resources/documents/a-to-z/r/robinson_2003.pdf

Robison, Richard. 2002. "What Sort of Democracy? Predatory and Neo-Liberal Agendas in Indonesia." In *Globalization and Democratization in Asia: The Construction of Identity*, edited by Catarina Kinnvall and Kristina Jönnson, 92–113. London: Routledge.

————. 2006. "Corruption, Collusion and Nepotism after Suharto: Indonesia's Past or Future?" *IIAS Newsletter* 40 (13).

Rose, Nikolas. 1996. "Death of the Social? Refiguring the Territory of Government." *Economy and Society* 25 (3): 327–56.

Rose-Ackerman, Susan. 1978. *Corruption: A Study in Political Economy.* New York: Academic Press.

————. 1999. *Corruption and Government: Causes, Consequences and Reform.* Cambridge: Cambridge University Press.

Rubinstein, William D., and Patrick von Maravić. 2010. "Max Weber, Bureaucracy, and Corruption." In *The Good Cause: Theoretical Perspectives on Corruption*, edited by Gjalt De Graaf, Patrick von Maravić, and Pieter Wagenaar, 21–35. Opladen: Verlag Barbara Budrich.

Rudnyckyj, Daromir. 2010. *Spiritual Economies: Islam, Globalization, and the Afterlife of Development.* Ithaca, NY: Cornell University Press.

Rutherford, Danilyn. 2003. *Raiding the Land of the Foreigners: The Limits of the Nation on an Indonesian Frontier.* Princeton, NJ: Princeton University Press.

STPDN. 2007. YouTube video. 2:44, April 9, 2007, accessed July 31, 2020, https://www.youtube.com/watch?v=9OqM0AOAKUA.

Sahlins, Marshall. 2013. *What Kinship Is—And Is Not.* Chicago: University of Chicago Press.

Sampson, Steven. 2005. "Integrity Warriors: Global Morality and the Anti-Corruption Movement in the Balkans." In *Corruption: Anthropological Perspectives*, edited by Dieter Haller and Cris Shore, 103–30. London: Pluto Press.

————. 2009. "Corruption and Anti-Corruption in Southeast Europe." In *Governments, NGOs and Anti-Corruption: The New Integrity Warriors*, edited by Luís de Sousa, Peter Larmour, and Barry Hindess, 168–85. London: Routledge.

Samuels, Annemarie. 2019. *After the Tsunami. Disaster Narratives and the Remaking of Everyday Life in Aceh.* Honolulu: University of Hawai'i Press.

Sanders, Todd, and Harry G. West. 2003. "Power Revealed and Concealed in the New World Order." In *Transparency and Conspiracy: Ethnographies of Suspicion in the New World Order*, edited by Harry G. West and Todd Sanders, 1–37. Durham, NC: Duke University Press.

Sannen, Ad M. H. 1983. "Mandors and Tukangs: The Functioning of Informal Sub-Contractors and Buildingworkers in the Construction Sector of Bandung." Ph.D diss, International Institute of Social Science.

Scherz, China. 2011. "Protecting Children, Preserving Families: Moral Conflict and Actuarial Science in a Problem of Contemporary Governance." *PoLAR: Political & Legal Anthropology Review* 34 (1): 33–51.

Schneider, Jane, and Peter Schneider. 2005. "Mafia, Antimafia, and the Plural Cultures of Sicily." *Current Anthropology* 46 (4): 501–20.

Schulte Nordholt, Henk. 2004. "Decentralisation in Indonesia: Less State, More Democracy?" In *Politicising Democracy. The New Local Politics of Democratisation*, edited by John Harriss, Kristian Stokke, and Olle Törnquist, 29–50. New York: Palgrave Macmillan.

Schulte Nordholt, Henk, and Irene Hoogenboom. 2006. *Indonesian Transitions*. Yogyakarta, Indonesia: Pustaka Pekajar.

Schulte Nordholt, H. G. 1971. *The Political System of the Atoni of Timor*. The Hague: Martinus Nijhoff.

Schwarz Wentzer, Thomas. 2018a. "Human, the Responding Being; Considerations Towards a Philosophical Anthropology of Responsiveness." In *Moral Engines: Exploring the Ethical Drives in Human Life*, 211–29. New York: Berghahn Books.

———. 2018b. "Selma's Response: A Case for Responsive Anthropology." *HAU: Journal of Ethnographic Theory* 8 (1/2): 211–22.

Scott, James. 1977. *The Moral Economy of the Peasant: Rebellion and Subsistence in Southeast Asia*. New Haven, CT: Yale University Press.

Scott, James C. 1998. *Seeing Like a State: How Certain Schemes to Improve the Human Condition Have Failed*. Yale Agrarian Studies, Yale ISPS Series. New Haven: Yale University Press.

Sharma, Aradhana. 2013. "State Transparency after the Neoliberal Turn: The Politics, Limits, and Paradoxes of India's Right to Information Law." *PoLAR: Political and Legal Anthropology Review* 36 (2): 308–25.

———. 2018. "New Brooms and Old: Sweeping Up Corruption in India, One Law at a Time." *Current Anthropology* 59 (S18): S72–82.

Sharma, Aradhana, and Akhil Gupta, eds. 2006. *The Anthropology of the State: A Reader*. Oxford: Blackwell.

Shiraishi, Saya S. 1997. *Young Heroes: The Indonesian Family in Politics*. Ithaca, NY: Southeast Asia Program.

Shore, Cris. 2005. "Culture and Corruption in the EU: Reflections on Fraud, Nepotism, and Cronyism in the European Commission." In *Cor-*

ruption: *Anthropological Perspectives*, edited by Dieter Haller and Cris Shore, 131–55. London: Pluto Press.

———. 2018. "How Corrupt Are Universities? Audit Culture, Fraud Prevention, and the Big Four Accountancy Firms." *Current Anthropology* 59 (S18): S92–104.

Shore, Cris, and Dieter Haller. 2005. "Introduction—Sharp Practice: Anthropology and the Study of Corruption." In *Corruption: Anthropological Perspectives*, edited by Dieter Haller and Cris Shore, 1–26. London: Pluto Press.

Siegel, James T. 1998. *A New Criminal Type in Jakarta: Counter-Revolution Today*. Durham, NC: Duke University Press.

Simandjuntak, Deasy. 2012. "Gifts and Promises: Patronage Democracy in a Decentralised Indonesia." *European Journal of East Asian Studies* 11 (1): 99–126.

Smart, Alan. 1998. "Guanxi, Gifts, and Learning from China: A Review Essay." *Anthropos* 93 (4/6): 559–65.

Smith, B. C. 2007. *Good Governance and Development*. Houndmills, UK: Palgrave Macmillan.

Smith, Daniel Jordan. 2007. *A Culture of Corruption in Nigeria: Everyday Deception and Discontent in Nigeria*. Princeton, NJ: Princeton University Press.

———. 2018. "Corruption and 'culture' in Anthropology and in Nigeria." *Current Anthropology* 59 (S18): S83–91.

Spyer, Patricia. 2002. "Fire without Smoke and Other Phantoms of Ambon's Violence: Media Effects, Agency, and the Work of Imagination." *Indonesia* 74: 21–37.

Stansbury, Neill. 2005. "Exposing the Foundations of Corruption in Construction." In *Global Corruption Report 2005*, 36–50. London: Pluto Press and Transparency International.

Stasch, Rupert. 2009. *Society of Others: Kinship and Mourning in a West Papuan Place*. Berkeley, CA: University of California Press.

Steedly, Mary. 2013. *Rifle Reports: A Story of Indonesian Independence*. Berkeley, CA: University of California Press.

Steijlen, Fridus, and Deasy Simandjuntak, dirs. 2011. *Performances of Authority*. Leiden: Royal Netherlands Institute of Southeast Asian and Caribbean Studies, Offstream Films.

Stevenson, Lisa. 2014. *Life Beside Itself Imagining Care in the Canadian Arctic*. Berkeley: University of California Press.

Strassler, Karen. 2010. *Refracted Visions: Popular Photography and National Modernity in Java*. Durham: Duke University Press.

———. 2020. *Demanding Images: Democracy, Mediation, and the Image-Event in Indonesia*. Durham, NC: Duke University Press.

Strathern, Marilyn. 2006. "Bullet-Proofing: A Tale from the United Kingdom." In *Documents: Artifacts of Modern Knowledge*, edited by Annelise Riles, 181–205. Ann Arbor: University of Michigan Press.

Suparlan, Parsudi. 1985. "Kebudayaan Timor [Timorese culture]." In *Manusia dan kebudayaan di Indonesia* [Peoples and cultures in Indonesia], edited by R. M. Koentjaraningrat, 205–221. Jakarta: Djambatan.

Suryakusuma, Julia I. 1996. "The State and Sexuality in New Order Indonesia." In *Fantasizing the Feminine in Indonesia*, edited by Laurie J. Sears, 92–119. Durham, NC: Duke University Press.

Tanzi, Vito. 1998. "Corruption Around the World: Causes, Consequences, Scope and Cures." Working Paper 00/182. Washington, DC: IMF.

———. 2000. *Policies, Institutions and the Dark Side of Economics*. Cheltenham, UK: Edward Elgar.

Tarlo, Emma. 2001. "Paper Truths: The Emergency and Slum Clearance through Forgotten Files." In *The Everyday State and Society in Modern India*, edited by C. J. Fuller and Véronique Bénéï, 68–90. London: Hurst.

Taussig, Michael. 1999. *Defacement: Public Secrecy and the Labor of the Negative*. Stanford, CA: Stanford University Press.

Tempo. 2003. "Satu lagi korban kekerasan STPDN bicara [Another victim of STPDN violence speaks up]," *Tempo News*, September 26, 2003.

———. 2009. "Kupang, Kota Paling Korup Di Indonesia [The city of Kupang is the most corrupt in Indonesia]." *Tempo News*, January 21, 2009.

Ticktin, Miriam I. 2011. *Casualties of Care Immigration and the Politics of Humanitarianism in France*. Berkeley: University of California Press.

Tidey, Sylvia. 2010. "Problematizing 'Ethnicity' in Informal Preferencing in Civil Service: Cases from Kupang, Eastern Indonesia." *Journal of Asia Pacific Studies* 1 (3): 545–69.

———. 2012. "A Divided Provincial Town: The Development from Ethnic to Class Segmentation in Kupang, West Timor." *City & Society* 24 (3): 302–20.

———. 2016. "Between the Ethical and the Right Thing." *American Ethnologist* 43 (4): 663–76.

————. 2018. "A Tale of Two Mayors: Configurations of Care and Corruption in Eastern Indonesian Direct District Head Elections." *Current Anthropology* 59 (S18): S117–27.

Törnquist, Olle. 2008. "How Far to a Meaningful Democracy–2." *Inside Indonesia*, April 20, 2008.

Transparency International. 2008. *Bribe Payers Index 2008*. Berlin: Transparency International.

————. 2009. *Global Corruption Report 2009*. Berlin: Transparency International.

Trouillot, Michel-Rolph. 2001. "The Anthropology of the State in the Age of Globalization: Close Encounters of the Deceptive Kind." *Current Anthropology* 42 (1): 125–38.

Van Beek, Ursula, ed. 2019. *Democracy Under Threat: A Crisis of Legitimacy?* London: Palgrave Macmillan.

Van Klinken, Gerry. 2005. "New Actors, New Identities: Post-Suharto Ethnic Violence in Indonesia." In *Violent Internal Conflicts in Asia Pacific. Histories, Political Economies and Politics*, edited by D. F. Anwar, 79–100. Jakarta: Yayasan Obor Indonesia.

————. 2007. *Communal Violence and Democratization in Indonesia: Small Town Wars*. London: Routledge.

————. 2014. *The Making of Middle Indonesia: Middle Classes in Kupang Town, 1930s–1980s*. Leiden: Brill.

Van Klinken, Gerry, and Edward Aspinall. 2011. "Building Relations: Corruption, Competition and Cooperation in the Construction Industry." In *State and Illegality in Indonesia*, edited by Edward Aspinall and Gerry Van Klinken, 139–64. Leiden: KITLV Press.

Van Leur, J. C. 1967. *Indonesian Trade and Society: Essays in Asian Social and Economic History*. The Hague: W. van Hoeve Publishers.

Vel, Jacqueline. 2009. "Reading Politics from a Book of Donations: The Moral Economy of the Political Class in Sumba." In *State of Authority: State in Society in Indonesia*, edited by Gerry Van Klinken and Joshua Barker, 117–48. Ithaca, NY: Cornell University Press.

Waldenfels, Bernhard. 1994. *Phenomenology of the Alien: Basic Concepts*. Evanston, IL: Northwestern University Press.

Waterson, Roxana. 1990. *The Living House: An Anthropology of Architecture*. Singapore: Oxford University Press.

Webber, Douglas. 2006. "Consolidated Patrimonial Democracy? Democratization in Post Suharto Indonesia." *Democratization* 13 (3): 396–420.

Weber, Max. 1946. "Politics as a Vocation." In *From Max Weber: Essays in Sociology*, edited and translated by H. H. Gerth and C. Wright Mills, 77–128. New York: Oxford University Press.

———. 1968. On Charisma and Institution Building. Edited by S. N. Eisenstadt. Chicago: University of Chicago Press.

———. 1978. *Economy and Society: An Outline of Interpretive Sociology*. Edited by Guenther Roth and Claus Wittich. Translated by Ephraim Fischoff. Berkeley: University of California Press.

———. 2006. "Bureaucracy." In *The Anthropology of the State: A Reader*, edited by Aradhana Sharma and Akhil Gupta, 49–70. Oxford: Blackwell.

Williams, Mark S. 2017. *Indonesia, Islam, and the International Political Economy: Clash or Cooperation?* London: Routledge.

World Bank. 2001. "Indonesia; Country Procurement Assessment Report—Reforming the Public Procurement System." Jakarta: East Asia and Pacific Region: World Bank Office Jakarta, Operational Service Unit.

WFP Indonesia. 2013. "East Nusa Tenggara (NTT) Profile." Jakarta: World Food Program Indonesia.

Yan, Yunxiang. 1996. "The Culture of Guanxi in a North China Village." *The China Journal* 35: 1–25.

Yang, Mayfair Mei-hui. 1994. *Gifts, Favors, and Banquets: The Art of Social Relations in China*. Ithaca, NY: Cornell University Press.

Yurchak, Alexei. 2006. *Everything Was Forever, Until It Was No More: The Last Soviet Generation*. Princeton, NJ: Princeton University Press.

Zigon, Jarrett. 2007. "Moral Breakdown and the Ethical Demand." *Anthropological Theory* 7 (2): 131–50.

———. 2009. "Within a Range of Possibilities: Morality and Ethics in Social Life." *Ethnos* 74 (2): 251–76.

———. 2011a. "A Moral and Ethical Assemblage in Russian Orthodox Drug Rehabilitation." *Ethos* 39 (1): 30–50.

———. 2011b. *HIV Is God's Blessing: Rehabilitating Morality in Neoliberal Russia*. Berkeley: University of California Press.

———. 2013a. "Human Rights as Moral Progress?" *Cultural Anthropology* 28 (4): 216–23.

———. 2013b. "On Love: Remaking Moral Subjectivity in Postrehabilitation Russia." *American Ethnologist* 40 (1): 201–16.

———. 2017. *Disappointment: Toward a Critical Hermeneutics of World-building.* New York, NY: Fordham University Press.

———. 2019. *A War on People Drug User Politics and a New Ethics of Community.* Berkeley: University of California Press.

Zinn, Dorothy L. 2019. *Raccomandazione: Clientelism and Connections in Italy.* New York: Berghahn Books.

Index

195

Buchan, Bruce, 10
Buddhism, 35
Budi, 99–100, 102, 115
bureaucracy, 121, 142; ethnographic studies of, 21, 21n12; modern bureaucratic institutions, 107; post-*reformasi* bureaucracy, 99, 116, 122; "symbolic roots of Western bureaucracy," 147. *See also* bureaucracy, merit, and the KKN
bureaucracy, merit, and the KKN, 98–103; tension between merit and the KKN, 99–100

C

Cahaya, Hiasan, 152–53
camouflage, 134–35
care/caring, 25–26; caring responsibility toward family, 115; connection between corruption and care, 158–60, 162–63; ethical implications to understanding care, 26; friction between caring impulses and situated notions of what counts as a good life, 24–25, 24n13; governmental good grounded in care, 165–68; policing of caring behavior, 24; uneasy boundary between corruption and care, 64–65; visualizations and materializations of the caring responsibility, 89–90. *See also* narratives, of kin and care
Carsten, Janet, 73–74n9
charity boxes, 95–96; decorative words written on (*sumbangan*

sukarela [voluntary contribution]), 95
civil servants, 30, 90–91, 98, 118, 122, 126, 159, 162, 164, 170; civil servants involved in hiring, 131–32; conflict between the professional legitimacy of and their social intimacy, 105; embodied morality of, 115; ethical dilemmas faced by, 110–11; exploitations of, 129, 134–35; moratorium on the hiring of, 52; *Pendidikan dan Pelatihan Prajabatan* civil service training course, 114; in post-*reformasi* Kupang, 99; role of in the New Order regime, 109; and the space between civil servants and citizens, 129–30; training of including elite civil servants, 96–97, 112–17; and the transformative power of a civil service job, 31; vertical civil servants, 48. See also *Performances of Authority*
civil service, 107; Rotenese and Savunese last names as the most dominant in Kupang's civil service, 75. See also *diklat*
Civil Service Corps of the Republic of Indonesia (KORPI), 43, 109
Civil Service Testing Procedure, 131–32
cleanliness, performing of, 130–33
clientelism, 5, 7, 12, 18, 42, 99, 165, 166
Cloke, Jonathan, 14
Cold War, the, 9

Collier, Stephen, 17
colonialism, 11
concealment and unconcealment, 135–37
corruption, 116, 162; connection between corruption and care, 158–60, 162–63; cross-cultural concerns with, 67–68; definitions of, 10, 10n8, 12, 16; different types of, 18; novel forms of, 4–5; opportunities for, 13; perceptions of, 123–24; poetic aspect of, 20; as political failure, 5–8; post-*refromasi* approach to, 94; post-*refromasi* definition of, 70; in post-*reformasi* Kupang, 162–63; public-office understanding of, 94; relational view of, 65–70, 91; scrutiny of, 23; transgressive character of, 8, 91; uneasy boundary between corruption and care, 64–65; in Western liberal democracies, 12. *See also* corruption, in the construction sector; corruption, vernacular terms similar to
corruption, in the construction sector, 48–49, 139–40, 141; attempts to curb corruption in the industry, 143–44, 143n1, 143–44n3; and the circulation of money among contractors, 156–57; and "construction customs," 49; and granting of contracts to family members, 157–58; in local construction projects (the local bribery system), 49–50; and the tendering

process, 157, 158; and the Windmill Project, 50–51. *See also* bidding books; lobbying
corruption, vernacular terms similar of, 18–19; Indian, 19; Nigerian, 19; Russian, 19
Corruption Action Plan Working Group, 9
Corruption Eradication Commission (KPK), 3, 13, 94, 123
Corruption Perceptions Index (Transparency International), 12, 13, 32, 124

D

Das, Vena, 151
débrouiller (ability of French villagers in dealing with the state), 124–25
decentralization, 162; post-*reformasi*, 46–47, 52, 101–2
decolonization, 11–12
democracy: across the globe, 3; liberal, 4, 7, 97, 166; promotion of, 15
democracies, Western, 4, 168
democratization, 3, 5, 7, 12, 162
Department of Governance, 110
Department of Human Resources, 134, 135
Department of Motor Vehicles, 123, 125, 126
Department of Public Works, 111, 124, 139, 142, 143, 145–46, 148–49, 150, 158–60, 163. *See also* bidding books; lobbying
development, 12; post-Cold War, 11

Index

the giving city, 51–52; and parading personhood, 43–46. *See also* corruption, in the construction sector

P

Pak Calvin, 55, 57
Pak Levy, 54–55
Pak Marinus, 30–31, 104
Pak Yohanes, 54–55
Pardo, Italo, 16–17, 168
Partai Komunis Indonesia (PKI [Communist Party of Indonesia]), 38n8, 40
Pater Paulus, 93–94
patrimonialism, 7, 9n7; neo-patrimonialism, 7, 9n7, 12
Pengadilan Tindak Pidana Korupsi (*TiPiKor*), 1n1
Perkembangan, Pengharapan, 152, 153
perfection, 116, 118; New Order perfection, 110, 115
Performances of Authority, 114–15
Permesta rebellion, 42
Perserikatan Kebangsaan Timor (Union of the Timorese People), 38n8
Perserikatan Timor (Timor Union), 38n8
personhood, 41; giving personhood, 58–59; Indonesian national personhood, 109
Philp, Mark, 65–66; on political scientists in the 1960s and 1970s, 67n2
Pierce, Steven, 19
Piliavsky, Anastasia, 25

poetics, 124–30; experience in social poetics (*débrouillardise*), 128–29
political economy, 11
political orders, 10n8
political pluralism, 14
politics: decentralized Indonesian politics, 7, 101–2; modern, liberal conceptions of, 18; in post-Suharto Indonesia, 102–3
Portuguese, the, 36
Pos Kupang, 1, 15
Povinelli, Elizabeth, 23–24
power: asymmetrical power relations, 7; global political-economic power dynamics, 8; and politics, 7; Thai forms of, 94–95n1
prejudices, Orientalist, 11
public administration accountability, 15
public interests, 67
public secrets (*rahasia umum*), and intimate knowledge, 119–22; of KKN, 124, 135–36. *See also* transparency
Purnama, Basuki Tjahaja, 39n10

R

racommandazione, Italian practice of, 20
Radio Republik Indonesia (RRI), 130–31, 133
Rais, Amien, 68–69
Reed-Danahay, Deborah, 124–25, 129n2
reformasi, 7, 27; post-*reformasi* good government efforts, 22;